T0190022

CPTED and Traditional Security Countermeasures

150 Things You Should Know

CPTED and Traditional Security Countermeasures

150 Things You Should Know

Lawrence J. Fennelly
Marianna A. Perry

CRC Press
Taylor & Francis Group
Boca Raton London New York

CRC Press is an imprint of the
Taylor & Francis Group, an **informa** business

CRC Press
Taylor & Francis Group
6000 Broken Sound Parkway NW, Suite 300
Boca Raton, FL 33487-2742

ISBN-13: 978-1-138-48974-5 (hbk)
ISBN-13: 978-1-138-50173-7 (pbk)

Library of Congress Cataloging-in-Publication Data

Names: Fennelly, Lawrence J., 1940- author. | Perry, Marianna A., author.
Title: CPTED and traditional security countermeasures : 150 things you should know / Lawrence J. Fennelly and Marianna A. Perry.
Description: Boca Raton, FL : CRC Press, 2018.
Identifiers: LCCN 2017056319| ISBN 9781138489745 (hardback : alk. paper) | ISBN 9781138501737 (pbk. : alk. paper) | ISBN 9781315144528 (ebook)
Subjects: LCSH: Crime prevention and architectural design. | Buildings--Security measures. | Crime prevention.
Classification: LCC HV7431 .F397 2018 | DDC 364.4/9--dc23
LC record available at https://lccn.loc.gov/2017056319

Cover image word art courtesy: Karen Camilovic with Camilovic Creative.

I wish to dedicate this book to my granddaughter, Emma Marie Agnes Fennelly, who is one of our five beautiful granddaughters.

Lawrence J. Fennelly

This book is dedicated to all the men and women who are serving or have served in the U.S. Military; especially my son, Captain Andrew Agee. Thank you for your service. Stay safe.

Marianna A. Perry

We both wish to give a special thanks to Rich Arrington who works in the Virginia State Training Office and who has trained hundreds of law enforcement officers in Crime Prevention and CPTED Strategies.

Contents

Preface

What is crime prevention through environmental design (CPTED)?
CPTED (pronounced sep-ted) is a short form for the proactive crime-fighting technique known as crime prevention through environmental design.[1]
There are different, yet similar definitions of CPTED:

> CPTED is a proactive design philosophy built around a core set of principles that is based on the belief that the proper design and effective use of the built environment can lead to a reduction in the fear and incidence of crime as well as an improvement in the quality of life.[2]

> Crime Prevention through Environmental Design (CPTED) is defined as a multi-disciplinary approach to deterring criminal behavior through environmental design. CPTED strategies rely upon the ability to influence offender decisions that precede criminal acts by affecting the built, social and administrative environment.[3]

> CPTED Is Based upon the Theory That: the proper design and effective use of the built environment can lead to a reduction in the incidence and fear of crime, and an improvement in the quality of life.[4]

CPTED's emphasis is based on the design and the use of the environment. It is different from the traditional target-hardening approach to crime prevention. Traditionally, the target-hardening approach focused on denying access to a crime target through physical barriers, such as locks, alarms, fences, and gates. Target hardening often overlooked the opportunities for natural access control and

---

[1] What is CPTED? Retrieved on April 23, 2017, from: https://www.peelpolice.ca/en/crimeprevention/resources/whatiscpted.pdf

[2] Crime Prevention Through Environmental Design. Retrieved on April 23, 2017, from: http://cptedontario.ca/mission/what-is-cpted/

[3] The International CPTED Association. Retrieved on April 23, 2017, from: http://www.cpted.net/

[4] What is CPTED? Retrieved on April 23, 2017, from: https://www.peelpolice.ca/en/crimeprevention/resources/whatiscpted.pdf

surveillance. The emphasis was on controlling the use, access, and enjoyment of the "hardened" environment. CPTED overcomes this "hardened" environment with the original three overlapping CPTED strategies of

- *Natural surveillance*—a design strategy with the purpose of observing intruders
- *Natural access control*—a design strategy with the purpose of decreasing the opportunity for crime
- *Territorial reinforcement*—a design strategy that uses physical design for the purpose of increasing a sense of proprietorship or territoriality

If you Google CPTED, you will find an endless source of information on this topic. We recently found *A Basic Training Manual* material on CPTED by Timothy D. Crowe that we would like to share with you. Keep in mind that it is from the early 1990s, when training or lecturing was done using overlays that projected the presentation on a screen, similar to PowerPoint. The actual overlays are as follows:

First overlay: Definition of CPTED—Proper design and effective use of the built environment can lead to a reduction in the incidence and fear of crime and an improvement in the quality of life.
Second overlay: CPTED Emphasis—Physical Environment, Behavior of People, Productive use of space and Crime/loss prevention.
Third overlay: CPTED Actors—Normal users, Abnormal Users, Observers.
Fourth overlay: Relationship Between Man and the Environment—Human Reactional Elements, Temperature, Pressure, Humidity, Light, Sound, Gravity (with nine words around a box). Perceptual system: Sight, Hearing, Smell, Touch, Taste and Gravitational Orientation (words inside the box).
Fifth overlay: Key CPTED Concepts—Natural Surveillance, Natural Access Control and Territorial Behavior.
Sixth overlay: CPTED Strategies,
  - Provide clear border definition of controlled space
  - Provide clearly marked transitional zones that indicate movement from public to semi-public to private space
  - Relocate gathering areas to locations with natural surveillance and access control or to locations away from the view of would-be offenders
  - Place safe activities in unsafe locations to promote the natural surveillance of these activities to increase the perception of safety for normal users and risk for offenders
  - Place unsafe activities in safe spots to overcome the vulnerability of these activities with the natural surveillance and access control of the safe area
  - Reallocate the use of space to provide natural barriers to conflicting activities
  - Improve the scheduling of space to allow for effective use, appropriate *"critical intensity,"* and temporal definition of accepted behaviors

- Redesign and revamp space to increase the perception or reality of natural surveillance
- Overcome distance and isolation through improved communication and design efficiencies

Seventh overlay: The Three D's of CPTED—Definition, Designation and Design.

Timothy D. Crowe, Former Director (1950–2009)
National Crime Prevention Institute

Authors

Lawrence J. Fennelly is an internationally recognized authority on crime prevention, security planning and analysis, and on the study of how environmental factors (CPTED)—and lacking physical hardware, alarms, lighting, site design, management practices, security policies and procedures, and guard management—can contribute to criminal victimization.

He is a frequent speaker and lecturer on CPTED, physical security, school crime, and other issues. He serves as an expert witness who works closely with attorneys in defense as well as plaintiff cases, assisting in case preparation, offering knowledgeable questions to ask the opposing side, etc. He has done a considerable amount of consulting work throughout the United States.

Marianna A. Perry is a Certified Protection Professional (CPP) through ASIS International and has more than 35 years of progressive experience in law enforcement, physical security, safety, and loss control. She received her bachelor's degree from Bellarmine University (Louisville, Kentucky) and her master's degree from Eastern Kentucky University. She is a safety and security consultant and is a frequent presenter at the annual ASIS International Seminar. Perry is a former trooper and detective with the Kentucky State Police and was previously the director of the National Crime Prevention Institute (NCPI) at the University of Louisville. She is a member of the ASIS International School Safety and Security Council as well as the Women in Security Council. Her recent books (with Larry Fennelly) are titled, *Investigations: 150 Things You Should Know, 2nd Ed.*, *150 Things You Should Know about Security, 2nd Ed.*, *Physical Security: 150 Things You Should Know, 2nd Ed.*, *Security in 2025, 2nd Ed.*, *The Handbook for School Safety and Security* and *Security for Colleges and Universities.*

Introduction

We conducted a tremendous amount of research not only on crime prevention through environmental design (CPTED) but on designing out crime, as well. Our research led us to security professionals and CPTED experts around the world. We communicated with friends like Rick Draper in Australia and Dylan Gwinn in the United Kingdom. We actually looked very closely at first-, second-, and third-generation CPTED.

We learned several aspects of CPTED:

1. In first-generation CPTED, there are now seven strategies, which have been recognized for years, and it is time for everyone to redesign their programs. We learned that CPTED has a huge following in Australia and New Zealand, where it is used in schools throughout those countries, in hospitals, in shopping malls, and even in country clubs. Plus, under each category is a separate set of guidelines and direction when discussing natural surveillance, natural access control, and territoriality.
2. Traditional security countermeasures and security deterrents play a large role in the success of CPTED. Specific deterrents are effective and must be in place in order to see a reduction in crime.
3. We recommend a total update of all crime prevention programs, websites, apps, and newsletters. This is the twenty-first century, and crime prevention strategies need to move out of the dark ages.
4. We also recommend a total update and redesign of the Neighborhood Watch Program.
5. We are living in the age of technology—social media, websites, QR Codes, newsletters, webinars, and so on. Basically, mass media is upon us. Crime prevention programs should be embracing technology, and to coin a familiar phrase, "We all need to be thinking outside the box more."
6. CPTED initially grew because Tim Crowe's material was available and basically copyright free. However, we also realize times have changed, and we also must change or be left behind the curve.

7. We commend the many countries, cities, towns, law enforcement agencies, and schools for your hard work and effort for doing everything possible to reduce not only crime, but the fear of crime as well.

8. We are not criminologists or sociologists, and we certainly do not sit behind a desk all day. We consider ourselves security professionals who are crime prevention practitioners. We work in the field conducting assessments, training individuals and law enforcement officers, and so on.

9. *YES, we are raising the bar for* CPTED *and you should too!* Within the next decade or by possibly 2027–2030, law enforcement and security will be something that we cannot even imagine today. Everything will be different. Weapons, vehicles, GPS tracking devices, and predictive analysis will come of age. We have to change our thinking now to be prepared to move ahead.

10. The study of CPTED is not a simple process; it requires in-depth knowledge of all security concepts and strategies in order to work efficiently and effectively.

Security professionals . . . the future is yours! We welcome your comments at:

Lawrence J. Fennelly, CPO, CSS
lafenn@aol.com

Marianna A. Perry, CPP, CPO
mariannaperry@lpsm.us

Chapter 1

Who Is Jane Jacobs?

Jane Jacobs wrote extensively on urban studies and was a woman ahead of her time. Many consider her the first woman in the security profession. She wrote, *The Death and Life of Great American Cities* (1961), which *The New York Times* said was "Perhaps the most influential single work in the history of town planning."[1]

She recommended "four generators of diversity" for cities and economic developments that "create effective economic pools of use":

- Mixed primary uses, activating streets at different times of the day
- Short blocks, allowing high pedestrian permeability
- Buildings of various ages and states of repair
- Density[2]

The book covers such topics as the use of sidewalks, their safety, and the public assimilating them to children's activities—and that was just the first 88 pages. Next, Jacobs covered the use of neighborhood parks and the use of city neighborhoods. Chapter 22 is titled, "The Kind of Problem a City Is." It begins, "Thinking has its strategies and tactics too, much as other forms of action have. Merely to think about cities and get somewhere, one of the main things to know is what kind of problems cities pose, for all the problems cannot be thought about the same way."

---

[1] When Jane Jacobs Took on the World. Retrieved on April 28, 2017, from: http://www.nytimes.com/books/01/04/08/specials/jacobs.html

[2] *The Death and Life of Great American Cities.* https://en.wikipedia.org/wiki/The_Death_and_Life_of_Great_American_Cities; Aaron M. Renn. On Jane Jacobs: "Generating and Preserving Diversity." http://www.newgeography.com/content/002711-on-jane-jacobs-generating-and-preserving-diversity

There is something very pure about Jacob's style of writing. It is much deeper than it initially appeared, and reading *The Death and Life of Great American Cities*[3] will require you to think about the implications of her thoughts on urban planning, even though she was not an architect or a city planner. We highly recommend this work.

---

[3] A pdf of Jane Jacobs book, *The Death and Life of Great American Cities* is available at: https://www.buurtwijs.nl/sites/default/files/buurtwijs/bestanden/jane_jacobs_the_death_and_life_of_great_american.pdf

Chapter 2

Defensible Space Theory and CPTED

Oscar Newman, an architect and city planner, developed the *Defensible Space Theory* in the early 1970s to encompass ideas about crime prevention and neighborhood safety.[1] Newman's book, *Defensible Space* was written in 1972. The book contains a study from New York that discusses how higher crime rates existed in high-rise apartment buildings than in lower housing projects. His conclusion was that an area was safer when people felt a sense of ownership and responsibility for the property. Fear was higher in an area where residents had no control or personal responsibility for an area occupied by so many people. Newman's focus was on social control, crime prevention, and public health in relation to community design.

Theory

Newman's book, *Design Guidelines for Creating Defensible Space*, defined *defensible space* as "a residential environment whose physical characteristics—building layout and site plan—function to allow inhabitants themselves to become the key agents in ensuring their own security" (p. 118). He goes on to explain that a housing development is only defensible if residents intend to adopt this role, which is defined by good design: "Defensible space therefore is a socio-physical phenomenon," says Newman. Both society and physical elements are parts of a successful defensible space.

The theory argues that an area is safer when people feel a sense of ownership and responsibility for the area. Newman's ideas include that "the criminal is isolated

[1] Defensible Space Theory. Retrieved on January 15, 2017, from: https://en.wikipedia.org/wiki/Defensible_space_theory

because his turf is removed" when each space in an area is owned and cared for by a responsible party. If an intruder can sense a watchful community, the intruder feels less secure committing his or her crime. The idea is that crime and delinquency can be controlled and mitigated through environmental design.

There are five factors that make a space defensible:

1. *Territoriality*—the idea that one's home is sacred.
2. *Natural Surveillance*—the link between an area's physical characteristics and the residents' ability to see what is happening.
3. *Image*—the capacity of the physical design to impart a sense of security.
4. *Milieu*—other features that may affect security, such as proximity to a police substation or busy commercial area.
5. *Safe Adjoining Areas*—for better security, residents obtain higher ability to surveil the adjoining area through designing the adjoining area.

The concept of defensible space is controversial. A U.S. Department of Justice experiment in Hartford, Connecticut, closed streets and assigned police teams to certain neighborhoods. New public housing projects were designed around ideas of limited access to the neighborhoods, but Hartford did not show any dramatic drop in crime. The same scenario in a community in St. Louis had much lower crime than in the public streets. The reason appears to be that in St. Louis, people had the capacity and incentives to defend their spaces. The residents had the right to ask an unwelcome individual, such as someone who was not a resident or guest, to leave the street because they jointly owned it. On public streets, one cannot legally act against someone until that person has committed a crime.

Intention

The goal of physical features is to create a sense of *territorialism* in a community, so members can ensure a safe living environment for those who care for it. Defensible space works within the hierarchy of living and community spaces. Housing developments that evoke territorialism are "the strongest deterrents to criminal and vandal activity." Housing should be grouped in such a way to deter crime. In other words, areas should be defined for function. Paths should be defined for movement. Outdoor areas should be juxtaposed with homes, and indoor spaces should visually provide for close watch of outside areas.

Newman states that through good design, people should not only feel comfortable questioning what is happening in their surroundings, but they should feel obligated to do so. Any intruder should be able to sense the existence of a watchful community and avoid the situation altogether. Criminals fear the likelihood that a resident, upon viewing the intrusion, would then question their actions. This is highly effective in neighborhoods that cannot afford professional security.

The defensible space theory can be applied to any type of planned space, and the key is the development of a communal area in which residents can "extend the realm of their homes and the zone of felt responsibility." Circulation paths and common entry are also important aspects of defensible design. Residents must extend their protective attitudes to locations where property and urban streets and surroundings connect. The goal is an interface between private property and community space.

Newman's intent in creating the theory of defensible space is to give the residents of a community control of *public spaces* that they formerly felt were out of reach. In effect, residents care enough for their entire area to protect it from crime as they would protect their own private property.

Principles

Oscar Newman's basic five principles of designing defensible space as quoted in *Design Guidelines for Creating Defensible Space* are as follows:

1. The assignment to different resident groups and the specific environments they are best able to utilize and control, as determined by their ages, lifestyles, socializing proclivities, backgrounds, incomes, and family structures.
2. The territorial definition of space in residential developments to reflect the zone of influence of specific inhabitants. Residential environments should be subdivided into zones toward which adjacent residents can easily adopt proprietary attitudes.
3. The juxtaposition of dwelling interiors with exterior spaces and the placement of windows to allow residents to naturally survey the exterior and interior public areas of their living environments and the areas assigned for their use.
4. The juxtaposition of dwellings—their entries and amenities—with city streets so as to incorporate the streets within the sphere of influence of the residential environment.
5. The adoption of building forms and idioms that avoids the stigma of peculiarity that allows others to perceive the vulnerability and isolation of a particular group of inhabitants.

To create a defensible space community, residential areas should be subdivided into smaller entities of similar families because this way control is enhanced. Responsibility for the area is more easily assumed in a smaller group of families as opposed to a larger community. Smaller groups more frequently use an area geared toward them. The number of activities in the space is increased; thus, a feeling of ownership and a need to protect the property follows. On the other hand, when larger groups use a community space, no one has control over the area, and an agreement over its acceptable uses is often in dispute.

Chapter 3

Natural Surveillance

It is important to remember that the concepts that are expressed through crime prevention through environmental design (CPTED) are derived from a criminology-based approach to a safer environment.[1] These concepts can be blended with other sound urban design principles but are not intended to be a complete representation of good urban design. Components or strategies of CPTED and some of the underlying philosophies are provided in the following sections.

Natural Surveillance

This design concept is directed primarily at discouraging criminal activity by ensuring that public spaces are easily observable. Formal surveillance techniques may involve hidden cameras and security personnel, but physical features that maximize the visibility of people, parking areas, and building entrances can be just as effective. Examples include the following:

- Doors and windows that look out onto streets and parking areas.
- Sidewalks and streets that are open and inviting to pedestrians.
- Unobstructed sight lines.
- Open design concepts (e.g., that do not create hidden spaces).
- Front porches and activity areas in front of buildings to encourage a visual connection with the street.
- Adequate nighttime lighting.

The overall sense of safety improves when people can easily see others and be seen. With proper use of natural surveillance, formal surveillance may only be necessary in vulnerable locations such as elevators and interior corridors.

---

[1] Crime Prevention through Environmental Design, City of Kelowna, Australia, Planning and Development Services, Community Planning Division, 1999.

CPTED Guidelines: Comprehensively Planned Residential Areas

Natural Surveillance

- Landscaping should not create blind spots or hiding places.
- Motion lighting in lanes can improve safety of pedestrians and reduce break-ins, if there is also surveillance from nearby homes.
- Open green spaces, children's play areas, and recreational areas should be located so that they can be observed from nearby homes.
- Children's play areas should be located far enough from the street to protect children from traffic or abduction by strangers (in the worst-case scenario).
- Pedestrian-scale street lighting should be used in high pedestrian traffic areas.
- Not all public areas should be lit, as this promotes a false sense of security for those passing through at night (parks are a good example).
- Storm-water retention areas should be visible from the homes or street—they should be visual amenities, not hedged in or fenced off.

CPTED Guidelines Offices

Natural Surveillance

- Windows and doors should have views into hallways.
- Entrances to washroom facilities should be observable from nearby offices.
- All exterior doors should be well lit.
- Hallways should be well lit.
- Dumpsters should not create blind spots or hiding areas.
- Shrubbery should be kept under 3 feet in height for visibility.
- The lower branches of existing trees should be kept at least 7–8 feet off of the ground.
- Windows should not be obstructed with signs.
- Windows and exterior doors should be visible from the street or by neighbors.
- All four facades should have windows.
- Parking spaces should be assigned to each employee and visitor.
- Parking and entrances should be observable by as many people as possible.
- Parking areas and walkways should be well lit.
- Parking areas should be visible from windows; side parking areas should be visible from the street.
- Dumpsters should be clearly visible from windows.

Chapter 4

Natural Access Control

Natural access control is a design concept directed primarily at decreasing crime opportunities by discouraging access to crime targets and creating a perception of risk to offenders.[1] This is a logical extension of the idea of territorial reinforcement. It is gained by designing streets, sidewalks, building entrances, and neighborhood gateways to clearly indicate public routes, and by discouraging access to private areas with structural elements. There are positive ways to achieve this without creating fortresses with walls and gates.

Natural Access Control in Neighborhoods

- Avoid walling off an entire development, as it increases fear by reducing ownership and surveillance of the street.
- Access should be limited (without completely disconnecting the subdivision from adjacent development).
- Streets should be designed to discourage speeding and nonlocal traffic.
- Paving treatments, plantings, and architectural design features, such as a columnar gateway, guide visitors away from private areas.
- Walkways should be easy to identify, located in such a way as to direct pedestrian traffic, and visible from the street, homes, or parking areas.

---

[1] Crime Prevention through Environmental Design, City of Kelowna, Australia, Planning and Development Services, Community Planning Division, 1999.

Block Watch

The premise behind Block Watch is neighbors getting to know each other, and watching out for one another.[2] The families on a block form a communication chain added by a block map of names, telephone numbers, and addresses. They watch out for each other's homes and report suspicious activities to the police and each other to reduce the likelihood of residential crime.

Block Watch also provides tips on a better way to secure your home, information on how to mark your property, protective window stickers, and crime prevention strategies.

To get involved and join Block Watch, contact your nearest Community Police Station. There may be a Block Watch team in your area that you can join, or start your own team.

---

[2] This section was reproduced from Delta Police, Block Watch. http://deltapolice.ca/services/residential/blockwatch/ accessed on August 23, 2017.

Chapter 5

Target Hardening

Target hardening is the last resort to resist crime by increasing physical security and is a more recognizable, traditional way to discourage crime. Target hardening is accomplished by features that prohibit entry or access, such as window locks, dead bolts for doors, and interior door hinges. This method of crime prevention is most effective when combined with the strategies identified above, so as to achieve a balanced approach.

Opportunities to implement crime prevention through environmental design (CPTED) strategies come with any proposal that involves new construction; revitalization, particularly in a downtown area or existing residential neighborhood; renovation of individual buildings; and repairs to buildings and structures. At the proposal stage, or when reviewing development plans, the application of CPTED can incrementally help to generate a greater level of safety in our communities. The best opportunities for safety, however, come with the establishment of good communities, where neighbors interact effectively and are committed to ensuring that their environments are positive. The rest of this text gives examples and provides guidelines on how to apply these CPTED strategies in different urban areas.

Target Hardening Is Not a Fortress Mentality

In 2015, Dr. Jennifer Hesterman wrote, *Soft Target Hardening: Protecting People from Attack*. The amount of research she did far surpassed other books in the security field, and this is a must-read for practitioners.

Target hardening is not a fortress mentality concept; it is a good security practice (M. Perry, NCPI 2012). Marianna and I both live in gated communities, where access is limited by two entrances. Families are aware of who the neighbors are and who drives what vehicles.

In Cape Cod, Massachusetts, some homes have rolling shutters for protection from storms when homeowners are away, but they also work well as security devices. The majority of neighbors have good locks on doors and windows, follow good landscape principles, do not have walls that obstruct visibility, and some have 6-foot, white, vinyl fences according to town code. The residents are constantly walking back and forth from their homes to the beach, and most carry cell phones.

The community has zero to very little crime because of the property image and the maintenance provided to all townhouses and homes. Additionally, there are several law enforcement retirees who actually patrol the neighborhood before and after running errands. Nearly everyone now has a cell phone, and yes, it is a crime prevention device to call for help and assistance.

Offices

Office buildings are places of work where many people spend much of their day. With a little foresight, these buildings can be designed to be safer environments for both workers and office clientele. A little influence over the surrounding community to enable crime prevention can be accomplished as well.

Chapter 6

Territorial Reinforcement

The historical basis of the idea of territorial reinforcement lies in the need to defend an environment against attack.[1] Physical design can create or extend a sphere of influence. Users then develop a sense of territorial control, while potential offenders, perceiving this control, are discouraged. This strategy is promoted by features that define property lines and distinguish private spaces from public spaces. Ways of doing this include using landscape plantings, pavement designs, gateway treatments, and fences, which create boundaries without compromising natural surveillance. This is further enhanced by a sense of pride or ownership, which is demonstrated by the way in which a space is cared for or maintained. By contrast, poorly maintained areas offer an invitation to criminal activity.

Defensible space is another criminology-based way of describing this strategy. Part of the strategy involves creating recognizable public, semiprivate, and private zones or spaces:

- Public zones are generally open to anyone and are best suited to natural surveillance approaches to create a safe environment.
- Semiprivate zones create a buffer between public and private zones and may serve as common use spaces, such as an interior courtyard. Although accessible to the public, separation is provided by using design features, such as landscaping, that establish definite transitional boundaries.
- Private zones are areas of restricted entry. Access is controlled and limited to specific individuals or groups. A private residence is a clear example.

---

[1] Crime Prevention through Environmental Design, City of Kelowna, Australia, Planning and Development Services, Community Planning Division, 1999.

Residential Territorial Reinforcement

- ■ Lots, streets, and houses should be designed to encourage interaction between neighbors, with elements such as front porches, windows overlooking the street, and landscaping that identifies public, private, and semiprivate spaces without erecting high walls, fences, or hedges.
- ■ Entrances should be accentuated with different paving materials, changes in street elevation, and architectural and landscape design so as to establish areas of influence and the impression of ownership. Walling off an area not only leaves the streets less safe and without surveillance, but provides cover for those breaking in once they are over the wall.
- ■ Residences should be clearly identified by street address numbers that are a minimum of 5 inches (12.5 cm) high and are well lit at night.
- ■ Property lines should be defined with fencing (that does not create a visual barrier), gates, and plantings to direct pedestrian traffic. (This helps to define private, public, and semiprivate areas.)
- ■ All off-street parking spaces should be assigned, so that visitors are acknowledged.

Chapter 7

Maintenance and Image

Maintenance and image are characteristics of an environment that express ownership of the property.[1] Deterioration of a property indicates less ownership involvement, which can result in more vandalism, also known as the Broken Window Theory.[2] If a window is broken and remains unfixed for a length of time, vandals will break more windows. Crime is more prevalent in areas that are not maintained; as a result, law-abiding persons do not feel safe and do not want to frequent those areas.

Milieu

This feature is generally associated with environmental land use and reflects adjoining land uses and the ways in which a site can be protected by specific design styles.[3] For example, a diverse housing mix is more likely to have people present at all times of the day, and bedroom communities are more likely to be vacant during various times of the day. Because criminals know their neighborhoods and potential targets of crime, they are more likely to strike at times when they will not be discovered, and possibly apprehended. Another concept that can be implemented, as required, in addition to the three other crime prevention through environmental design (CPTED) principles is target hardening.

---

[1] CPTED Security. Crime Prevention Through Environmental Design Guidelines. http://www.cptedsecurity.com/cpted_design_guidelines.html

[2] James Q. Wilson and George L. Kelling. Broken Windows. http://www.cptedsecurity.com/broken_windows_theory.htm

[3] Greg Saville and Gerry Cleveland. 2nd Generation CPTED: An Antidote to the Social Y2K Virus of Urban Design, March 13, 2008.

Target Hardening

The use of mechanical devices (locks, security systems, alarms, and monitoring equipment) and organized crime prevention strategies (security patrols and law enforcement) make an area harder to access but may have a tendency to make the inhabitants "feel" unsafe. This technique is the opposite of "natural," which reflects crime prevention as a by-product of normal and routine use of an environment. Target hardening often happens after crime has been committed. The integration of similar, but customer service-oriented CPTED strategies in the initial environmental design may be as effective, but less threatening.

Maintenance and Image

We recently conducted an assessment of several housing and urban development (HUD) properties in the northeast area. Some properties were in fairly good shape, and some were in deplorable conditions.

The following is information on the worst HUD property we assessed:

■ Roughly over 2000 pieces of litter were on the ground.
■ This complex had 250 units with only two small dumpsters on each side of the complex.
■ Four sets of old mattresses and box springs were resting up against a fence in the dumpster area.
■ Drug dealers were openly selling drugs at 3:30 p.m., and individuals who appeared to be under the influence were outside of buildings and sitting on the steps.
■ The homeless were at the top of the street and had been given cell phones and would call the drug dealers if they saw law enforcement coming down the street.

We have a question. What do you think about the maintenance and image of this complex? You cannot get to the next security level until you fix this mess:

■ Keep trees and shrubs trimmed back from windows, doors, and walkways. Keep shrubs trimmed to 3 feet, and prune lower branches of trees up to 8 feet to maintain clear visibility.
■ Use exterior lighting at night, and keep it in working order.
■ Enforce deed restrictions and covenants, in addition to all county codes. Disregarding these issues makes a site appear uncared for and less secure.
■ Maintain signs and fencing, and remove graffiti promptly.
■ Maintain parking areas to high standards without potholes or trash.

Milieu/Management

- Interaction between neighbors is vital to the awareness of persons and activities in the area. Management may need to create opportunities for neighbors to get to know one another.
- If security systems are utilized, ensure all employees and other authorized persons are familiar with the security system to avoid false alarms.
- Set operating hours to coincide with those of neighboring businesses.
- Avoid shifts and situations where only one employee is present.
- Fully illuminate interior spaces.
- Business associations should work together to promote shopper and business safety and the appearance of safety.

An environment with CPTED design principles does not guarantee an absence of crime and vandalism. To be effective and truly implement the CPTED principles, the design (industrial) factors must be blended with the social (human) factors of the environment.

Activity Support

The concept of activity support is to deliberately design formal and informal support for increasing the levels of human activity in particular spaces as a crime prevention strategy.[4]

How do we accomplish this strategy? First, review how the complex is being used, and then add, if necessary, bus stops, community gardens, food trucks, children's playgrounds, cement tables and seats for playing chess or checkers. The use of the grounds will bring the community together for a positive purpose.

---

[4] Paul M. Cozens. 2016. *Think Crime! Using Evidence, Theory, and CPTED for Planning Safer Cities.* Quinns Rocks, Western Australia: Praxis Education.

Chapter 8

Geographical Juxtaposition

By definition, *geographical juxtaposition* (Newman, 1974)[1] is assessing the potential influence on crime levels of proximal land users that may generate crime.[2]

We suggest that you read closely in this book Tim Crowe's CPTED Strategy and 3-D Concept. This material has been updated based on the past writings and newly discovered material of Crowe's found in 2016.[3]

We see crime prevention through environmental design (CPTED) as a process of a series of concepts and strategies that address risk, reduce crime and the fear of crime, and improve the quality of life for our communities.

---

[1] Lewis H. LaRue, *Defensible Space*, By Oscar Newman, 31 Wash. & Lee L. Rev. 809, 1974. http://scholarlycommons.law.wlu.edu/wlulr/vol31/iss3/16

[2] http://criminology.oxfordre.com/view/10.1093/acrefore/9780190264079.001.0001/acrefore-9780190264079-e-2

[3] Timothy D. Crowe, Revised by Lawrence J. Fennelly, 1940. *Crime Prevention Through Environmental Design*, 3rd Edition. Waltham, MA: Elsevier, 2013.

Chapter 9

Defensible Space: The Concept

All defensible space programs have a common purpose: they restructure the physical layout of communities to allow residents to control the areas around their homes.[1] This includes the streets and grounds outside of their buildings and the lobbies and corridors within them. The programs help people preserve those areas in which they can realize their commonly held values and lifestyles.

Defensible space relies on self-help rather than on government intervention, and so it is not vulnerable to government's withdrawal of support. It depends on resident involvement to reduce crime and remove the presence of criminals. It has the ability to bring people of different incomes and race together in a mutually beneficial union. For those with low incomes, defensible space can provide an introduction to the benefits of mainstream life and an opportunity to see how their own actions can better the world around them and lead to upward mobility.

Defensible space technology can be used to enable residents to take control of their neighborhoods, to reduce crime, and to stimulate private reinvestment. The process will also produce inexpensive ways to create housing for the poor, often without government assistance.

---

[1] Oscar Newman. *Creating Defensible Space*. April 1996. U.S. Department of Housing and Urban Development, Office of Policy Development and Research. https://huduser.gov/publications/pdf/def.pdf

Today

Oscar Newman's defensible space theory was largely popular in city design from its emergence until the 1980s. Some of his basic ideas are still taken into consideration. Even though changes were made in the implementation of the theory in the 1990s, and the twenty-first century, Newman's basic principles still exist in design.

Chapter 10

First-Generation CPTED

The theory of Crime Prevention Through Environmental Design is based on one simple idea: that crime results partly from the opportunities presented by physical environment. This being the case, it should be possible to alter the physical environment so that crime is less likely to occur.[1]

Ronald V. Clarke

The definition of crime prevention through environmental design (CPTED) is as follows:

The proper design and effective use of the built environment that can lead to a reduction in the fear and incidence of crime and an improvement in the quality of life. The goal of CPTED is to reduce opportunities for crime that may be inherent in the design of structures or in the design of neighborhoods.[2]

The first generation of CPTED is a collection of strategies and concepts to discourage crime.

First-generation CPTED principles like natural access control and natural surveillance provide a clear line of sight to discourage criminals from using the safe zone for their activities.

---

[1] https://pdfs.semanticscholar.org/4a94/e72074e829aba49ff001e177870d37be13d5.pdf
[2] T. Crowe. 2000. *Crime Prevention through Environmental Design* (2nd ed.). Burlington, MA: Elsevier.

First Generation

CPTED is defined as the use of a built environment where that environment acts to prevent or reduce the incidence of crime and the fear of crime, and to improve the quality of life (Jefferies and Crowe, 1991).[3]

In its first-generation form, CPTED theory is underpinned by the three requirements of natural surveillance, natural access control, and territorial reinforcement.[4]

Simple ploys such as playing classical music in front of shopping centers to persuade young skateboarders away from loitering are useful starting points in understanding the possibilities of using a CPTED approach. First-generation CPTED involves the application of physical design principles to an area in order to minimize the environmental support for criminal behavior.[5]

It also serves to reinforce positive behavior from the same design philosophy. When designed properly, CPTED environments lead to a reduction in crime and the fear of crime.[6]

First-generation CPTED differs from the defense in depth strategy, which entails a series of physical barriers to limit access to potential crime targets, by focusing on the design of physical space to encourage legitimate use and deter criminal activity.

First-generation CPTED draws criticism from criminologists who argue that many environmental strategies only shift criminal behavior rather than reducing it.[7] Additionally, it is limited as it is designed around a rational mindset that assumes criminal behavior is always committed through rational choice.[8] It is further limited as a stand-alone strategy when applied to applications that are events rather than being property focused.

Some examples of the application of first-generation CPTED include the maintenance of facilities to portray the message that they are owned and cared for; adequate signage to deter intruders and criminal activity by reinforcing ownership and legitimate use; satisfactory lighting; closed-circuit television (CCTV); and open space environments to promote surveillance and increase the perceived risk

---

[3] http://criminology.oxfordre.com/view/10.1093/acrefore/9780190264079.001.0001/acrefore-9780190264079-e-2

[4] O. Newman. 1972. *Defensible Space: Crime Prevention through Urban Design*. New York, NY: Macmillan.

[5] Western Australia Planning Guidelines. 2006. Perth Western Australia: Western Australia Planning Commission.

[6] P.M. Cozens, G. Saville, and D. Hillier. 2005. CPTED: A Review and Modern Bibliography. *Property Management* 23(5):328–356; R. Wortley and L.G. Nazerolle. 2008. *Environmental Criminology and Crime Analysis*. Cullompton, England: Wilan.

[7] R.I. Atlas. 2008. *21st Century Security and CPTED*. Boca Raton, FL: CRC Press.

[8] G. Saville and G. Cleveland. 1999. 2nd Generation CPTED: An Antidote to the Social Y2K Virus of Urban Design. Unpublished manuscript.

of criminals being caught. The human space in CPTED must have a designated function. It must be defined and supported by the design of the location.[9]

Second-generation CPTED is defined as a supplemental extension to first-generation CPTED that focuses on explicit social and cultural dynamics in each individual neighborhood.[10] It is not a replacement for first-generation CPTED. Instead, it is intended to augment physical environmental design through the addition of a socially cohesive stratagem. To further characterize second-generation beyond this simple definition, it is necessary to consider crime prevention over a period of time, rather than as a moment in time. First-generation CPTED is about design strategies to prevent criminals from entering an area.[11]

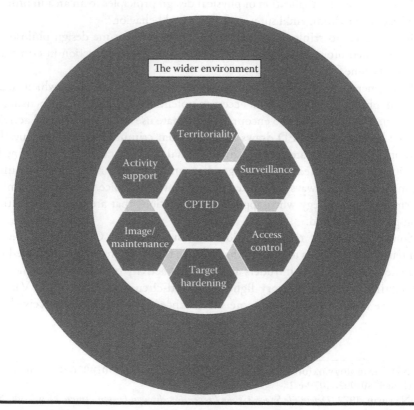

Figure 10.1 Design prepared by Marianna Perry, CPP. (Adapted from Moffat, 1983, p. 23. http://www.emeraldinsight.com/fig/1130230502001.pmg)

---

[9] T. Crowe. 2000. *Crime Prevention through Environmental Design* (2nd ed.). Burlington, MA: Elsevier.

[10] R.I. Atlas. 2008. *21st Century Security and CPTED*. Boca Raton, FL: CRC Press.

[11] G. Saville and G. Cleveland. 1999. 2nd Generation CPTED: An Antidote to the Social Y2K Virus of Urban Design. Unpublished manuscript.

Following is a breakdown of concepts:

1. Territoriality
2. Natural surveillance (both formal and informal)
3. Natural access control[12]
4. Image and/or maintenance
5. Activity program support
6. Target hardening
7. Geographical juxtaposition (wider environment)

Concepts

We all need to be on the same page, and we are not. Tim Crowe had three concepts, but the fourth on the list above was always part of territoriality. As security practitioners conducted assessments, concepts four, five, and six were developed by Ian A. Moffett, chief of police and district security for the Miami-Dade Police Department. Chief Moffatt wrote a paper where the information in Figure 10.1 was listed.

It is important to say, "As times change, we also must change or be left behind the curve." Paul Cozens also endorsed these concepts in his paper, "Designing Out Crime: From Evidence to Action" (2005, pp. 328–356) and also in his book, *Think Crime* (2016, p. 18), which states: "Following two extensive reviews of CPTED (Cozens and Love, 2015; Cozens, Saville, and Hillier, 2005). The seven concepts of CPTED are:" [as stated in previous section][13] (Figure 10.1).

---

[12]Crowe and Fennelly. 2013. *CPTED* (3rd ed.).
[13]Paul Cozens. 2016. *Think Crime* (2nd ed.). Perth Western Australia: Praxis Education.

Chapter 11

First-Generation CPTED Breakdown

1. Natural Surveillance
   a. Clear windows
   b. Law enforcement
   c. Delineate boundaries

2. Natural Access Control
   a. Security awareness
   b. Reporting and reactive
   c. Reducing the number of entrances and access

3. Territoriality Reinforcement
   a. Sphere of influence
   b. Physical design
   c. Maintenance

4. Image Management
   a. Positive and negative indicators
   b. Perception of space
   c. Behavioral effects

5. Activity Program Support
   a. Space to reduce crime
   b. Increasing the level of human activity in a particular space
   c. Additional eyes on the street

6. Target Hardening
   a. Securing of property
   b. Installation of physical security devices
   c. Use of security officers or law enforcement

7. Geographical Juxtaposition (Wider Environment)[1]
   a. Land use
   b. Vacant or derelict sites
   c. Lack of pedestrian movement

Description of the First Generation of CPTED

First-generation CPTED focuses on 12 strategies and concepts that will reduce and discourage criminal opportunity:

- Defines boundaries
- Clear line of sight
- Users of space
- Urban zones prone to criminal activity
- Street lighting
- Security surveillance systems (CCTV)
- Digitally administered makes the offender visible to others (digital sign)
- Proper maintenance of space signifies a sense of ownership that is influential in reducing fear of crime
- Spatial design
- Reinforcing positive behavior within the physical space through the use of physical attribute
- Public and private space
- Acceptable patterns of usage[2]

---

[1] Paul Cozen & Love 2015, Cozen, Saville & Hiller, 2005. Adapted from Cozens et al., 2005, pp. 328–356. http://criminology.oxfordre.com/view/10.1093/acrefore/9780190264079.001.0001/acrefore-9780190264079-e-2

[2] This is based on the UN Interregional Crime and Justice Research Institute text titled, *New Energy for Urban Security—Improving Urban Security through Green Environmental Design.*

Chapter 12

Second-Generation CPTED: Part 1

Second-generation crime prevention through environmental design (CPTED) is about preventing crime from growing within an area.[1] Second-generation CPTED extends beyond basic physical design and focuses on the various social issues within society as well as other situational factors. This approach offers the promise of more enhanced and realistic crime prevention strategies. In the past, the rational offender theory applied to traditional CPTED strategies has been offender focused, rather than victim focused. Second-generation CPTED and Designing Out Crime strategies are designed to expand on this perspective to incorporate a more holistic approach to crime prevention within the community.[2] Without second-generation CPTED, factors such as adolescent isolation (from parents and older peers) remain as untreated risks. Key dynamics behind the requirement for second-generation CPTED strategies include their application to alcohol-related crime, such as public disorder and antisocial behavior, where "rationality" is often relatively absent due to intoxication.[3] Second-generation CPTED is a more reliable strategy for changing an offender's character or motivation. This is more beneficial

---

[1] J. Letch, E. McGlinn, J.F. Bell, E. Downing, and D.M. Cook. 2011. An Exploration of 1st and 2nd Generation CPTED for End of Year School Leavers at Rottnest Island. Perth Western Australia: Edith Cowan University. http://ro.ecu.edu.au/cgi/viewcontent.cgi?article=1012&context=asi

[2] J. Letch, E. McGlinn, J.F. Bell, E. Downing, and D.M. Cook. 2011. An Exploration of 1st and 2nd Generation CPTED for End of Year School Leavers at Rottnest Island. Perth Western Australia: Edith Cowan University. http://ro.ecu.edu.au/cgi/viewcontent.cgi?article=1012&context=asi

[3] Designing Out Crime Research Centre. 2011. Physical Surveillance CCTV.

to longer-term and more practical solutions in preventing crime.[4] Overall, it is the social interaction and cohesion among all stakeholders that enables a more holistic (and therefore successful) approach. Social cohesion promotes the idea of legitimate users taking responsibility and being involved in an ongoing manner. This can be achieved by mutually supported social events, joint meetings and discussions, and awareness programs. In many instances, these additional concepts require high-level connectivity with local authorities, law enforcement, and agencies from a broad church of relations. In combination, these requirements demand an understanding of the threshold or capacity that the local community can tolerate and deliver. This is particularly difficult in built environments where the normal purpose of the environment is uniquely different from the social makeup that defines a particular event.[5]

[4] S. Geason and P. Wilson. 1990. *Crime Prevention: Theory and Practice, Australian Institute of Criminology*, Canberra.

[5] R.I. Atlas. 2008. *21st Century Security and CPTED*. Boca Raton, FL: CRC Press.

Chapter 13

Second-Generation CPTED: Part 2

Second-generation CPTED "seeks to cultivate while building or rebuilding our Urban Areas".[1,2]

There are few opportunities for positive and social interactions between people and groups within the community (Green et al., 1998; Saville and Clear, 2000).[3]

There are four second-generation CPTED concepts:

1. Social Cohesion
2. Connectivity
3. Community Culture
4. Threshold Capacity

Second-generation CPTED reduces crime motives by dealing with the cultural, social, and emotional needs of people at the specific locales where crime is or may be most acute.

---

[1] G. Saville and G. Cleveland. 1999. *2nd Generation CPTED: An Antidote to the Social Y2K Virus of Urban Design.* Unpublished manuscript.

[2] G. Saville and G. Cleveland. 1999. *2nd Generation CPTED: An Antidote to the Social Y2K Virus of Urban Design.* http://www.veilig-ontwerp-beheer.nl/publicaties/2nd-generation-cpted-an-antidote-to-the-social-y2k-virus-of-urban-design/view

[3] D.P. Green, D.Z. Strolovitch, and J.S. Wong. 1998. Defending neighborhoods, integration, and racially motivated crime. *American Journal of Sociology* 104(2): 372–403; G. Saville and T. Clear. 2000. Community renaissance with community justice. *The Neighborworks Journal* 18: 18–24.

Social Cohesion

A few of the characteristics that define social cohesion include the following:

- Participation in local events and organizations
- Presence of self-directed community problem solving
- Extent to which conflicts are positively resolved within the community (e.g., restorative justice programs)
- Prevalence of friendship networks within the community
- Extensive positive relations between friendship networks

Connectivity

Connectivity means the neighborhood has positive relations and influence with external agencies such as government funding sources.

Some characteristics of connectivity include the following:

- Existence of networks with outside agencies, for example, shared websites
- Grant writer or access to a grant writing service
- Formal activities with outside groups, organizations, and neighborhood
- Adequate transport facilities (ride sharing, bicycle paths, public transit) linking to outside areas

Community Culture

CPTED practitioners sometimes forget what is significant about Jacob's "eyes in the street"—not the sight lines or the streets, but the eyes. We do not need neighborhoods of watchers; we need a sense of community where people care about whom they are watching. Community culture brings people together in a common purpose. This is how local residents begin to share a sense of place and why they bother to exert territorial control in the first place (Adams and Goldbard, 2001).[4]

A few characteristics that define culture within a community include the following:

- Presence and effectiveness of gender and minority equality strategies
- Gender-based programs, for example, violence against women
- Extent of social and cultural diversity within a neighborhood
- Prevalence of special places, festivals, and events

---

[4] D. Adams and A. Goldbard. 2001. *Creative Community: The Art of Cultural Development.* New York, NY: Rockefeller Foundation.

- Extent of community traditions and cultural activities, for example, arts fairs and sports role models
- A unique sense of pride or distinctiveness based on the attributes or characteristics of the residents, occupants, or users of the space involved

Threshold Capacity

Second-generation CPTED seizes on the concept of social ecology. Although first-generation CPTED works to minimize crime opportunities through design, second-generation CPTED establishes balanced land uses and social stabilizers. Stabilizers include safe congregation areas or events for young people while minimizing destabilizing activities that tip an area into crime, such as illegal pawn shops and abandoned buildings.[5]

The concept of the tipping point is another threshold idea (Saville, 1996; Saville and Wong, 1994).[6] The movement toward "community imbalance" is colloquially described as "tipping." This refers to the capacity of any given activity or space to properly support the intended use. Too many abandoned homes in a neighborhood have been shown to act as a magnet for certain types of crime (Spellman, 1993). Too many bars in a small area can generate an exorbitant number of bar-related problems such as assaults, drunk driving, and disorder incidents (Saville and Wong, 1994).[7]

Characteristics of Capacity

- Human-scale, land use density, and maximum diversity
- Balance of social stabilizers, for example, community gardens, street entertainment, and street food venders for downtown lunches
- Minimal congestion versus economic resources
- Crime generators below critical threshold, for example, number of abandoned homes per neighborhood and number of bars in an area

Summary

If you begin to employ second-generation CPTED strategies and teach the essentials of the four Cs, you will arm yourself and your community against violence, social

---

[5] Ibid.

[6] G. Saville. 1996. Searching for a Neighborhood's Crime Threshold. Subject to debate (10 [10]). Washington, DC: Police Executive Forum; G. Saville and P. Wong. 1994. Exceeding the Crime Threshold: The Carrying Capacity of Neighborhoods. Presented at the 53rd Annual Meeting of the American Society of Criminology, Miami, FL.

[7] G. Saville and P. Wong. 1994. Exceeding the Crime Threshold: The Carrying Capacity of Neighborhoods. Presented at the 53rd Annual Meeting of the American Society of Criminology, Miami, FL.

conflict, and emotional detachment. For those persons and professionals interested and involved in making engaging and sustaining community involvement, we believe there is no better way than to incorporate the concepts of second-generation CPTED to the basics of first-generation CPTED.

Developing and sustaining a sense of community and involvement by the legitimate users of the built environment is the best insurance against social detachment, crime inflation, and occupant apathy.[8]

Author's Comments

1. In our opinion, Adams and Goldbard have misinterpreted some of the key concepts outlined by Jane Jacobs in her book, *The Death and Life of Great American Cities* (1961), when she first introduced "eyes on the street." Jacobs supported the concept of Neighborhood Watch within the community, and she wanted the community to come together and to report suspicious activity to the police as a means of creating a safer environment. This is the same concept currently being used by the Department of Homeland Security campaign, "If You See Something, Say Something." Adams and Goldbard failed to state the facts of what neighbors should do if they see something suspicious.

2. Saville and Cleveland's second generation may not apply in every situation, but you need to know about their methods and how to use them for your benefit.

---

[8] G. Saville and G. Cleveland. 2008. Second Generation CPTED, the rise and fall of opportunity theory. In R. Atlas (Ed.), *21st Century Security and CPTED*. Boca Raton, FL: CRC Press.

Chapter 14

Third-Generation CPTED

The third generation of crime prevention through environmental design (CPTED) envisions a green sustainable approach to enhance the living standards of urbanites and improve the image of the city as user friendly, safe, and secure.[1] It also aims to create a sense of belonging and membership to a greater community of soliciting citizen engagement and participation in improving the conditions of urban living.

Third-generation CPTED focuses on three main methodological branches that suggest to the urban policymakers an approach to be adopted when planning the security policies of the respective cities:

1. Anticipate the dynamics of the city
2. Collaborate on improving standards of living

The green environment design must lead to a more secure and safer environment. The city's budget has to be managed in a way to achieve multiple results through more intelligent and efficient policies.

The third generation of CPTED that is the subject of investigation and contemplation in this report adds another dimension to the discourse, which is that of the synergies among CPTED, urban sustainability, technology, and the potential of networks.[2]

---

[1] UN Interregional Crime and Justice Research Institute. Improving Security Through Green Environmental Design. MIT. Retrieved July 10, 2017, from: http://www.unicri.it/news/files/2011-04-01_110414_CRA_Urban_Security_sm.pdf

[2] P.M. Cozens. 2002. Sustainable urban development and crime prevention through environmental design for the British City. Towards an effective urban environmentalism for the 21st Century. *Cities: The International Journal of Urban Policy and Planning* 19(2): 129–137.

The Premise of Third-Generation CPTED

The premise of third-generation CPTED is that a sustainable green urbanity is perceived by its members and outsiders as safe. With the focus on sustainable green environmental design strategies, the perception of urban space as safe

1. Addresses energy crisis, urban pollution, recycling, and minimizing waste
2. Reprograms the physical space and material, based on consumption, online services, and cyberfunctionality
    a. Green
    b. Natural energy as a power source

The Third Generation of CPTED Strategies

1. Reprograming urban space
2. Urban-scale green urbanism and green space
3. Design strategies
4. Portal of digital information
5. Smart signs
6. Perception of safety and security
7. Recycle of waste

Chapter 15

Designing Security, Designing Out Crime, and Working with Architects

Architecture is not just a matter of style, image and comfort. It can create encounter crime—and prevent it ... with crime prevention through environmental design.

Oscar Newman 1972

Today, it is critical to include security designers at the beginning of any new construction project or the renovation of an existing structure. Doing so will save your organization a great deal of money and time in doing what could have been done in the early stages of a project. Architects are experts in building design and construction but often do not consider the security needs of the population the building will ultimately serve. Different groups have different needs that must be considered during the planning stages, so that the building does not have to be retrofitted with physical security measures not previously considered. All of this causes extra time, material, and money to complete. And, all of this ultimately needs to be integrated with existing systems, which are not always compatible.[1]

As with crime prevention through environmental design (CPTED), some of the leadership in energy and environmental design (LEED) concepts complement security concerns, whereas others conflict with physical security principles. The

---

[1] R. Hurley. 2017. Designing security and working with architects. In L.J. Fennelly (Ed.), *Effective Physical Security* (5th ed., p. 291). Boston, MA: Elsevier.

LEED Green Building Rating System represents the U.S. Green Building Council's (USGBC) effort to provide a national standard for what constitutes a "green building." Through its use as a design guideline and third-party certification tool, it aims to improve occupant well-being, environmental performance, and economic returns of buildings using established and innovative practices, standards, and technologies.[2] LEED is a voluntary building assessment tool that is most applicable to commercial, institutional, and high-rise residential construction. Owners, architects, and engineers must work together to strike a balance between building design objectives.[3]

Recently, we had a discussion about why a building did not turn out as originally stated. The contractor and architect were in the planning meetings, but the subcontractors were not. Working with architects is like doing a risk assessment on paper; you need to spell out what you want, for example, type of lighting and foot-candles needed, alarm system and type of control panel and other components, as well as where and what you need protected. Granted the list would be long, but so is not the assessment?

Additionally, you need to educate your committee, the architects, the contractors, and the subcontractors on CPTED concepts—why natural surveillance is important, and why access control, both natural and mechanical surveillance needs to be incorporated into the design process. You may find that many of the things on your list have already been included in the project but just need to be tweaked a bit more specifically.

Our experiences with planners over the years have been more positive than negative. An architect/planner stated once, "It's in the plans to install a fire and intrusion alarm but I had no specific panel in mind, what do you suggest?" A secret that has worked for us over the years is to write a private report after every meeting and list questions that were asked and answered, including needed research for the next meeting that is to be done. By integrating multiple security systems in a layered effect—including CPTED and environmental security, critical infrastructure protection, building designs, interior/exterior layout, detection systems, structural barriers, access controls, communications, and security surveillance systems (closed-circuit television [CCTV])—assessment contributes to the protection of assets as well as the control and reduction of losses and improves the quality of life within the complex.[4]

---

[2] Green Building Rating System 2.1 Announced (November 19, 2002). Retrieved July 11, 2017, from: http://www.buildings.com/news/industry-news/articleid/1115/title/green-building-rating-system-2-1-announced
[3] L.J. Fennelly and M.A. Perry. 2017. Designing security and working with architects. In L.J. Fennelly and M.A. Perry (Eds.), *Physical Security: 150 Things You Should Know* (2nd ed.). Cambridge, MA: Elsevier.
[4] U.S. Green Building Council. LEED Green Building Z Rating, System for new construction and major renovation version 2.1. http://www.usgbc.org; November 2002.

Chapter 16

The Four Basic Layers
of Physical Security

The four basic layers of physical security are design, control, detection, and identification.[1] For each of these layers, there are different options that can be utilized for security. In order to maximize protection, the idea is to use a holistic approach.

Physical Security Design

Physical security design refers to any structure that can be built or installed to deter, impede, or stop an attack from occurring. These structures may be walls, fences, barbed wire, vehicle barriers, speed bumps, gated windows, and so on. Limiting the number of building entrances, channeling movement through the building to go through security checkpoints with security officers or locking devices, are all part of the physical security design of a building. Reinforcing the building structure with additional steel or concrete to withstand various types of attacks can all be considered before construction begins.

Physical Security Control

Physical security controls refer to all control capabilities in a building, from mechanical and electronic to procedural, that limit access to certain areas. This can

---

[1] Elert and Associates. The Four Necessary Basic Layers Required for Proper Physical Security. Retrieved on May 28, 2017, from: http://www.elert.com/ the-four-necessary-basic-layers-required-for-proper-physical-security/

entail key locked and key coded doors, electronic card access, or security or access control checkpoints.

Physical Security Detection

There are different forms of detection from intrusion detection (alarm) systems with audible alerts, motion sensors and lights, to video surveillance and security officers. Video surveillance is now considered an essential layer of physical security and can be monitored live by security officers for suspicious activity or recorded to be reviewed at a later time.

Physical Security Identification

When access to certain areas is limited, it is crucial that there is a system to identify who should and should not have access. Biometrics is becoming more common through fingerprint or hand geometry, voice recognition, or retinal scans. Electronic fob/card access or mechanical keys can be used as well as security checkpoints where security officers can verify identification.

Chapter 17

CPTED Strategies for Parking Lots and Parking Garages

Parking lots and parking garages must have natural surveillance and natural access control.[1] Routes of travel for vehicles and pedestrians should be clearly identified and marked. Surveillance by both casual observers and law enforcement will help to create a surface parking lot or parking garage that "feels" safe to legitimate users. Proper landscaping design and principles can certainly make the difference toward creating an "open" parking garage or surface parking lot and a "closed" parking garage or surface parking lot. Parking lots or parking garages that have dark areas because there is not adequate lighting are considered "closed" environments that do not "feel" safe. They may have enclosed stairwells or tall bushes that have not been maintained that create hiding places. Additionally, many times there is no security presence, and this may cause users to "feel" unsafe and vulnerable.

Some of the concepts that follow apply to parking garages as well as surface parking lots:[2]

---

[1] L.J. Fennelly and M.A. Perry. 2017. 101, Parking lots and garages. In L.J. Fennelly and M.A. Perry (Eds.), *Physical Security: 150 Things You Should Know* (2nd ed., pp. 111, 112). Cambridge, MA: Elsevier.

[2] Adapted from M.S. Smith. April 1996. National Institute of Justice, Research in Brief: Crime Prevention through Environmental Design in Parking Facilities. Retrieved July 11, 2017, from: http://www.popcenter.org/problems/residential_car_theft/pdfs/smith.pdf

- A well-distributed security surveillance system can monitor drive paths, parking spaces, elevator lobbies, and stairwells.
- Access control and perimeter security should always be considered in the initial design stage.
- Video surveillance for parking facilities that is implemented as a retrofit is typically twice as expensive.
- Consider mobile cameras that ride on tracks back and forth down the length of parking aisles and can see between parked vehicles.
- Emergency call buttons (blue light phones) should be placed for emergency assistance at vulnerable areas, especially in elevators and on each level of the parking structure (Photo 17.1).
- Elevator lobbies and stairs in open garages should be clear to the parking area except at the roof levels, where glass enclosures may be provided for weather protection.
- The ideal solution for a stair or elevator waiting area is to have it totally open to the exterior or parking area.
- Pedestrian paths should be carefully planned to concentrate egress. For example, taking all pedestrians through one exit rather than allowing them to disperse in a number of directions improves the likelihood of seeing and being seen by others.
- Locate attendant booths, parking offices, and security stations where attendants can directly monitor activity.
- Avoid dead-end parking areas, as well as nooks and crannies, in the general design of the parking facility.
- Plant shrubbery away from the facility and keep it trimmed to eliminate hiding places.

Photo 17.1 Cabling used in a parking garage, instead of solid walls, to increase natural surveillance and safety. (Photo taken by Marianna Perry, CPP.)

- Provide security screening or fencing at points of low activity to discourage individuals from entering these areas of the facility on foot. Make sure such areas maintain openness and natural surveillance.
- A system of fencing, grilles, and doors also may be designed to completely shut down access to the facility during unattended hours.
- Close off potential hiding places below stairs.
- Maximize flat parking areas and minimize ramps.
- Openness enhances natural surveillance.
- Long-span construction and high ceilings create openness and aid in lighting the facility.
- Ground-level pedestrian exits that open into nonsecure areas should be emergency exits only and fitted with panic bar hardware.
- To help direct patrons and allow them to move quickly in and out of the parking facility, use care when placing signs and graphics. Use color coding and unique memory aids to help patrons quickly locate their parked vehicles.
- Place clear, visible signage at all entrances and exits.
- Open stairways to have a clear line of sight from the outside.
- Set up regular patrols by uniformed security or law enforcement (or both) utilizing a guard tour system to document varying routes.
- Limit entry points for pedestrians and vehicles.
- Ensure walls and ceilings are bright with colorful décor or painted white walls and ceilings to enhance reflectivity (Photo 17.2).
- Parking garages should have raised ceiling heights to enhance openness as well as signage that indicates the floor-to-ceiling height clearance.

Photo 17.2 Painted white walls and ceiling used to reflect light in the stairwell of a parking garage. (Photo taken by Marianna Perry, CPP.)

- Design pedestrian entranceways with transparent glass to allow clear observation.
- Use directional signage indicating the locations of exits and elevators, and which floor the patron is on.
- Effective lighting should be properly maintained with upgrades to LED lights that operate with motion detectors, which will increase the level of light as the pedestrian walks closer to or under the fixture.

According to lighting recommendations by the Illuminating Engineering Society of North America (IESNA),[3]

- Covered parking structures and pedestrian entrances should be illuminated to 5 fc and garage elevators and stairs to 10 fc.
- An open parking lot should be illuminated to 0.20–0.90 fc.
- It must meet the lighting standards of the IESNA. The top three and the most critical mistakes in lighting design are (1) lack of understanding in the industry standards, (2) inadequate vertical illuminating, and (3) poor lighting uniformity.

Typical Concepts and Strategies

Traditionally, access control and surveillance, as design concepts, have emphasized mechanical or crime prevention techniques and overlooked or minimized attitudes, motivation, and use of the physical environment. More recent approaches to the physical design of environments have shifted the emphasis to natural crime prevention techniques by using natural opportunities for crime prevention. This shift in emphasis led to the concept of territoriality.[4]

Parking Structures

Studies show that in both urban and suburban environments, parking structures are problematic.[5] These structures isolate people. Many structures are not only badly designed, with many blind spots and hiding areas, but badly maintained as well.

[3] https://www.ies.org/standards/
[4] International CPTED Association. *CPTED Perspective* vol. 12, January/September, 2015; L.J. Fennelly and M.A. Perry, CPTED, *NIJ* April 1996, p. 10, updated October 2016. http://journals.sagepub.com/doi/abs/10.1177/0885412215595440
[5] General Guidelines for Designing Safer Communities. City of Virginia Beach. January 2000. https://www.vbgov.com/government/departments/planning/areaplans/Documents/Citywide/Cpted.pdf

Crime prevention through environmental design (CPTED) strategies can improve parking lot and parking structure safety without tremendous costs. For example, with the simple addition of high-intensity lighting, a parking lot or parking garage not only can become a much safer area, but people using the facilities will "feel" much safer also.

Parking Lot and Parking Garage Safety Tips

Parking areas can be potentially dangerous during nighttime hours as they many times afford cover for criminals who understand the vulnerability of individuals returning to their cars. For this reason, it is important to park as near as possible to the parking lot attendant's office, if one exists. If there is no attendant on duty, it is critical that you surveil the parking lot area as much as possible upon entry using your headlights. If you observe any suspicious activities or persons in the area, exit the lot immediately.

- When returning to your vehicle, always look in and around your car before getting in.
- Always try to park in well-lighted areas with good visibility.
- Never leave valuables visible in the car. Leave them in the trunk, if necessary.
- Personal items have your personal information on them, so avoid leaving mail, checkbooks, or your day timer in the car, which would show your gender, marital status, and address.
- Avoid bumper stickers that reveal personal information.
- Trust your instincts. If you feel uncomfortable walking to your car alone for any reason, ask security personnel or another person to walk with you.
- Find the panic button on your car's remote device and learn to use it.
- No property is worth risking your life for, so if a thief approaches, cooperate to avoid injury.
- Upon returning to your vehicle, it is important that you have your keys in your hand versus looking for them in your pockets, jacket, or purse. Such fumbling for keys, no matter how short in time, leaves you unnecessarily vulnerable to attack.
- If your vehicle is equipped with an alarm system, do not deactivate it until you are within a few feet of it. The noise (and blinking lights) triggered by a car alarm system being deactivated can alert criminals to the fact that a potential victim is in the immediate vicinity. Wait until the last minute to deactivate the alarm, get in the vehicle, lock the door, and exit the area immediately.
- Only press the "unlock" button on your keyless entry one time, so only the driver's door unlocks. (If you press it more than once, all of the doors in the vehicle will unlock, and someone may use an unlocked door to get in the vehicle with you.)

Chapter 18

The Grove Parking Garage: A Los Angeles Example

When the company, Caruso Affiliated, was designing The Grove, an innovative shopping district near Los Angeles' old Farmers Market, they decided they wanted the "best parking garage in Los Angeles."[1] They recognized the need for extensive redesign of their existing plans, and turned to crime prevention through environmental design (CPTED) to solve the traditional problems with garage design and construction. As a result, the garage turned out to be an exemplary design employing many CPTED and conscientious operational components:

- Limited access points for pedestrians and cars
- Bright walls and ceilings, and colorful décor
- Exemplary lighting with metal halite luminaries
- Raised ceiling heights
- Very large and furnished elevator lobbies on each floor
- Moderate but well-distributed camera systems and call boxes
- Very long and wide open sight lines
- Traffic-oriented entries and exits
- Open stairways
- Regular security patrols

---

[1] International CPTED Association. *CPTED Perspective* 12(1), January/September 2015.

Some municipalities do have some limited design strategies, such as video surveillance, lighting, or security patrols, and the National Institute of Building Sciences posts a few examples as well. There are CPTED books that promote good parking lot design, but CPTED practitioners must ensure these practices are actually implemented. As cities construct more covered parking in the twenty-first century, CPTED must play a significant role in assuring safety and security in these potentially vulnerable spaces.

Chapter 19

CPTED in Tacoma, Washington

Crime prevention through environmental design (CPTED) can help reduce the chance of criminal activity and can provide guidelines for property owners that will lower or prevent environmental factors from creating an opportunity for crime.[1]

To reduce opportunities for crime, ensure your property has the following:

- Secure fencing/barriers
- Securely locked entry points for pedestrians and vehicles
- Good visibility around entire perimeter of your property
- Buildings, sheds, and trailers that are locked
- Entrances clear of shrubberies and items that reduce visibility
- Clean structures—with no graffiti
- Bins, dumpsters, crates, or other items moved away from the building
- Sufficient and working lighting to eliminate shadows and increase visibility
- Surveillance cameras functional with clear view
- Visible signage—no parking, no trespassing, surveillance, hours of operation (commercial properties)
- Commercial buildings coated with antigraffiti sealer
- Commercial windows clean and uncovered

---

[1] CPTED, City of Tacoma, Washington, 2013. http://www.cityoftacoma.org/cms/One.aspx?pageId=94670 retrieved July 12, 2017.

Chapter 20

CPTED Elements

The maintenance and activity support aspects of crime prevention through environmental design (CPTED) are often treated separately because they are not physical design elements within the built environment.[1]

Maintenance

Maintenance is an expression of the ownership of property. Deterioration indicates less control by the intended users of a site and a greater tolerance of disorder. The broken windows theory describes the importance of maintenance to deter crime and supports a zero tolerance approach to property maintenance, observing that the presence of a single broken window will entice vandals to break more windows in the vicinity. The sooner broken windows are fixed, the less likely it is that such vandalism will occur in the future.

Activity Support

Activity support increases the use of a built environment for safe activities with the intent of increasing the risk of detection of criminal and undesirable activities. Natural surveillance by the intended users is casual, and there is no specific plan for people to watch out for criminal activity.

---

[1] CPTED: Wikis. Retrieved on July 12, 2017, from: http://www.thefullwiki.org/CPTED

There are four primary obstacles to the adoption of CPTED:

■ First is a lack of knowledge of CPTED by environmental designers, land managers, and individual community members. For this reason, allocating substantial resources to community educational programs is often required.
■ The second major obstacle is resistance to change. Many specifically resist the type of cooperative planning that is required to use CPTED. Beyond that, skeptics reject the research and historic precedents that support the validity of CPTED concepts.
■ The third obstacle is the perception that CPTED claims to be a panacea for crime that will be used to displace other more traditional approaches rather than a small, but important, complementary tool in deterring offender behavior.
■ The fourth obstacle is that many existing built areas were not designed with CPTED in mind, and modification would be expensive, be politically difficult, or require significant changes in some areas of the existing built environment.

Chapter 21

Controlling Physical Deterioration and Disorder

Physical deterioration, wear and tear, and large-scale accumulations of graffiti and trash routinely occur in many older, urban neighborhoods.[1] If people or public agencies do not do anything for a significant period about such deterioration or accumulations, residents and businesses owners will feel increasingly vulnerable.

Feeling more concerned for their personal safety, residents and business owners will participate less in the maintenance of order in public places. They are less likely to stop teens or adults who are "messing around," "being rowdy," or "hassling people."

Sensing fewer "eyes on the street" (Jacobs, 1961, 1968),[2] delinquent preteens and teens in the neighborhood become emboldened and harass or vandalize more frequently. Increasingly convinced they can get away with it, delinquents commit more minor crimes, and youths become increasingly disorderly.

Residents, sensing that some local youths are becoming increasingly troublesome, withdraw further from the public spaces in the neighborhood and become more concerned about protecting their own safety and personal property.

At this point, potential offenders from outside the neighborhood sense the area is vulnerable. They are drawn into the neighborhood because crimes committed

---

[1] National Institute of Justice. *Research Report: Physical Environment and Crime.* May 1996. https://www.ncjrs.gov/pdffiles/physenv.pdf

[2] J. Jacobs. 1961. *The Death and Life of the American City.* New York, NY: Vintage; J. Jacobs. 1968. Community on the city streets. In E.D. Baltzell (Ed.), *The Search for Community in Modern America* (pp. 74–93). New York, NY: Harper and Row.

there are less likely to be detected and responded to, so the neighborhood crime rate increases dramatically.

Following are six points of the broken window theory:

1. Increase in unrepaired physical deterioration.
2. Increased concern for personal safety among residents and proprietors.
3. Decreased participation in maintaining order on the street.
4. Increased delinquency, rowdiness, vandalism, and disorderly behavior among locals.
5. Further increase in deterioration and further withdrawal from the streets by residents and other locals.
6. Potential offenders from outside the neighborhood, attracted by vulnerability, move into the area.

Crime prevention through environmental design (CPTED) and the broken window theory[3] suggests that one "broken window" or nuisance, if allowed to exist, will lead to others and ultimately to the decline of an entire neighborhood. Neglected and poorly maintained properties are breeding grounds for criminal activity. It is important to develop a formal CPTED-based maintenance plan to help preserve the property value and make it a safer place.

[3] Retrieved on July 13, 2017, from: http://cptedsecurity.com/cpted_design_guidelines.htm

Chapter 22

Digital Intelligence

To fully understand "digital intelligence," we discuss how it is utilized in law enforcement, the security industry, and also the business industry.

From a law enforcement or security viewpoint, digital intelligence involves computer forensics that are used to analyze technical evidence for a variety of cases that may involve technology, including homicide, narcotics, gambling, theft, pedophilia, child pornography, embezzlement, destruction of data, and medical assistance fraud. International, federal, state, and local law enforcement officers and other experts can be trained in the basics of seizure, investigation, analysis, and prosecution of high-technology crimes.[1] It is critical that law enforcement officers in the field and their support personnel have digital forensic knowledge and forensic software proficiency that can be used in the investigation of crimes involving computers, smartphones, and other technology.

The mission of the CERT Software Engineering Institute at Carnegie Mellon University[2] is to conduct research and develop technologies, capabilities, and practices that can be used to facilitate forensics investigations. Current tools and processes are inadequate for responding to increasingly sophisticated attackers and cybercrimes. The Digital Intelligence and Investigation Directorate (DIID) is addressing that problem by conducting research and developing technologies and capabilities that organizations can use to develop incident response capabilities and facilitate forensics investigations. DIID team members also develop advanced tools and techniques to address gaps that are not covered by existing resources. Their research includes leveraging social media to discover malicious activity, protecting

---

[1] Digital Intelligence. Computer Forensics Training. Retrieved on January 24, 2017, from: http://www.digitalintelligence.com/forensictraining.php

[2] CERT Software Engineering Institute. Retrieved on January 24, 2017, from: https://www.cert.org/digital-intelligence/

mobile devices from unknown malware attacks, and improving automated text extraction and video exploitation. Basically, tools are developed to help members of the law enforcement community solve crimes where technology is used in the commission of an offense.[3]

In the business community, Forrester Research is one of the leading research and advisory firms in the world. Forrester works with businesses and technology leaders to develop customer strategies that drive growth. Digital intelligence is a framework with analysis techniques to help support decision-making in the digital environment. Digital intelligence is the next natural evolutionary stage in web analytics. Forrester calls this updated approach to marketing analytics "digital intelligence," which is defined as follows:

> The capture, management, and analysis of data to provide a holistic view of the digital customer experience that drives the measurement, optimization, and execution of marketing tactics and business strategies.[4]

Forrester Research analyzes digital data to help businesses be successful in a customer-driven market so they can respond quickly to changes and stay competitive in the market.

---

[3] Ibid.
[4] J. Stanhope. Welcome to the Era of Digital Intelligence. Retrieved on January 24, 2017, from: https://go.forrester.com/blogs/12-02-17-welcome_to_the_era_of_digital_intelligence/

Chapter 23

Digital Signage

Quite simply, digital signage is a different form of visual communication using signage. Digital signage is considered "place-based media" that relays pertinent information at the right time, in the right place, and to the right audience. Digital signage displays are used to deliver content with a targeted message.[1]

Digital signs rely on one or more display screens, one or more media players, and a content management server. Stand-alone digital sign devices combine all three functions in one device, and no network connection is needed.[2]

Digital sign displays may be LCD or plasma screens, LED boards, projection screens, or other emerging display types like interactive surfaces or organic LED screens (OLEDs). An array of these displays is known as a video wall.[3]

Organizations can create, deploy, and manage multiple visual communications applications on thousands of screens using a single enterprise software solution with live data integrations, powerful wayfinding solutions, and dynamic scheduling.[4]

[1] HIS Markit. Digital Signage Industry Market Tracker. Retrieved on January 26, 2017, from: https://technology.ihs.com/593762/digital-signage-industry-market-tracker-q2-2017

[2] Digital Signage. https://en.wikipedia.org/wiki/Digital_signage

[3] D. Nystedt. Wall Street Beat: Time to Put Off Buying LCD TVs and Displays. *The New York Times.* Retrieved on January 26, 2017, from: http://www.nytimes.com/idg/IDG_852573C40 069388048257498001FBEC6.html?partner=rssnyt&emc=rss

[4] POPAI. Digital Signage Device RS-232 Control Standard. Retrieved on January 27, 2017, from: https://web.archive.org/web/20110221085001/http://popai.com/docs/DS/POPAI%20 Digital%20Signage%20Device%20RS-232%20Standard-Rev%201-1.pdf; Four Winds Interactive. http://www2.fourwindsinteractive.com/generic-landing

The following digital signage terms were created by the members of the POPAI Digital Signage Standards Committee to establish an industry-accepted set of terms for communicating and describing the digital signage industry.[5]

Digital signage is a network of digital displays that are centrally managed and addressable for targeted information, entertainment, merchandising, and advertising. It is not television or broadcasting; this type of message board has become a great awareness tool in crime prevention.

A *content distribution server* is a computer, server, or device that stores the contents that are distributed to the player.

An *A/V distribution system* refers to the distribution of multimedia content from the player to the display device.

Display devices can be CRT, flat-panel LCD, plasma, projector, or other device that is the endpoint of a digital signage system.

A *player* is used for distribution of A/V content to display.

A *multichannel player* is a digital signage player that is capable of outputting multiple streams of unique content to multiple display devices.

Content broadly describes the media, clips, text, video, and audio that is delivered to display devices by a digital signage system.

The *playlog* is a record of information created from the digital signage system that reflects the content played, the system performance, and other data.

The *playlist* is composed of a list of clips and their play order by time or other heuristics.

The *channel* is a script that has been published in such a way that when its contents change, the updated material is forwarded to machines running the viewer that has subscribed to the channel.

Digital signs can be used for many different purposes, and there is no definitive list. Following are some of the most common applications of digital signage[6]:

1. *Public information*—news, weather, traffic, and local (location-specific) information, such as building directory with map, fire exits, and traveler information (Photos 23.1 and 23.2).

   AMBER Alerts are broadcast as public information on digital signs throughout the United States. The AMBER Alert Program, a voluntary partnership between law enforcement agencies, broadcasters, transportation agencies, and the wireless industry, is used to activate urgent information in the most serious child-abduction cases. The goal of the AMBER Alert

---

[5] POPAI. Digital Signage Group Standard Terminology. Retrieved on January 26, 2017, from: https://web.archive.org/web/20110221084749/http://popai.com/docs/DS/POPAI%20 DigSignage%20Standard%20TermsRev%201_0.pdf; https://www.digitalsignagetoday.com/ news/popai-digital-signage-standards-group-expands/

[6] Digital Signage. Retrieved on January 26, 2017, from: https://en.wikipedia.org/wiki/ Digital_signage

Photo 23.1 Informational digital signage for motorists. (Photo taken by Marianna Perry.)

Photo 23.2 Digital signage for a change in traffic patterns. (Photo taken by Marianna Perry.)

Program is to instantly involve the community to assist in the search for and the safe recovery of the child.[7]

2. *Internal information*—corporate messages, such as health and safety items, news, and so forth.

---

[7] U.S. Department of Justice. AMBER Alert. Retrieved on June 2, 2017, from: https://www.amberalert.gov/

3. *Product information*—pricing, photos, raw materials or ingredients, suggested applications, and other product information—especially useful in food marketing where signage may include nutritional facts.
4. *Advertising and promotion*—promoting products or services, may be related to the location of the sign or using the screen's audience reach for general advertising.
5. *Brand building*—in retail stores, a digital sign may be used to promote the brand and build a brand identity.
6. *Influencing customer behavior*—directing customers to different areas, increasing the "dwell time" in different areas to influence behavior.
7. *Influencing product or brand decision-making*—signage at the point of sale designed to influence choice.
8. *Enhancing customer experience*—applications include the reduction of perceived wait time in the waiting areas of restaurants and other retail operations, bank queues, and similar circumstances.
9. *Navigation*—with interactive screens (in the floor, e.g., as with "informational footsteps" found in some tourist attractions, museums, and the like) or with other means of "dynamic wayfinding."

Wayfinding is an element of territorial reinforcement when utilizing crime prevention through environmental design (CPTED) measures. Territorial reinforcement may be physical or symbolic. "Color, texture, surface variations, signage and wayfinding systems are all a part of territoriality and boundary setting."[8]

For additional information on digital signage, visit: https://web.archive.org/web/20110312031101/http://popai.com/about-us//

Navigo Active Signage Systems can provide the following[9]:

■ Customized, multimedia messaging to display important information regarding the facility, services, employees, general information, donors, and so on.
■ Scrolling text or ticker information in real time.
■ All information can be posted in multiple languages and dialects.
■ Instantly update your system as advertisements are renewed, departments move, important announcements are released, new areas are constructed, events change, and so on.

Navigo can offer a variety of capabilities to effectively communicate to target audiences[10]:

---

[8] M.E. Knoke. 2015. Physical Security Principles. Alexandria, VA: ASIS International.
[9] Navigo Touchscreen Systems. Retrieved on January 24, 2017, from: http://www.itouchinc.com/navigo-active-signage-system/
[10] Ibid.

Photo 23.3 Surface change in texture for a pedestrian crosswalk.

- Directory listings
- Cable TV broadcasts
- Current events

Low fencing or bushes, gates, signage, different pavement textures, or other landscape design features show the CPTED principle of territoriality by visually defining a transition between areas that are used for different purposes.

Different types of digital signage can be used for an effective means of communication as part of a wayfinding system (Photos 23.3 and 23.4).

Photo 23.4 Traditional directional signage for vehicles.

Chapter 24

Addressing Crime and Other Problems Using the SARA Process and CPTED Strategies

The problem-solving process used in crime prevention through environmental design (CPTED) is a series of steps designed to answer four questions:

1. What is the problem?
2. Why here?
3. What can be done to solve the problem?
4. How well are we doing?

Each question represents a phase in the SARA process: scanning, analysis, response, and assessment.[1] SARA serves as a framework for action; while SARA is a good place to start, the process may need to be modified and adapted to the specific location and circumstances. The actual process depends on a variety of factors. In the case of a specific crime problem in a single location, the process need not include time to define or refine the problem. Analysis focuses on a single type of crime and, because crime data are already available for the problem site, the analysis can begin immediately.

---

[1] Center for Problem-Oriented Policing. Responding to Crime and Other Problems Using CPTED. http://www.popcenter.org/tools/cpted/2; D. Zahm. 2007. *Using Crime Prevention through Environmental Design in Problem-Solving. Problem-Oriented Guides for Police Problem-Solving Tools Series. Guide No. 8.* Washington, DC: U.S. Department of Justice, Office of Community Oriented Policing Services.

For more information, see the description of the SARA process at: http://www.popcenter.org/about/?p=sara

Additional time is required as issues become more complex and impact larger geographic areas and greater numbers of stakeholders. In such instances, it takes time to organize a problem-solving team and to collect data. It is also more difficult to find a solution that both addresses the problem and satisfies all stakeholders.

One of the key constraints may be the cost of implementation. Although many CPTED strategies are relatively cost-free and easy to accomplish in a short time frame (e.g., changes to policies), other projects may require significant investments of capital and phased implementation over several years.

A general description of the four SARA phases and the steps that might be included as part of a CPTED problem-solving process are outlined in Table 24.1. Each phase addresses one or more aspects of the environment that are critical for employing CPTED strategies to solve the problem.

In *A Manual for Crime Prevention through Planning and Design* (Kruger, Landman and Liebermann, 2001) suggest a plan based on

1. Urgency or need
2. The likelihood for success
3. The potential for positive impacts in other areas
4. Cost
5. Resource availability

Defining and Understanding the Problem

One unique aspect of using CPTED for problem-solving is the array of data and information that must be gathered and analyzed.

While crime, fear, and victimization are critical considerations, an environmental evaluation needs to include information that is neither law enforcement based nor crime related, for example, land use and zoning, housing code or health code violations, or traffic volumes and pedestrian activity.

Quality-of-life issues such as trash and litter, weeds, vacant lots, and declining property values are also considered, as these problems often have a more debilitating impact on a community on a day-to-day basis. They can also be symptoms of, or precursors to, crime.

The purpose of the environmental evaluation is twofold[2]:

1. It is required in order to precisely define the problem.
2. Data analysis results in a better understanding of the building, site, or neighborhood context—the environmental conditions in which the problem is situated.

---

[2] http://www.popcenter.org/tools/cpted/2

Table 24.1   Problem-Solving with Crime Prevention through Environmental Design

The SARA Process
Scanning
1. Identify, define, and investigate an existing or emerging problem. 2. Identify the stakeholders who should be engaged in problem-solving. 3. Decide on the combination of meetings and activities that will be necessary for problem-solving, and create a schedule for working through the process. 4. Meet with stakeholders to clarify the problem and to define the goals and objectives for the process.
Analysis
1. Collect and analyze data and information about the problem. 2. Evaluate any connections or relationships between the problem(s) and environmental conditions. 3. Establish the goals to be achieved through the implementation of crime prevention through environmental design or other strategies. 4. Identify alternative strategies for achieving the implementation goals. 5. Evaluate the social, political, legal, financial, or technological feasibility of implementing each strategy. 6. Select the most promising strategies, and create and adopt a plan for improvement that identifies specific strategies, defines financial and other resource requirements, assigns responsibility for implementation and oversight, outlines a schedule for plan implementation, and establishes indicators of success.
Response
1. Put the most promising and feasible measure(s) into place. A combination of immediate responses, short-term improvements, and long-term investment may be required. 2. Monitor progress relative to the indicators of success specified in step 10.
Assessment
1. Decide if the process needs to be repeated due to lack of progress or the emergence of new problems.

The intricacy of the analysis ultimately depends on three conditions, which are described in greater detail as follows:

▪ *First, data and information requirements will be determined by the circumstances surrounding, and the setting of, an existing or emerging crime problem.*

Various types of information may become part of an environmental evaluation. Some data and information are available from existing sources and agency records;

however, significant and necessary pieces of information can sometimes only be obtained through interviews, surveys, and observations. Safety audits and security surveys need to be specifically tailored to the facility, the site, or the neighborhood, and in most cases, must be handled by someone who is knowledgeable about locks, lighting, or other aspects of security. The overall goal is to inventory existing conditions and document emerging trends related to a specific problem in a specific location—to answer the question, *why here?* Four types of scenarios are possible, and each suggests a different kind of data collection strategy:

1. A specific crime or other problem is occurring at a single location (e.g., school vandalism, graffiti, and ATM robbery cases), or a crime problem is occurring at a specific type of facility (e.g., robbery at several convenience stores).
2. A specific crime or other problem is limited to a defined geographic area.
3. A general crime problem or an array of problems is experienced by residents and businesses in a particular geographic area.
4. The potential for future problems emerges as an outcome of proposed development or facility redesign.

■ *Second, the amount of data that can be collected and analyzed is a function of the amount of time allotted for the analysis.*

Data collection and analysis can be a time-consuming process, and adequate time is not always available. In some instances, public or other pressures for an immediate response to the problem will strip away any opportunity for analysis. In such cases, evaluation becomes even more critical, to understand the impact of the intervention and to give greater definition to the original problem or any other issues that emerge as a result of the decision to intervene.

■ *Third, support resources like staff and funding must be available for the analysis.*

Crime prevention through environmental design is best undertaken by a team of departments and individuals in collaboration with community representatives. Experience has shown that CPTED strategies are most effective when those who are impacted by the problem are engaged in problem-solving and take ownership for the solution. The entire problem-solving process is enhanced when stakeholders are included early on, for example, by organizing a CPTED task force or by using community volunteers to help with data collection.

Chapter 25

Using CPTED for Problem-Solving at a Building or Facility

The following outlines a process for completing an environmental evaluation when the problem is limited to a single building or facility.[1] The process is divided into three phases related to a site visit and period of observation.

Activities before the site visit are focused on understanding the problem and the situation. This includes an examination of crime data, plans and policies, and organizational structures, all of which lead to the identification of key stakeholders who need to provide information and advice.

The site visit includes an orientation period, with a "tabletop" exercise, using a floor plan and site plan to review the structure of the facility and to identify the problem location or locations as well as safe and unsafe places. Facility tours are conducted with stakeholders, and then the crime prevention through environmental design (CPTED) evaluator observes behavior and use independently for several days, at various times of the day, and on several days during a week to address changing activity schedules.

The process concludes with the development of recommendations and a report documenting the site visit and the findings.

---

[1] Center for Problem-Oriented Policing. Using CPTED for Problem Solving at a Building or Facility. http://www.popcenter.org/tools/cpted/6; D. Zahm. 2007. *Using Crime Prevention through Environmental Design in Problem-Solving. Problem-Oriented Guides for Police Problem-Solving Tools Series. Guide No. 8*. Washington, DC: U.S. Department of Justice, Office of Community Oriented Policing Services.

Although the process as it is outlined here implies the work can be completed by a single person, most buildings and facilities are large enough to warrant a team approach.

Crime Prevention through Environmental Design Facility SARA Process	
Before the Site Visit	*Request and Review Information* • Administrative organization (to identify appropriate contacts) • Relevant statutes, ordinances, codes, policies, and procedures • Site and facility background (maps, plans, manuals, design/development review and approval processes, maintenance procedures, etc.) • Police/security calls for service and crime data
	Develop an Evaluation Strategy and Schedule Appointments with Owner/Manager Orientation to CPTED and the Evaluation Process Evaluator Orientation
During the Site Visit	• Overview of the organization • "Tabletop" exercise of location, site, and facility (assignment of spaces, activities and schedules, etc.), noting problem areas
	Constituent/Stakeholder Meetings and Facility Tours Independent Facility Examination (without stakeholders) • Morning, afternoon, evening, and night • Multiple weekday and weekend visits
	[*Break*—to organize materials, analyze data, identify information needs, document the process, and reflect on observations, if needed]
	[*Return Visit*—to fill gaps in data and information, to reconsider the findings from an earlier visit, to evaluate the facility during an alternate schedule, etc., if needed]
	Client Debrief

Following the Site Visit	Review Data and Other Materials (photographs, floor plans, notes) Develop Recommendations
	• Changes to physical design and layout
	• Modifications to laws, rules, regulations, policies, and procedures
	• Target hardening/security enhancements
	• Community and social programs and activities
	• Crime prevention education and awareness
	Draft the Report
	• Introduction to the problem and report overview
	• Description of methods (data collection and analysis, survey and interview protocols, site and facility evaluation activities, dates and times)
	• Discussion of issues and findings
	• Recommendations for future action (including additional or follow-up evaluation)
	• Supporting documentation in appendixes
	• Disclaimer**
	Submit Draft Report for Review and Comment (specifically, for factual accuracy) *Redraft, Re-Review, and Rewrite Present and Deliver Final Report*

** *Example Disclaimer:* The recommendations outlined in this report are based on research and experience that suggest certain design and policy approaches can be adopted to reduce opportunities for crime. It is not possible to guarantee that actual crime will be reduced or eliminated if these recommendations are implemented.

Chapter 26

Crime and the Fear of Crime Are Endemic Concerns in Contemporary Urbanized Societies

Crime prevention through environmental design (CPTED) is a branch of spatial practices that looks at interventions focused on place-based strategies for reducing crime, and the enhancement of spatial cognition as it relates to the perception of safety and security. The underlying premise of CPTED is that for any crime, there are four dimensions to be considered: the law, the offender, the target, and the location.[1] Place-based strategies for reducing crime and the fear of crime focus on the site of crime as it relates to the spatial aspects of the target and the location that facilitates the criminal activity, and how both of these factors generate fear in the general populace, discouraging those who perceive themselves as the potential targets of a crime.[2] Location is an important dimension of crime because crime is

---

[1] P.J. Brantingham and P.L. Brantingham. 1981. *Environmental Criminology*. Beverly Hills, CA: Sage Publications.

[2] A. Erdoan. 2010. What do place-based crime prevention strategies mean for the Turkish planning system and urban transformation? *Journal of Geography and Regional Planning* 3(11): 271–296. http://citeseerx.ist.psu.edu/viewdoc/download?doi=10.1.1.822.7436&rep=rep1&type=pdf

not randomly distributed in contemporary urbanized areas: there are particular zones in every city that are identified both by the public and the administration as "hot spots" of crime, and therefore unsafe.[3] If a phenomenon has such a prominent locational specificity, it is just common sense to assume that spatial design has a direct influence on either its enhancement or reduction, and that "the proper design and effective use of the built environment can lead to a reduction in the fear and incidence of crime, and an improvement in the quality of life."[4] Such an assumption has led to numerous studies on the subject since the mid-twentieth century.[5]

In its first generation, CPTED includes individual components such as territoriality, surveillance, image/maintenance, access control, activity program support, and target hardening.[6] Territoriality, access control, program support, and target hardening look at techniques of clearly defining boundaries and the preferred use of a given space. Surveillance, whether naturally, mechanically, or digitally administered, makes the offenders visible to others, which implies to the potential offender that he or she is more at risk of observation and apprehension. Natural surveillance is a result of clear lines of sight and public intervisibility, as well as an optimal relationship between the number of users of a space, its size, and the proper density of a given zone within an urban area. This means that isolated urban zones that are less populated are more prone to criminal activity, and such areas are more

---

[3] For more information, please see: A.M. Guerry. 1833. *Essai Sur la Statistique Morale de la France avec Cartes*, Paris: Crouchard; J.E. Eck, S. Chainey, J.G. Cameron, M. Leitner, and R.E. Wilson. August 2005. *Mapping Crime: Understanding Hot Spots*. National Institute of Justice Special Report. Washington, DC: U.S. Department of Justice. https://www.ncjrs. gov/pdffiles1/nij/209393.pdf; J. Fletcher. 1849. Moral statistics of England and Wales. *Journal of Royal Statistical Society of London* 12(3): 151–181; H. Mayhew. 1862. *London Labour and the Condition of the London Poor*. Bohn: Griffin; J.L. Nasar and B. Fisher. 1993. 'Hot spots' of fear and crime: A multi-method investigation. *Journal of Environmental Psychology* 13(2): 187–206; D. Lupton. 1999. Dangerous places and the unpredictable stranger: Constructions of fear of crime. *Australian and New Zealand Journal of Criminology* 32(1): 1–15.

[4] T. Crowe. 2000. *Crime Prevention through Environmental Design: Applications of Architectural Design and Space Management Concepts*. Oxford: Butterworth-Heinemann, p. 46.

[5] For more information, please see: K. Lynch. 1960. *The Image of the City*. Cambridge, MA: MIT Press; J. Jacobs. 1961. *The Death and Life of Great American Cities*. New York, NY: Vintage Books; L. Segato. 2009. Urban spaces—Enhancing the attractiveness and quality of the urban environment. WP3 Joint Strategy, Activity 3.2 Criteria and Principles, Sub-activity 3.2.4 Security and Social Cohesion criteria. http://www.central2013.eu/fileadmin/user_upload/ Downloads/outputlib/Urbspace_3.2.4_Security_and_social_aspects_PR2.pdf

[6] For more information, please see: O. Newman. 1973. *Defensible Space People and Design in the Violent City*. London: Architectural Press; R. Moffat. 1983. Crime prevention through environmental design—A management perspective. *Canadian Journal of Criminology* 25(4): 19–31.

feared by those who perceive themselves as potential targets of criminal activity.[7] Examples of mechanical surveillance are street lighting and video surveillance. An example of digitally administered surveillance is the grassroots reporting/streaming of criminal activity by citizens with handheld devices equipped with capturing and connectivity behavior, demographic profiling, and active community participation. These are added to the pallet of tools that can be utilized by designers.[8] If first-generation CPTED is focused on location, second-generation CPTED is more concerned with situation—that is, the multifaceted context of crime and fear that encompasses the locational, the social, the cultural, and the political subtexts of the reality and the perception of crime in an urban context. For example, in terms of surveillance, second-generation CPTED is focused on techniques that engender positive social activities and diversity to encourage the public to take ownership of their space and take advantage of natural surveillance, as opposed to a mere insistence on intensifying the mechanically administered methods of surveillance. Second-generation CPTED is designed to support social interaction and promote "eyes on the street" activity, relying on a triad of community culture, cohesion, and connectivity.[9]

The second generation of CPTED recognized that the most important measure is creating sustainable communities by looking at all issues in a holistic way, and especially through engaging the local people. To this effect, the initial task is to create and enhance a sense of belonging to a greater community, where a useful definition of *community* as a concept and a framework for intervention through design can be: "The web of personal relationships, groups, networks, traditions and patterns of behavior that exist amongst those who share physical neighborhoods, socio-economic conditions of common understanding and interests." This web can include extended families, networks of neighbors, community groups, religious organizations, local businesses and public services, youth clubs, parent/teacher associations, playgroups, elderly people's groups, and many more. The driving force beyond second-generation CPTED is the fact that these webs coming together in the interest of the community as a whole is vital to its sustainability. To this

[7] K. Painter and N. Tilley. 1999. *Surveillance of Public Space: CCTV, Street Lighting and Crime Prevention*, Monsey, NY: Criminal Justice Press. On relation of proper level of street activity and density and its preventive impact on crime and image of crime, more information can be found in A. Loukaitou-Sideris. 1999. Hot spots of bus stop crime: The importance of environmental attributes. *Journal of the American Planning Association* 65(4): 395–412. http://www.tandfonline.com/doi/abs/10.1080/01944369908976070

[8] For more information, see: J.L. Nasar and B. Fisher. 1993. 'Hot spots' of fear and crime: A multi-method investigation. *Journal of Environmental Psychology* 13(2): 187–206; R.B. Taylor and A.V. Harrell. 1996. *Physical Environment and Crime*. Washington, DC: National Institute of Justice, U.S. Department of Justice, p. 9. https://www.ncjrs.gov/pdffiles/physenv.pdf

[9] T. Crowe. 2000. *Crime Prevention through Environmental Design: Applications of Architectural Design and Space Management Concepts*. Oxford: Butterworth-Heinemann, p. 37; D. Perkins and R. Taylor. 1996. Ecological assessments of community disorder: Their relationship to fear of crime and theoretical implications. *American Journal of Community Psychology* 24(1): 63–107.

effect, second-generation CPTED supports institutions such as community forums, neighborhood management committees, and Development Trusts as venues for facilitating a civilized life and enjoying the benefits of being a part of a lively society.

In 1987, the UN World Commission under G. Harlem Brundtland created the Environmental and Development Report, which provided the guideline for the second generation of CPTED to take full advantage of what it defined as resources: social resources (people), economic resources (making best use of them), technological resources (ensuring sustainable development), environmental resources (making the best use of natural resources), and ecological resources (protecting and making the best of habitats, species, and ecosystems).

By utilizing these resources, second-generation CPTED focused on creating "balanced, mixed-use, walk-able neighborhoods."

Furthermore, proper maintenance of a space signifies a sense of ownership that is influential in reducing the fear of crime. Through proper spatial design, physical features of the environment can be arranged to offer a high probability of refuge and escape for the potential target of the crime, and a low probability of refuge and escape for the potential offender, reducing both risk and fear of crime.[10] The first generation of CPTED focuses on reinforcing positive behavior within the physical space through the use of physical attributes to separate public, public-private, and private space. These strategies define ownership and acceptable patterns of usage, in addition to promoting opportunities for surveillance that facilitate institutional control, and promote legitimate users' informal social control.[11]

First-generation CPTED insists on the principle of eliminating any unassigned spaces, ensuring that all spaces have a clearly defined and designated purpose, and are routinely cared for and monitored.[12] For example, improved lighting in public, open spaces has been categorized as being an effective intervention that "works."[13] Related to this approach is promoting design strategies that create more pedestrian-friendly

[10] J. Ratcliffe. 2003. *Suburb Boundaries and Residential Burglars*. Trends and Issues in Crime and Criminal Justice No. 246. Canberra: Australian Institute of Criminology. http://www.aic.gov.au/media_library/publications/tandi_pdf/tandi246.pdf; B. Brown. 2001. New homes/old homes: Physical environment and residential psychology predicting crime. *Proceedings of the International CPTED Conference*, September 24–27. Brisbane, Australia, pp. 167–177.

[11] J. Eck. 1997. *Preventing Crime at Places: Why Places Are Important*; L.W. Sherman, D.C. Gottfredson, D.L. MacKenzie, J. Eck, P. Reuter, and S.D. Bushway. July 1998. *Preventing Crime: What Works, What Doesn't, What's Promising*. National Institute of Justice Research in Brief. Washington, DC: U.S. Department of Justice. https://www.ncjrs.gov/pdffiles/171676.PDF

[12] D. Sorensen. The Nature and Prevention of Residential Burglary: A Review of the International Literature with an Eye towards Prevention in Denmark. http://research.ku.dk/search/?pure=en/publications/the-nature-and-prevention-of-residential-burglary-a-review-of-the-international-literature-with-an-eye-toward-prevention-in-denmark(901faf20-74c0-11db-bee9-02004c4f4f50)/export.html

[13] S. Merry. 1981. Defensible space undefended: Social factors in crime prevention through environmental design. *Urban Affairs Quarterly* 16(3): 397–422.

public or semipublic zones within the city. These areas that welcome more public use are less likely to host criminal activities because of the natural surveillance resulting from a significant public presence within a shared space.[14]

Although first-generation CPTED has proven effective in several cases, there are also various shortcomings. First, "irrational" offenders—those intoxicated by drugs and alcohol—are potentially less likely to be deterred by first-generation CPTED strategies. Second, negative socioeconomic and demographic dynamics can reduce the efficacy of CPTED strategies: on one hand, social conditions may nurture fear, reduce the inclination to intervene, and result in an individual withdrawing into the home that is heavily fortified.[15] That is, when CPTED is applied without sufficient community participation and becomes overly reliant on target hardening, mechanical and formal surveillance, access control, and the intensification of a "fortress mentality," the result can be citizens withdrawing behind walls, fences, and fortified homes. On the other hand, first-generation CPTED principles like access control, surveillance, clean lines of sight, and so on, can be used by criminals to create safe zones for their operations.[16] Furthermore, the implementation of crime prevention measures in one area can "displace" existing crime in terms of location, time, tactics, targets, and type of crime, instead of reducing criminal activity or the fear thereof in empirical, absolute terms.[17]

While first-generation CPTED exclusively focuses on space and location to reduce crime, second-generation CPTED extends beyond mere physical design to include social factors by adding risk assessments, socioeconomic factors, and demographics as a new model for urban communities. To this effect, second-generation CPTED offered both social and physical planning as possible tools to create communities that are balanced in terms of age, profile tenure, and so on. The main suggestions for accomplishing this goal were as follows:

1. Do not build concentrations of single-tenure social housing.
2. Bring private ownership into public housing areas.

---

[14] R. Atlas. March 1991. The other side of defensible space. *Security Management* 636 and https://www.ncjrs.gov/App/Publications/abstract.aspx?ID=143812

[15] S. Hakim and G.F. Rengert. 1981. *Crime Spillover*. Beverly Hills, CA: Sage. https://www.ncjrs.gov/App/publications/abstract.aspx?I85381

[16] S. Plaster Carter. 2002. Community CPTED. *Journal of the International Crime Prevention Through Environmental Design Association* 1(1): 15–24; A. Zelinka and D. Brennan. 2001. *Safescape: Creating Safer, More Livable Communities through Planning Design*. Chicago, IL: Planners Press and http://www.unicri.it/news/files/2011-04-01_110414_CRA_Urban_Security_sm.pdf

[17] G. Saville and G. Cleveland. 2003. An introduction to 2nd Generation CPTED: Part 1. *CPTED Perspectives* 6(2): 4–8; G. Saville and G. Cleveland. 2003. An introduction to 2nd Generation CPTED: Part 2. *CPTED Perspectives* 6(1): 7–9; A.L. Dannenberg et al. 2003. The impact of community design and land-use choices on public health: A scientific research agenda. *American Journal of Public Health* 93(9): 1500–1508. https://www.ncbi.nlm.nih.gov/pmc/articles/PMC1448000/

3. Build a substantial proportion of affordable housing and low-energy design in all new developments.
4. Invest at reasonable levels to ensure quality development based on specificities of the site.
5. Recognize the relationship between housing and schools, and the role that schools play in improving educational opportunities for young people and contributing to social desegregation.
6. Recognize the direct relationship between housing conditions and health.
7. Introduce "magnet policies" to attract active people with spending power back to socially isolated areas in poor condition.
8. Develop walk-able streets that are pedestrian friendly and promote sociability, community surveillance, and human interaction.
9. In laying out master plans, provide careful treatment of corners and vistas and landmarks to make the urban space more readable to the occupants.
10. Create mixed-use spaces by incorporating residential, workspace, shops, studios, and performance areas.
11. Provide living space over shops to contribute to 24/7 activity in the city and enhance the perception of safety and security.
12. Provide optimum density in urban areas, and do not leave un-maintained, un-attended, and isolated zones.
13. Focus on energy efficiency, waste minimization, and the optimum use of resources.
14. Foster community and social welfare.
15. Enhance economic prosperity, especially employment and education.
16. Create neighborhoods that are close to shops, public transport, activities, schools, and recreational opportunities.
17. Provide social structures for communities' social-political activism that offer opportunities for citizen participation and social influence on their own environment.
18. Pay attention to the accessibility of space for people with impaired mobility, as well as those who require care and attention.

All of the above are guidelines for creating mixed-use, mixed tenure, walk-able communities, and have great advantages from a crime prevention perspective. It is safe to claim that instead of the vision of segregated, fortified, gated communities that is the subtext of strategies promoted by first-generation CPTED theory and practice, second-generation CPTED is focused on bringing diverse social groups together and providing the social-political and physical backbone for them to coexist in a peaceful manner and conform to accepted behaviors.

The first generation of CPTED was a collection of strategies to discourage crime.

The second generation of CPTED focused on strategies to eliminate the reasons for criminal behavior via sustainable, livable environments.

The third generation of CPTED that is the subject of investigation and contemplation adds another dimension to the discourse, which is that of the synergies among CPTED, urban sustainability, technology, and the potential of networks.[18] The premise of third-generation CPTED is that a sustainable, green urbanity is perceived by its members and the outsiders as safe. Third-generation CPTED's focus on sustainable green environmental design strategies insists on practical measures, physically or cybernetically enhanced, that foster the perception of urban space as safe beyond mere concerns about crime. Furthermore, whereas first- and second-generation CPTED were of a more local nature, third-generation CPTED looks at security as a global issue and tries to provide a manual that can be utilized across geopolitical and social-political divisions.

---

[18] P.M. Cozens. 2002. Sustainable urban development and crime prevention through environmental design for the British City. Towards an effective urban environmentalism for the 21st Century. *Cities: International Journal of Urban Policy and Planning* 19(2): 129–137; A.L. Dannenberg et al. 2003. The impact of community design and land-use choices on public health: A scientific research agenda. *American Journal of Public Health* 93(9): 1500–1508. https://www.ncbi.nlm.nih.gov/pmc/articles/PMC1448000/

Chapter 27

Neighborhood Watch

Neighborhood Watch is one of the most effective crime prevention programs in the United States. It brings citizens and law enforcement together to deter crime and make communities safer. Sponsored by the National Sheriff's Association (NSA), it was developed in response to requests from sheriffs and police chiefs who were looking for a crime prevention program that would involve citizens. Neighborhood Watch, which began in 1972, encourages citizens to organize themselves and be the eyes and ears of their communities and work with law enforcement. Neighborhood Watch is an effective crime prevention program because it reduces opportunities for crime to occur, and it does not rely on changing a criminal's behavior or motivation.[1]

Communication through Neighborhood Watch group members has changed since 1972 because of new methods of communication. Previously, information was shared through newsletters, phone calls, and meetings. Now, Neighborhood Watch has embraced social media. Facebook, Twitter, and Instagram are a few of the modes of electronic communication being used by Neighborhood Watch members because of the importance of community members being notified quickly when there is an issue in their neighborhood.

Nextdoor is the private social network for neighborhoods and is an effective way to know what is going on in your neighborhood, whether an upcoming event or break-ins that are occurring in the area. To stay connected to your neighborhood, The *Nextdoor* app is now available for mobile devices. "It is the best way for you and your neighbors to hear what's happening in your local community. When neighbors start talking, good things happen."[2]

---

[1] Retrieved on June 2, 2017, from: https://www.ncpc.org/resources/home-neighborhood-safety/
neighborhood-watch/

[2] Retrieved on June 2, 2017, from: https://itunes.apple.com/us/app/nextdoor/id640360962?mt=8

Reporting suspicious behavior is an important part of being involved in a Neighborhood Watch Program, so be alert for the following:

- A stranger entering a neighbor's house when the neighbor is not home
- Unusual noises, like a scream, breaking glass, or an explosion
- People, male or female, in your neighborhood who do not live there
- Someone going door-to-door in your neighborhood, if he or she tries to open the doors or goes into the backyard, especially if a companion waits out front or a car follows close behind
- Someone trying to force entry into a home, even if wearing a uniform
- A person running, especially if carrying something of value[3]

Anyone who sees something suspicious should call the police immediately. Give the responding officers a physical description of the person and license plate number of the car. Even if it ends up that nothing is wrong, such alertness is appreciated by law enforcement. Research has shown that the value of citizen participation programs tends to decrease over time unless there are planned activities to keep the program operating effectively and consistently.

1. *Security assessments.* Many police departments have trained crime prevention officers who can provide security survey assistance to residents, enabling citizens to better protect their family, home, and environment. Security professionals are also available to conduct assessments.
2. *Citizen patrols.* Citizen patrols are reported to be increasing in a number of suburban communities and cities across the United States and are seen ideally as performing a relatively simple and narrowly defined role—to deter criminal activity by their presence. Their function should be that of a passive guard—to watch for criminal or suspicious activity and alert the police when they see it. Drawing on information that exists about current citizen groups, the advantages of these patrols over other protective measures include that they
   a. Are relatively inexpensive
   b. Perform a surveillance function effectively
   c. Take advantage of existing behavior patterns
   d. Can improve an individual's ability to deal with crime
   e. Contribute to other desirable social goals related to neighborhood cohesiveness and the provision of a desirable alternative to less acceptable activity

---

[3] L.J. Fennelly. 2012. *Handbook of Loss Prevention and Crime Prevention* (5th ed.). Cambridge, MA: Elsevier; L.J. Fennelly. 2012. *Effective Physical Security* (4th ed.). Cambridge, MA: Elsevier.

In practice, however, citizen patrols exhibit serious shortcomings:

■ The typical citizen patrol is formed in response to a serious incident or heightened level of fear about crime. The ensuing pattern is cyclic: increased membership; success in reducing criminal activity at least in a specific area; boredom; decreasing membership; dissolution. As a result, patrols tend to be short lived.

■ The passive role of a citizen patrol is difficult to maintain without at least a paid, part-time coordinator.

■ The police are reluctant to cooperate with a citizen patrol and may even oppose it.

■ The citizen patrol may aggravate community tensions. The principal problems of patrols relate to their inability to sustain the narrow, anticrime role they initially stress. They may be an effective temporary measure to deal with criminal activity in a particular area, but over the longer term, the inherent risks may outweigh the continued benefits. The increased number of citizen patrols in recent years is evidence that there is a need, but it should be recognized that citizen patrols are no substitute for adequate police protection.

Residential security can best be obtained by getting the facts on what you can do to secure your home, deciding what will work best for you, and then implementing effective security measures.[4]

---

[4] Ibid.

Chapter 28

Managing Risk: CPTED Strategies for Multifamily Structures

Multifamily homes (townhomes, duplexes, triplexes and condos, apartment complexes, and smart homes) pose the same problems as single-family structures, although these problems can be compounded by the number of dwellings and residents.[1] Public areas—shared hallways, elevators, laundry rooms, and parking areas—present a design challenge for crime prevention.

There is a certain amount of truth to the saying "there's safety in numbers." Management may need to create opportunities for neighbors to get to know one another and create Neighborhood Watch programs. When neighbors take responsibility for themselves and each other, it creates a safer environment.

Natural Access Control

- Keep balcony railings and patio enclosures as low as possible using opaque materials.
- When addressing railing heights and construction features, comply with local building codes.

---

[1] Crime Prevention through Environmental Design, General Guidelines for Designing Safer Communities, City of Virginia Beach Municipal Center, January 20, 2000, updated in 2017. https://www.vbgov.com/government/departments/planning/areaplans/Documents/Citywide/Cpted.pdf

- Define entrances to the site and each parking lot with landscaping, architectural design, or symbolic gateways.
- Block off dead-end spaces with fences or gates.
- Discourage loitering by nonresidents; enforce occupancy provisions of leases.
- Use devices that automatically lock upon closing on common building entrances.
- Provide good illumination in hallways.
- Allow no more than four apartments to share the same entrance; individual entrances are recommended.

Natural Surveillance

- Design buildings so that exterior doors are visible from the street or by neighbors.
- Use good lighting at all doors that open to the outside.
- Install windows on all four facades of buildings to allow good surveillance.
- Assign parking spaces to residents. Locate the spaces next to the resident's unit, but mark them with their unit number. This makes unauthorized parking easier to identify and less likely to happen.
- Designate visitor parking.
- Make parking areas visible from windows and doors.
- Adequately illuminate parking areas and pedestrian walkways. Position recreational areas (pools, tennis courts, and clubhouses) to be visible from many of the unit's windows and doors.
- Screen or conceal dumpsters, but avoid creating blind spots and hiding places.
- Build elevators and stairwells in locations that are clearly visible from windows and doors.
- Prevent shrubbery from being no more than 3 feet high for clear visibility in vulnerable areas.
- Site buildings so that the windows and doors of one unit are visible from another (although not directly opposite).
- Locate elevators and stairwells to be open and well lit.
- Place playgrounds where they are clearly visible from units, but not next to parking lots or streets.

Territorial Reinforcement

- Define property lines with landscaping or decorative fencing.
- Use low shrubbery, 3 feet maximum, and fences to allow visibility from the street.

- Accentuate building entrances with architectural elements, lighting, and/or landscaping.
- Clearly identify all buildings and residential units using street numbers that are easily observed from the street. Use Arabic numerals at least 3 inches (76 mm) high with a half inch (13 mm) stroke.
- Where possible, locate individually locked mailboxes next to the appropriate units.

Maintenance/Image

- Maintain all common areas to very high standards, including entrances and right-of-way.
- Prune trees and shrubs back from windows, doors, and walkways.
- Use and maintain exterior lighting.
- Strictly enforce rules regarding junk vehicles and inappropriate outdoor storage.
- Do not allow the site to appear uncared for and less secure.

Chapter 29

Managing Risk: CPTED Strategies for Neighborhoods

Crime prevention through environmental design (CPTED) guidelines can be used in neighborhoods and can help create a safe environment—without the use of intimidating methods such as high fences.[1] For instance, streets designed with gateway treatments, roundabouts, speed humps, and other "traffic calming" devices establish territories and discourage speeding and cut-through traffic. By keeping public areas observable, you are telling potential offenders that they should think twice before committing a crime. Criminals prefer low-risk situations, and public visibility increases the chances a perpetrator will be caught.

These measures are simple, inexpensive to implement, and will have a much more positive effect on residents than high fences and bars on the windows.

Natural Access Control

- Limit access without completely disconnecting the subdivision from adjacent subdivisions.
- Design streets to discourage cut-through or high-speed traffic.

---

[1] Crime Prevention through Environmental Design, General Guidelines for Designing Safer Communities, City of Virginia Beach Municipal Center, January 20, 2000, updated in 2017. https://www.vbgov.com/government/departments/planning/areaplans/Documents/Citywide/Cpted.pdf

■ Install plantings and architectural design features such as a columned gateway to guide visitors to desired entrances and away from private areas.
■ Install walkways in locations safe for pedestrians, and use them to define pedestrian bounds.

Natural Surveillance

■ Avoid landscaping that might create blind spots or hiding places.
■ Locate open green spaces and recreational areas so that they are visible from nearby homes and streets.
■ Use pedestrian-scale street lighting in high pedestrian traffic areas to help people recognize potential threats at night.

Territorial Reinforcement

■ Design lots, streets, and houses to encourage interaction between neighbors.
■ Accentuate entrances with the subdivision name, different paving material, changes in street elevation, and architectural and landscape design.
■ Clearly identify residential buildings using street numbers that are easily observed from the street. Provide Arabic numerals at least 3 inches (76 mm) high with a half inch (13 mm) stroke.
■ Define property lines with post and pillar fencing and gates, and plantings to direct pedestrian traffic to desired points of access only.

Maintenance/Image

■ Maintain all common areas to very high standards, including entrances and right-of-way.
■ Enforce deed restrictions and city codes.

Chapter 30

Managing Risk: Office Buildings and Other Commercial Properties

Office Buildings

As office buildings grow in size and pedestrian and vehicle traffic increases, safety becomes an extremely important issue.[1] Regardless of the size of the structure being built, it can be safe and secure:

- All tenants must show photo identification upon entering.
- Metal grills with letter-sized slits should cover mail slots.
- Garages and loading areas should be secured by steel, anti-ram barricades.

It is important to avoid the adverse images that come with fortress hardware, but recognizable security should be present.

Natural Access Control

- Clearly define public entrances with architectural elements, lighting, landscaping, paving, and signage.
- Reduce the number of public access points to those that are watched by guards, receptionists, nearby tenants, or passing traffic.

---

[1] Crime Prevention through Environmental Design, General Guidelines for Designing Safer Communities, City of Virginia Beach Municipal Center, January 20, 2000, updated in 2017. https://www.vbgov.com/government/departments/planning/areaplans/Documents/Citywide/Cpted.pdf

Natural Surveillance

- Position restrooms to be observed from nearby offices.
- Install and use good lighting at all exterior doors, common areas, and hallways.
- Keep dumpsters visible and avoid creating blind spots or hiding places, or place them in secured, locked areas.
- Design windows and exterior doors so that they are visible from the street or by neighboring buildings.
- Install windows into all facades except where in conflict with building code.
- Place parking as to be visible from windows.
- Keep shrubbery under 3 feet in height for visibility.
- Prune the lower branches of trees to at least 7–8 feet off the ground.
- Do not obstruct views from windows.

Territorial Reinforcement

- Manned guardhouses allow for both access control and surveillance.
- Define perimeters with landscaping or fencing.
- Design fences to maintain visibility from the street.
- Differentiate exterior private areas from public areas.
- Position security and reception areas at all entrances.

Maintenance

- Keep all exterior areas neat and clean.
- Keep all plantings looking well managed.

Industrial Properties

In most industrial site designs, the most important issue is the safety of those who will be working or traveling to the site. Unfortunately, safety regarding crime is often given little consideration. After work hours, industrial areas are, for the most part, badly illuminated, seldom under any type of surveillance, and virtually deserted, which in itself can be a problem. Add to this isolation blind alleys and expansive parking areas, and you have the potential for an extremely unsafe environment.

Natural Access Control

- Avoid dead-end driveways, and design streets to increase surveillance opportunities from passing traffic and patrols.
- Use easily securable site entrances.

- Install entrance controls to employee parking areas (fence, gate, attendant, etc.).
- Assign parking by shifts, and appoint late night workers with closed-in spaces.
- Plan storage yards for vehicular or visual access by patrol cars.
- Restrict access to roofs by way of dumpsters, loading docks, stacked items, ladders, and so on.
- Keep building entrances to a minimum, and monitor them.
- Use a separate, well-marked, monitored entrance for deliveries.
- Have the employee entrance close to the employee parking and workstations.
- Keep nighttime parking separate from service areas.
- Provide access to both the front and back of the site so that the grounds can be patrolled.
- Use separate docks for shipping and receiving.

Natural Surveillance

- Illuminate and define all entrances so that they are visible to the public and patrol vehicles.
- Make parking areas visible to patrol cars, pedestrians, parking attendants, and building personnel.
- Position parking attendants for maximum visibility of property.
- Open stairs provide good visibility from the entrance as well as the parking area.
- Design the reception area to have a view of the parking areas, especially the visitor's parking.
- Use walls only where necessary and, if used, make them high enough to prevent circumvention.
- Avoid creating hiding places in alleys, storage yards, loading docks, and so on.

Territorial Reinforcement

- Create a well-defined entrance or gateway with plantings, fences, gates, and so on.
- Limit deliveries to daylight hours only, if possible.
- Define vehicle entrances with different paving materials and signage.
- Separate visitor parking from employee parking and shipping and receiving areas.

Maintenance

- Keep all exterior areas neat and clean.
- Keep all plantings looking well managed and well maintained.

Chapter 31

Environmental Design to Positively Affect Behavior

Crime prevention through environmental design offers many methods to interfere with offenders stalking victims. Communities can locate women's washrooms away from telephones, light up suspicious areas, open up blind spots, and place legitimate businesses in areas formerly used for criminal approach. The point is to give offenders a smaller window of opportunity.

Marcus Felson[1]

The term *design* includes physical, social, management, and law enforcement directives that seek to positively affect human behavior as people interact with their environment.

Crime prevention through environmental design (CPTED) programs seek to prevent certain specified crimes (and the fear attributed to them) within a specifically defined environment by manipulating variables that are closely related to the environment.

The program does not purport to develop crime prevention solutions in a broad universe of human behavior but rather solutions limited to variables that can be manipulated and evaluated in the specified human and environment relationship. CPTED involves the design of physical space in the context of the needs of legitimate users of the space (physical, social, and psychological needs), the normal and expected (or intended) use of the space (the activity or absence of activity planned for the space), and the predictable behavior of both legitimate users and offenders.

---

[1] Felson, M. 2006. *Crime and Nature.* Thousand Oaks, CA: Sage Publications, p. 240.

In the CPTED approach, a design is proper if it recognizes the designated use of the space, defines the crime problem incidental to and the solution compatible with the designated use, and incorporates the crime prevention strategies that enhance (or at least do not impair) the effective use of the space. CPTED draws not only on physical and urban design but also on contemporary thinking in behavioral and social science, law enforcement, and community organization.

Target Hardening

The emphasis on design and use deviates from the traditional target-hardening approach to crime prevention. Traditional target hardening focuses predominantly on denying access to a crime target through physical or artificial barrier techniques (such as locks, alarms, fences, and gates). Target hardening often leads to constraints on use, access, and enjoyment of the hardened environment. Moreover, the traditional approach tends to overlook opportunities for natural access control and surveillance. The term *natural* refers to deriving access control, and surveillance results as a by-product of the normal and routine use of the environment. It is possible to adapt normal and natural uses of the environment to accomplish the effects of artificial or mechanical hardening and surveillance. Nevertheless, CPTED employs pure target-hardening strategies, either to test their effectiveness as compared to natural strategies or when they appear to be justified as not unduly impairing the effective use of the environment.

As an example, a design strategy of improved street lighting must be planned, efficient, and evaluated in terms of the behavior it promotes or deters and the use impact of the lighted (and related) areas in terms of all users of the area (offenders, victims, and other permanent or casual users). Any strategies related to the lighting strategy (e.g., block watch or Neighborhood Watch, 911 emergency service, and police patrol) must be evaluated in the same regard. This reflects the comprehensiveness of the CPTED design approach in focusing on both the proper design and effective use of the physical environment. Additionally, the concept of proper design and effective use emphasizes the design relationship among strategies to ensure that the desired results are achieved. It has been observed that improved street lighting alone (a design strategy) is ineffective against crime without the conscious and active support of citizens (in reporting what they see) and of police (in responding and conducting surveillance). CPTED involves the effort to integrate design, citizen and community action, and law enforcement strategies to accomplish surveillance consistent with the design and use of the environment.

Chapter 32

Managing Risk: CPTED Strategies for Site Design of Schools

In site design of schools, the following crime prevention through environmental design (CPTED) strategies should be considered:[1]

Natural Access Control

- Clearly establish and define school property lines.
- Secure the site perimeter and limit access with selected entry points.
- Create boundaries that delineate public, semipublic, semiprivate, and private spaces.
- Establish clearly defined and secure boundaries between joint-use facilities and school.
- Where feasible, utilize fencing that does not permit footholds in order to deter unauthorized access.

---

[1] Florida Safe School Design Guidelines Strategies to Enhance Security and Reduce Vandalism, Florida Department of Education. 2003. http://www.k12.wa.us/SchFacilities/Advisory/pubdocs/2016April/FlSafeGuide2003.pdf; A. Wallis and D. Ford. 1980. Crime Prevention through Environmental Design: The School Demonstration in Broward County, Florida. Washington, DC: U.S. Department of Justice, National Institute of Justice. http://www.popcenter.org/library/scp/pdf/185-Wallis_and_Ford.pdf

Natural Surveillance

- Avoid blocking lines of sight with fencing, signage, and landscaping.
- Locate site entry points in areas of high visibility where they can be easily observed and monitored by staff and students in the course of their normal activities.

Territorial Integrity

- Maintain school property to help establish pride of place and a sense of ownership.
- Encourage activities on school grounds that promote community ownership and territorial integrity.

Management

- Utilize fencing materials that resist graffiti.
- The location of a school and its relationship to its immediate surroundings are critical in evaluating safety and security concerns. While there is evidence showing that, by and large, schools and community college campuses tend to be safer places than the neighborhoods in which they are located, crime rates and types of crimes in schools nevertheless are affected by their surrounding environment. Despite this, each campus is unique, and there are no formulas that can be applied to all. However, there are overarching design principles that are applicable to virtually all locations, whether rural or not. Secure the perimeter with limited entry and access points:
  - Bus drop-off
  - Parent drop-off
  - Service and delivery areas
  - Student parking
  - Staff parking

Joint Use Recreational Facilities—School or Community, Suburban, or Inner-City Urban Areas

These principles apply to the relation of the school at its perimeter, whether physical or perceptual, between the school and neighboring areas. These principles include maximizing natural surveillance opportunities onto school grounds from surrounding areas; controlling access into and out of the campus; increasing, whenever possible, the sense of ownership that students, staff, and neighbors have in the school; clearly demarcating boundaries and spaces; minimizing undefined and "unowned" spaces; properly maintaining the property and grounds so that strong signals are sent that "someone cares about this place"; and locating campus facilities and activities so that they are compatible with adjacent, off-site land uses and activities.

The site perimeter, which is the part of the school grounds that connects the street and adjacent property, defines the initial impression of a school. How a school's site responds to its immediate surroundings is evident in its treatment of its perimeter and edges. These edges communicate to the public messages of accessibility or inaccessibility. Therefore, a primary consideration in school site design is the clear definition of the school property lines. This definition can be achieved by utilizing layered edge treatments such as fencing, landscaping, and ground surface treatments. Symbolic markers such as archways, entry posts, and student artworks are also useful in creating psychological boundary delineations of the school's perimeter and edges.

Special consideration should be taken in the design of schools with joint-use or shared facilities such as playgrounds and recreational areas, which are accessible to the community during and after school hours. In such circumstances, it is critical to delineate internal boundaries between the community and the school by establishing a distinct perimeter for both the school and the joint-use facilities with separate and secure access points. Properly designed joint-use facilities can reinforce neighborhood connections, ownership, and territorial integrity.

Vehicular Routes and Parking Areas

Natural Access Control

- Restrict external access to parking areas to a limited number of controlled entrances.
- Close unsupervised entrances during low-use times to reinforce the idea that access and parking are for school business only.
- Provide clear signage and posted rules as to who is allowed to use parking facilities and when they are allowed to do so.
- Locate visitor parking directly adjacent to main entry and administration.
- Provide adequate space adjacent to the building for emergency vehicles.
- Establish separate vehicular circulation routes to service and delivery areas, visitor entry, bus drop-off, student parking, and staff parking.
- Prohibit through traffic on school campuses.
- Provide a secure caged area for off-hour deliveries.

Natural Surveillance

- Locate visitor parking areas in close proximity to school building or activity areas to facilitate natural surveillance.

- Provide windows in classrooms and administration areas that overlook parking areas.
- Provide adequate lighting in drop-off zones and parking areas.
- Utilize zoned parking in limited controlled areas when appropriate.
- Locate bus loading area so that it is visible to administration or adjacent to areas of surveillance.
- Locate access to public transportation in areas that promote natural surveillance.

Territorial Integrity

- Differentiate and identify parking spaces for students, faculty, staff, and visitors.
- Provide designated primary routes and parking lots for after-hours use when applicable.
- Clearly mark transition(s) from public street onto school entry routes and into parking areas.
- Provide clearly marked transitions from parking areas to pedestrian routes such as with protective barriers.
- Minimize ambiguous and unassigned spaces at entry and parking areas.
- Maintain a separation between pedestrian and vehicular traffic.
- Provide blue-light emergency phones in parking lots on community college campuses.

Management

- Supervise entrances and parking areas during peak use times.
- Utilize vandal-resistant lighting in parking areas and along vehicular routes.
- Design parking lots that reduce opportunities for high-speed activity.

Vehicular routes and parking areas include the primary entry drive, parking lots, bus loading zones, parent drop-off and pickup areas, and service and delivery sections. Vehicular routes and parking lots must be designed to handle the rush of people and vehicles at the peak unloading and loading times at the beginning and end of each day. Other times, these areas may be completely empty and unsupervised, potentially providing opportunities for unwanted access.

In general, the safety and security of vehicular routes and parking areas benefit from the following design considerations:

- They should not be isolated from the school but should be in close proximity to facilitate visual surveillance from classroom and administration areas.
- These areas, especially classrooms, should be provided with windows that overlook vehicular routes and parking areas.

■ External access to parking areas should be restricted to a limited number of controlled entrances.

■ Provisions must be made to ensure separation of vehicular and pedestrian circulation by creating barriers and well-defined routes.

■ Unassigned and "unowned" spaces should be minimized as much as possible, especially in student parking zones.

■ Entry areas and parking lots should have signs that spell out accepted usage and rules that describe what is and is not permitted.

■ Parking areas and vehicular routes should be adequately lit with vandal-resistant lighting.

For K-12 schools, the main entry drive area should be where visitors enter the school and parents pick up their children. This entry drive should be clearly visible from the administration office, where staff can keep an eye on who is coming and going during regular school hours. Also, it is important to provide a designated paved area adjacent to the building for emergency vehicles.

The bus loading area must be segregated from the main entry and other vehicular traffic according to code. However, when possible, the bus waiting area should still be visible from the administration area or some other point of natural surveillance, such as classrooms.

Parking lots are particularly susceptible to criminal activity. A primary factor is that these areas are typically the farthest from the central core of the campus. Because parking lots have been consistently identified by principals, school resource officers, and facility managers as venues for misbehavior, vandalism, and more serious crimes, adequate supervision is essential. While this is particularly important at peak use times, it should also be a priority, resources permitting, during off-peak periods since parking lots contain an enormous trove of valuable targets for motivated offenders.

Locating parking lots near areas that promote natural surveillance, such as classrooms, can help mitigate criminal activity. It is important to provide a sufficient number of windows in these areas for visibility of the parking lots. Provisions may have to be made for overflow lots to accommodate special and sporting events. When numerous lots exist, such as on large campuses, these lots should be clearly numbered or identified to avoid confusion. It is also recommended that designated parking lots be provided, especially for high schools, in order to monitor students who may leave campus during school hours. Such lots should be able to be secured and, if possible, supervised during peak use times. When designing parking lots, particularly those that will be used by students, avoid long, straight layouts that allow cars to speed through the lot endangering pedestrians. Traffic calming devices can greatly reduce the potential for high-speed activity.

Community colleges have unique vehicular route and parking requirements for several reasons. The bulk of the student population is no longer delivered in groups to specific entry points. Instead, these students typically arrive individually, are usually required to park in areas located a substantial distance from the implied security zones of campus buildings, and often leave school after dark. It is, therefore, imperative that areas used in these circumstances have appropriate levels of lighting and that potential hiding places be eliminated. In addition, in order to increase security on community college campuses, blue-light emergency phones should be located in all parking lots. It is important to place these phones in areas that are clearly visible and easily accessible.

For community colleges, public transportation also poses particular safety and security concerns. Public buses can provide a means to quickly enter and leave the campus undetected and unmonitored. Therefore, access points to public transportation should be located near areas that promote natural surveillance whenever possible. Colleges should also consider incorporating electronic surveillance, such as video surveillance, of these access points.

Service and delivery drives should be separated from other vehicular routes. These areas should be able to be secured and include a caged area for off-hour deliveries.

There are some key considerations regarding vehicular routes and parking areas when schools incorporate joint-use or shared facilities. Clearly marked designated parking lots should be provided for the public to avoid conflict and confusion. In addition, routes and access points for the community should be well defined and separated from the school.

Chapter 33

Modern Environmental Design

Modern environmental design still uses many concepts passed down from the ancients, and new technology and ideas continuously evolve. Various energy crises over the years have led architects and city planners to design buildings around the relative location of the sun and other natural formations like trees, mountains, and bodies of water in attempts to increase energy efficiency. Windows are oriented to allow maximum sunlight penetration in winter and minimum in summer to cut climate control costs. Large buildings in warm climates are built with stone floors to assist in cooling, and often have louvered windows that allow light to penetrate indirectly, keeping the heat outside.

This discipline applies to outdoor design as well. Responsible landscape designers will only use plants native to the region to avoid the invasion of foreign species, and desert gardens are likely to be xeriscaped, using cactus in rock and pebble beds to eliminate the need for irrigation. Thorny hedges under windows deter break-ins, and large shade trees outside large windows reduce energy needs. Outdoor lighting can easily contain a small solar panel that will collect enough energy during daylight hours to power it all night long without the use of electricity.

The United States Green Building Council began the Leadership in Energy and Environmental Design (LEED®) certification system in 1998 to recognize sustainably designed buildings. These buildings often incorporate solar energy, wind energy, and even geothermal energy to create a zero-emissions state, with the building itself producing all of the energy it needs to run. The most efficient of these actually produce more energy than they need, which they then sell to electric companies for use by consumers.

At its root, environmental design is not necessarily about new technology, although recent advances have furthered the field considerably. It is about using what is already there, instead of demolishing and leveling a building site, for example. Working with the imperfections and unique aspects of each individual site ultimately makes the end product operate more smoothly, at a lower cost.[1]

[1] Reprinted from wiseGEEK, What Is Environmental Design? http://www.wisegeek.org/what-is-environmental-design.htm

Chapter 34

Five Things about Design

The following are five essential factors in crime prevention through environmental design[1]:

1. Ensure that physical space is designed in the context of the needs of bona fide users of the space. The purpose is to properly match a space's physical design with its intended use. This can best be accomplished by matching the physical design of the space with the physical, social, and psychological needs of the space's bona fide users.
2. When designing and organizing space, its effective and productive use will create safe and critical intensity zones so that "abnormal users" will feel at greater risk from surveillance and intervention, and "normal users" will experience a reduced risk.
3. Design space to create natural surveillance and natural access control with windows, having a clear line of sight, and to promote space definition. This minimizes the perception of constraints on the enjoyments and use of the property, which is often found with traditional target hardening.
4. Strategically allocate safe activities within what would be considered unsafe or vulnerable areas, limited natural considered unsafe or vulnerable areas, limited natural surveillance or access control areas, and areas with a lack of territoriality. By identifying these areas, such as in public places and parking lots, this increases the benefits of safety for normal users of the space, and the

---

[1] http://www.lisc.org/media/filer_public/a5/4e/a54e1982-f2b4-4c3c-ac34-13c3f515679c/
cpted_more_than_just_locks_and_lights_rvp_2016_.pdf. Crime Prevention Through
Environmental Design Principles, January 2002.

perception of greater risk with a sense of supervision and intervention among abnormal users of the space.

5. Maps can be of immense benefit in locating natural boundaries, neighborhoods, land use, and pedestrian and traffic movement. Maps can be obtained from city planning departments, zoning boards, local council, and transport engineering council.

Chapter 35

Vandalism and Graffiti

Vandalism is a crime that is defined a bit differently among the 50 states, the hundreds of counties, and thousands of communities in the United States, and by federal statute, as well.[1] Generally, it can be described as the malicious or willful destruction or disfigurement of public or private property that does not belong to the vandal, without the consent of the property's owner. It is a crime, not a harmless prank. Vandalism costs millions of dollars of taxpayer money to counteract.

Significant Consequences

Vandalism may be thought of as a minor crime by some people, with a "boys will be boys" attitude, but they may be unaware that vandalism offenses are often punishable as misdemeanors or even felonies, with strict consequences, such as

- Fines
- Mandatory community service
- Incarceration (jail time)

---

[1] Reprinted from Criminal Law Lawyer Source. Vandalism. Retrieved November 2016 from: http://www.criminal-law-lawyer-source.com/terms/vandalism.html; Graffiti. Retrieved on July 30, 2017, from: http://en.wikipedia.org/wiki/Graffitti

Penalty Enhancement

Additional factors can make the punishment for vandalism more severe (sometimes called "penalty enhancement"). For instance, vandalism against the property of an individual because of their race, religion, sexual orientation, color, ancestry, disability, or national origin, if defined as hate crimes, may carry more serious penalties.

Types of Vandalism

Vandalism can take many forms, including

- Broken windows
- Graffiti, from insignificant scribbles to huge paintings on buildings, trains, and buses
- Theft of property
- Arson
- Posting leaflets and handbills
- Damage to mailboxes
- Destruction of playground equipment, library books, campground or beach facilities
- Defacing gravestones
- Egging or toilet papering property
- Littering

Vandalism of Federal Property

The U.S. federal government takes an especially dim view of vandalism. Although some teens think that trashing a public mailbox is funny, they are probably not aware that such a mailbox is federal property, and that the potential punishment for the destruction of federal property is rather severe. Vandalism at national parks, monuments, historic sites, military installations, and post offices will carry serious penalties.

Graffiti

Graffiti (including stickers) is illegal and can be defined as any marking placed on public or private property without the owner's permission.[2]

---

[2] Seattle.gov. Reporting Graffiti. http://www.seattle.gov/police/prevention/graffiti.htm

How to Report Graffiti

Graffiti is vandalism without permission. Graffiti is created to be seen by others, so the best thing you can do if it appears on your property is to report it, document it, and then clean it up thoroughly and immediately.

- To report an act of graffiti or vandalism in progress, call 9-1-1.
- To report graffiti noticed on somebody else's property or public property call the police at a nonemergency number.

How to Prevent Graffiti

For Business Owners

- Create or join an existing local chamber of commerce or business association to develop strategies to deal with this type of crime.
- Make sure a sign identifying the business is visibly displayed at each shop front.

For Residential Property Owners

- Keep the neighborhood clean to send the message that you care about the neighborhood.
- Join a Neighborhood Watch program.

3M.com

Vandalism can damage your image as well as being costly and disruptive.[3] 3M Anti-Graffiti Film can be removed and replaced quickly without the need to remove your windows. Vanquish vandals with graffiti protection.

- Protect your surfaces against most scratches, acid etching, gouges and tagging with 3M™ Anti-Graffiti Film
- Easy to remove and replace quickly—without the hassle of replacing your windows
- Money-saving option that's only a fraction of the cost of new glass
- Rejects 99% of the UV rays that cause fading, helping to extend the life of display merchandise

---

[3] Reprinted from https://www.3m.com/3M/en_US/company-us/all-3m-products/~/3M-Anti-Graffiti-Films/?N=5002385+3292716670&rt=rud; Graffiti. http://en.wikipedia.org/wiki/Graffiti

Chapter 36

CPTED Security Solutions: 10 Things You Need to Know

Following are 10 crime prevention through environmental design (CPTED) security solutions[1]:

1. Have a security professional conduct assessment of the property to identify potential security risks and vulnerabilities, to either eliminate the risk or reduce the impact if an incident does occur.
2. The assessment, along with the mission statement of the organization and a culture of security, should be a part of the overall security master plan.
3. This assessment should incorporate training and security awareness, to include scenarios, drills, and full-scale exercises with local first responders.
4. Review the policies and procedures of the organization and update them every 5 years, or more often if necessary. Organizational policies change less often than organizational procedures. Ensure that emergency procedures are a part of the policies and procedures of the organization.
5. Formulate partnerships with local first responders—law enforcement, fire department, emergency medical services, the state Homeland Security advisor, the Federal Emergency Management Agency (FEMA), and so on. Develop relationships with all resources that are available in the local area. Discuss security concerns and the daily operations of the organization with

[1] M.J. Fagel and J.L. Hesterman. 2017. *Soft Targets and Crisis Management: What Emergency Managers Need to Know.* Boca Raton, FL: CRC Press.

first responders and involve them in training and drills. The basic idea is plan, practice, and prepare.

6. Ensure that the organization has a visitor management program in place and that security officers and employees are trained to identify suspicious behavior and activity. This emphasizes the need to greet visitors and have someone available to answer questions and direct them to the proper location. Many retail establishments, healthcare facilities, and churches have greeters at their entrances to observe who is entering the facility.

7. If you have concerns with theft at your organization or are concerned about weapons being brought onto the property, consider the implementation of a "no bag" or "clear bag" policy to reduce the risk.

8. Security officers in plain clothes or trained employees are ideal for detecting suspicious behavior and activity.

9. Every organization should have redundant mass notification capabilities, by an announcement over the PA system, an automatic call to company telephones and/or registered cell phones, an e-mail, a pop-up message on all computers connected to the organization's intranet, a text message to a cell phone, or an audible siren or alarm. More than one of these means of communication can be used for notification. Some may indicate where in the building or property there is an issue and also include a photo. Ensure there are provisions for those who are physically, visually, or hearing impaired.

10. All security devices and systems should be inspected regularly to ensure they are operational. This can be the responsibility of security officers or a designated company employee, but ensure it is documented.

Chapter 37

Residential NFPA Safety Tips as Part of the Knowledge Required to Conduct a Residential CPTED Assessment

Begin developing a home fire escape plan with all members of your family.[1] Use this checklist to make sure your escape plan includes all the elements needed to ensure your family's safety from fire.

- Make a map of your home indicating all windows and doors that can be used to get outside if the smoke alarm sounds.
- The home fire escape plan includes two ways out of every room in the home (usually a door and a window).
- Routes out of each room and the home should be clear, free of clutter, and opened easily.

---

[1] National Fire Protection Association (NFPA). Keeping Your Community Safe with Home Fire Escape Planning. Retrieved on November 18, 2016, from: http://www.nfpa.org/public-education/resources/education-programs/community-tool-kits/keeping-your-community-safe-with-home-fire-escape-planning; https://www.ready.gov/make-a-plan; Department of Homeland Security. Make a Plan. http://www.ready.gov/make-a-plan

- Security bars on doors and windows should have a quick-release device on the inside, so they can be used to get outside in case of a fire.
- Your family should have a meeting place (a tree, neighbor's home, or street light) outside, in front of your home, where everyone knows to meet upon exiting.
- Your house number should be clearly seen from the street.
- Your plan should include the local emergency telephone number (or 9-1-1) to be contacted immediately upon leaving the home.
- There should be working smoke alarms in all required locations throughout your home and one on every level of the home (including the basement), outside all bedrooms and sleeping areas.
- Everyone should know what the smoke alarm sounds like, and what to do when they hear it.
- Your family should practice your home fire escape drill, and continue to do so at least twice a year.
- Everyone in your home should know how to get low and go under smoke, in case they need to escape through smoke.
- Everyone should know that if the smoke alarm sounds, to get outside of the home and stay outside, and understand that they should report to the fire department any people or pets trapped inside.
- Smoke alarms[2] are a key part of a home fire escape plan. When there is a fire, smoke spreads fast. Working smoke alarms give you early warning so you can get outside quickly.
- Large homes may need extra smoke alarms.
- It is best to use interconnected smoke alarms.
- When one smoke alarm sounds, they all sound.
- Test all smoke alarms at least once a month. Press the test button to be sure the alarm is working.
- There are two kinds of alarms. Ionization smoke alarms are quicker to warn about flaming fires. Photoelectric alarms are quicker to warn about smoldering fires. It is best to use both types of alarms in the home.
- A smoke alarm should be on the ceiling or high on a wall. Keep smoke alarms away from the kitchen to reduce false alarms. They should be at least 10 feet (3 meters) from the stove.
- People who are hard-of-hearing or deaf can use special alarms. These alarms have strobe lights and bed shakers.
- Replace all smoke alarms when they are 10 years old.
- Smoke alarms are an important part of a home fire escape plan.

---

[2] https://www.nfpa.org/Public-Education/By-topic/Smoke-alarms/Safety-messages-about-smoke-alarms; North Lauderdale, Florida. http://www.nlauderdale.org/department/fire_prevention/index.php; City of Brooklyn. Residential Home Security Tips (CPTED). http://www.cityofbrooklyncenter.org/index.aspx?NID=1077; ESFi. http://www.esfi.org/resource/smoke-alarms-carbon-monoxide-alarms-and-fire-escape-planning-185

Children and Smoke Alarms

The National Fire Protection Association (NFPA) is aware of research indicating that sleeping children do not always wake up when a smoke alarm activates.[3] While this research is worrisome, we should not allow them to obscure the fact that smoke alarms are highly effective at reducing fire deaths and injuries.

The NFPA reaffirms the value of the smoke alarms already available to protect people from home fire deaths and voice its concern about the number of U.S. households without these early warning devices. Ninety-six percent of American homes have at least one smoke alarm, but almost two-thirds of home fire deaths resulted from fires in homes with no smoke alarms or no working smoke alarms.

The NFPA emphasizes the need to continue planning and practicing home fire escape plans and to make sure everyone in a home can be awakened by the sound of the smoke alarm. The NFPA suggests practicing the escape plan during which the smoke alarm is activated so all family members know its sound.

Every home fire escape plan is different, and every family should know who will—and who will not—awaken at the sound of the smoke alarm. If someone does not wake up when the alarm sounds during a drill, the family should design an escape plan that assigns a grown-up who is easily awakened by the alarm to wake the sleepers, perhaps by yelling "FIRE," pounding on the wall or door, or blowing a whistle.

On each level of the dwelling unit including basements, but excluding crawl spaces and unfinished attics, at least one battery-operated or hard-wired smoke detector in proper operating condition must be present. Smoke detectors must be installed in accordance with and meet the requirements of the NFPA Standards 74 or its successor standards.

If a hearing-impaired person is occupying the dwelling unit, the smoke detectors must have an alarm system designed for hearing-impaired persons as specified in NFPA 74.

Reference: http://www.michigan.gov/som/0,4669,7-192-29943_34759-366431-,00.html and https://www.idahohousing.com/documents/chapter-13-inspection-policies-and-housing-quality-standards.pdf

---

[3] abcNEWS. March 15, 2017. Can Children Sleep through a Smoke Detector Alarm? http:abcnews.go.com/US/children-sleep-smoke-detectors-alarms/story?id=46133010; Preventfire.com. Children and Smoke Alarms. http://www.preventfire.com/adults/children-and-smoke-alarms.html; U.S. Fire Administration. Smoke Alarm Outreach Materials. http://www.usfa.fema.gov/prevention/outreach/smoke_alarms.html

Chapter 38

Partnerships to Reduce Crime

Much has been said and written about the topic of partnerships.[1] Neighborhoods shift from a dead zone to a livable space, whether you live in New York; New Haven, Connecticut; Kansas City or St. Louis, Missouri; Detroit, Michigan; or Chicago, Illinois. All have been referred to (and some still are) as "crime hot spots."

Why should communities formulate police-community partnerships[2] for problem-solving issues? The primary reason is in order to obtain results that will benefit the community through the partnership of public and private sectors, which will include a team of dedicated individuals who have the will and energy for this task.

Community leaders look toward crime prevention programs, crime prevention through environmental design (CPTED) principles and Neighborhood Watch to help with the development of crime-free zones.

Common goals are as follows:

- Reduction to removal of drug dealers
- Reduction to removal of crime and police calls
- Creation of safe housing
- Encouragement to address problem-solving issues

---

[1] B. Geller and L. Belsky. 2012. Building Our Way Out of Crime. http://www.olneyville.org/Geller-Belsky-case-study.pdf

[2] https://www.ncjrs.gov/pdffiles1/nij/247182.pdf

- Encouragement to upgrade neighborhoods with planning of trees and flowers
- Development of neighborhood pride
- Development of crime prevention workshops
- Building away crime
- Development of a checklist for direction

Chapter 39

Developing a Culture of Security with CPTED

Culture within CPTED

Culture is what gives a society, a nation, or a community its identity. Societies are indeed identifiable through their cultural expressions. Therefore, every society makes an effort to preserve its particular cultural heritage by ensuring that it is passed from one generation to the next.

What is meant by a "culture of violence" in a community? An example, in 2016 there were 762 murders in Chicago, Illinois. That is a more than 50% increase from 2015 to 2016.

Would it be fair to say that Chicago has a "culture of violence"?

This brings us to the next question. What is a "culture of security"? Whether they want to admit it or not, every company, organization, and community has a security culture. Many times, when someone says that they do not have a security culture, it is because they do not want to admit that they have a "bad" security culture. A company, organization, or community must make a conscious effort to invest in a security culture if it is to become sustainable, and it has to be more than a one-time event with its own life cycle. This way, there will be a return on investment (ROI). A culture of security has to become an integral part of everything that is done, and it is crucial that the security culture keep pace with any threats.

To determine what type of culture a company, organization, or community has, we suggest you start with a thorough risk assessment to identify issues with crime, personal safety concerns, as well as noncriminal issues. There has to be a social mechanism in place to support the development of a culture of security.

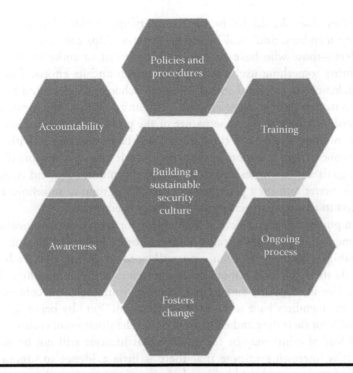

Figure 39.1 Building a sustainable security culture. (Created by Marianna Perry, CPP, 2017.)

As stated in Figure 39.1, a culture of security is part of an overall security master plan. Timothy Giles describes a security master plan as, "a document that delineates the organization's security philosophies, strategies, goals, programs, and processes. It is used to guide the organization's development and direction in these areas in a manner that is consistent with the company's overall business plan. It also provides a detailed outline of the risks and the mitigation plans for them in a way that creates a 5-year business plan."

A step-by-step process will define how the plan should be implemented and how the organization will reach its security goals. A vulnerability or risk assessment will identify issues to be addressed. It is important that a vulnerability or risk assessment be conducted by a trained security professional so the organization will know what assets they need to protect and what risks to retain, transfer, or mitigate. When the appropriate countermeasures are put into place, the emphasis will be on layers of security, security policies and procedures, and security education and training. It also may be helpful to have a safety and security committee.

The formulation of partnerships[1] is a problem-solving approach to the issues identified during the risk or vulnerability assessment. Identify key agencies

---

[1] http://www.popcenter.org/tools/partnering/

or businesses that should be in the partnership. Besides law enforcement, community members, and local businesses, partnerships can also include other stakeholders—those who have an identifiable interest or stake in the outcome and can bring something useful to the partnership and its efforts. Examples of possible stakeholders are social service agencies, schools, religious and faith-based organizations, government agencies, and community groups. The membership in the partnership will depend on the nature of the problem, but remember that the greater the number of partners, the harder it will be to organize activities or even to get everyone in the same room at the same time. It may also be more difficult to decide on goals and strategies and to maintain communication and cooperation. It is usually better to form a partnership with a core group of stakeholders and to invite others to join the partnership as situational needs arise.

It is important that you design a blueprint for what security measures will be implemented to address specific vulnerabilities identified during the risk or vulnerability assessment. Then, you will need to ensure that each partner understands their role and responsibilities to educate the community. In order to achieve buy-in, support, and participation in your plan, the community (or organization) members have to know what they will "get" by being involved, or what the ROI for their time and efforts will be. In the situation of criminal activity, a reduced fear of crime may be the goal so that lifestyle will not be negatively affected. It is interesting to note that there is little evidence to support a link between fear of crime and the likelihood of victimization, since there are so many variables involved. In Chicago, as in most cities, the fear of crime has been one of the most important factors "driving residents to the suburbs, encouraging race and class segregation and undermining the political importance of American cities."[2] Eighty-four percent of police officers who participated directly in community policing activities agree that reducing fear of crime should be just as high a priority as reducing the crime rate.[3]

Your security program, as a part of your overall culture of security, must be promoted so that it becomes ingrained within the company, organization, or community.

This brings us back to the question, "What is a culture of security?" A culture of security means that security procedures become unconsciously, instinctively, and essentially effortless because safe behavior will become a habit. It will become "just the way things are done around here," so that identified vulnerabilities are effectively mitigated. Remember that security policies and procedures have to effectively address the identified threats, so changes will need to be made from time to time so that you have a living, breathing culture of security.

Conclusion: *A culture of good security practices combining first-, second-, and third-generation crime prevention through environmental design (CPTED), followed by*

---

[2] http://www.popcenter.org/library/reading/PDFs/ReducingFearGuide.pdf
[3] Ibid.

Neighborhood Watch and community policing, will become effective as part of developing an impressive culture of security. Utilizing CPTED strategies will reduce the incidence of crime as well as the fear of crime.

As a side note, Chicago is starting to see some positive effects and a gradual decline in incidents of crime.

Chapter 40

Definition of CPTED and Lighting Terminology

CPTED Definitions

Following are definitions for common terms used in crime prevention through environmental design (CPTED)[1]:

Access Control—the general idea of access control is extremely simple: the offender should not dare—and/or be able—to get into an area, building, or space.

Activity Program Support—building design documentation consists of a set of documents that are required for the building and use of a construction project or part of such a project, including specifications, technical drawings, instructions on maintenance, and other relevant documents (such as explanatory diagrams, tables and charts for drawings, expert opinions and survey reports, and other documents). In addition to other information, building design documentation contains technical information that needs to be submitted to the local government when applying for written approval, a building permit, and a use and occupancy permit.

Buildings—estates, semidetached houses, the layout of single-family terraced houses, inner grounds, enclosed squares, and so on.

Certificate of Registration—a certificate for renting out a building or complex for applicants such as housing associations, groups of owners, or a pension fund.

Comprehensive Plan—which should be prepared for land owned by the state or by a county governmental body in order to establish the spatial concept for

---

[1] A. Levald et al. 2012. CPTED Manual for Police Officers. http://www.cpted.net/resources/documents/articles_resources/EU%20manual4police.pdf

the planned construction on that land and the principles of use and protection for that land. A comprehensive plan may also be prepared for the whole of the municipality or for part of it (such as a town or city).

Design—this is all about planning, design, and the management and/or maintenance of a city, a neighborhood, or a building with all of its physical features (bricks, mortar, concrete, and general form), as well as the people who live, stay, and reside there.

Detailed Plan—this is a land planning document that set out the land parcel boundaries, the land management process, and the land use regime (construction and other compulsory operating conditions). Detailed plans may be prepared for towns and for parts of cities (individual neighborhoods), plus villages and individual land parcels or groups of land parcels.

Environmental—the environment is essential for an increase or decrease in [the opportunities for] crime.

Facilitating Positive Use—this principle relates to the creation of an environment, which increases the likelihood that legitimate users will make use of an area.

CPTED—crime prevention through environmental design.

Crime—this includes "specific forms of crime" as well as fear of crime and feelings of insecurity. The specific forms of crime are often of an opportunistic nature. Crimes, as well as uncivil acts or antisocial behavior, can include burglary, theft, vandalism, street violence (as opposed to domestic violence), graffiti, littering, and so on.

Image/Maintenance—the principle is to keep an area free of litter, graffiti, vandalism, and damage.

Land Use Plan (Project)—a document for which the framework of the use of land in rural areas and its protection, as well as specific land-use planning measures, are established.

Local Planning—Wikipedia defines local planning as being a matter that is related to a local government or council that is empowered by law to exercise statutory town planning functions for a particular area.[2] At the level of comprehensive planning, eight types of urban environment can be identified in the sense of crime prevention. Each one of these types has an appropriate set of measures to prevent crime through urban planning and building design.[3]

National Planning—a spatial development strategy for the entire country has to contain a vision that foresees a settlement system that could provide a high-quality living environment that includes most general safety matters.

Private Space—the dwelling or a private garden.

Public Space—the roads, squares, and parks in a city.

Public Areas—public lighting, open air parking, private garages, playing facilities, tunnels and subways, bus stops, back alleys, with these areas requiring neighborhood management, maintenance, supervision, and so on.

---

[2] Local Planning Authority. http://en.wikipedia.org/wiki/local_planning.authority
[3] Comprehensive Planning. http://en.wikipedia.org/wiki/comprehensive_planning

Prevention—this concept implies that you act before a problem arises. Pro-action instead of reaction.

Regional Planning—this specifies the principles for a settlement system for the region and provides a direction for spatial development, serving as the basis for the preparation of comprehensive plans for rural municipalities and cities.

Semiprivate—the interior corridors in an apartment complex or a communal garden within an enclosed building block.

Semipublic Space—a hallway or front garden that is open to the general public.

Spatial Plan—this refers to a document that is drawn up as a result of the planning process. A spatial plan consists of text and technical drawings that complement each other and constitute a single whole. Special plans are prepared for specific purposes or themes, for instance, infrastructure objects, water and forest management, and so on.

Surveillance—a distinction must be made between natural surveillance by the residents of a particular district, the formal surveillance duties that are carried out by the police or by private security personnel, and semiformal observation that is carried out by the postman, a housekeeper or concierge, housing officials, and so on.

Target Hardening—physical security and design that are implemented in order to make it more difficult to enter a building or space or to vandalize an object.

Territoriality—ownership or a sense of ownership.

"Through"—a catchphrase for the way in which crime prevention is implemented and executed.

Urban Planning—Wikipedia defines urban planning as being a technical and political process that concerns the use of land and the design of the urban environment, including air, water, and the infrastructure that passes into and out of urban areas, such as transportation and distribution networks.

Urban Planning and Design—the size of the district, its density, height and scale, access to the district by car and bicycle, and so on.[4]

Lighting and Illumination Definitions

Following are definitions used in lighting and illumination[5]:

Ballast—a device that provides the necessary starting voltage and appropriate current to a fluorescent or high-intensity discharge (HID) luminaire.

CRI—Color Rendering Index, sometimes CIE. The ability of a light source to accurately render an object's color in comparison with a natural light source. Measured on a scale of 1–100 with 100 being the ideal.

---

[4] Urban Design. http://en.wikipedia.org/wiki/urban_design

[5] National Crime Prevention Institute, Louisville, Kentucky. Student handout, 2004, Marianna Perry, CPP; Retrieved on August 8, 2017, from: http://www.lrc.rpi.edu/programs/nlpip/lightinganswers/adaptableballasts/ballast.asp

Efficacy—the ratio of light output (in lumens) to input power (in watts, expressed as lumens per watt (LPW).

Foot-Candle (fc)—a measure of illuminance in lumens per square feet. One foot-candle equals 10.76 lux, although 10 lux is commonly used as the equivalent.

Illuminance—light arriving at a surface, expressed in lumens per unit area; 1 lumen per square foot equals 1 foot-candle, while 1 lumen per square meter equals 1 lux.

Lamp—the source of light in a fixture, colloquially called a "light bulb."

Lumen Depreciation—the decrease in lumen output of a light source over time; every lamp type has a unique lumen depreciation curve (sometimes called a lumen maintenance curve) depicting the pattern of decreasing light output.

Lumen—a unit of luminous flux; overall light output; quantity of light, expressed in lumens.

Luminaire—a complete lighting unit that contains a lamp, housing, ballast, sockets, and any other necessary components.

Chapter 41

The Psychological Properties of Colors

Following is a list of colors and their associated psychological properties[1]:

Red—Red is a powerful color. Its effect is physical, strong, and basic. Red is
stimulating and lively as well as friendly. A person wearing a red tie does so
because it is called a "power tie."
Positives: Physical, Courage, Strength, Warmth, Energy, Basic Survival, Fight
or Flight, Stimulation, Masculinity, Excitement.
Negatives: Defiance, Aggressive and Aggression, Visual Impact, Strain.

Blue—Blue is the color of the mind and is essentially soothing. It affects us
mentally, rather than the physical reaction we have to red. Strong blues will
stimulate clear thoughts, and lighter, soft blues will calm the mind and aid
concentration. The world's favorite color is blue, but it can be perceived as
cold, unemotional, and unfriendly.
Positives: Intellectual, Communication, Trust, Efficiency, Serenity, Duty,
Logic, Coolness, Reflection, Calm.
Negatives: Coldness, Aloofness, Lack of Emotion, Unfriendliness.

---

[1] Psychological Properties of Colours. Retrieved on May 14, 2016, from: http://www.colour-affects.co.uk/psychological-properties-of-colours; C. Shovlin. 2015. *Your True Colors: A Practical Guide to Color Psychology—Grow Your Color Sense and Shine.* Customer Interpreter Limited, CreateSpace Independent Publishing; J.U. McLeod. 2016. *Color Psychology Today.* Hants, United Kingdom: O-Books.

Yellow—The yellow wavelength is relatively long and essentially stimulating. The wrong color scheme with yellow can cause fear and anxiety.
  Positives: Emotional, Optimism, Confidence, Self-Esteem, Extraversion, Emotional Strength, Friendliness, Creativity.
  Negatives: Irrationality, Fear, Emotional Fragility, Depression, Anxiety, Suicide.

Green—If a green color scheme is used incorrectly it can indicate stagnation.
  Positives: Harmony, Balance, Refreshment, Universal Love, Rest, Restoration, Reassurance, Environmental Awareness, Equilibrium, Peace.
  Negatives: Boredom, Stagnation, Blandness, Enervation.

Violet—The excessive use of purple can bring about too much of the wrong tone faster than any other color if it communicates something cheap and nasty.
  Positives: Spiritual Awareness, Containment, Vision, Luxury, Authenticity, Truth, Quality.
  Negatives: Introversion, Suppression, Inferiority.

Orange—Orange focuses our minds on issues of physical comfort—food, warmth, shelter, and sensuality. It is a fun color. Too much orange suggests a lack of serious intellectual values.
  Positives: Physical Comfort, Food, Warmth, Security, Sensuality, Passion, Abundance, Fun.
  Negatives: Introversion, Decadence, Suppression, Inferiority.

Black—Black is all colors, totally absorbed. It creates barriers, as it absorbs all the energy coming toward you. *Black is the absence of light*. Many people are afraid of the dark. In cowboy movies, the good guys wear what color hats? The bad guys wear what color hats? We wear a black tie to a funeral. We wear black to look thinner, though in 2016 a fashion designer stated that multicolor clothing was the way to go. Black race horses look faster.
  Positives: Sophistication, Glamour, Security, Emotional Safety, Efficiency, Substance.
  Negatives: Oppression, Coldness, Menace, Heaviness.

Gray—The heavy use of gray usually indicates a lack of confidence and fear of exposure.
  Positives: Psychological Neutrality.
  Negatives: Lack of Confidence, Dampness, Lack of Energy, Depression, Hibernation.

Pink—Being a tint of red, pink also affects us physically, but it soothes rather than stimulates. Pink is a powerful color, psychologically.

Positives: Physical Comfort, Food, Warmth, Security, Sensuality, Passion, Abundance, Fun.
Negatives: Inhibition, Emotional Claustrophobia, Emasculation, Physical Weakness.

White—White is total reflection. It reflects the full force of the spectrum to the eyes. White is purity, the negative effect of white on warm colors is to make them look and feel garish.
Positives: Hygiene, Sterility, Clarity, Purity, Cleanness, Simplicity, Sophistication, Efficiency.
Negatives: Sterility, Coldness, Barriers, Unfriendliness, Elitism. White is total reflection.

Brown—Brown usually consists of red and yellow with a large percentage of black.
Positives: Seriousness, Warmth, Nature, Earthiness, Reliability, Support.
Negatives: Lack of Humor, Heaviness, Lack of Sophistication.

Purple—Throughout her 2016 presidential campaign, Hillary Clinton's clothing was symbolic. A popular color for her was white; the color of the suffragette movement.[2] She wore it when she accepted the nomination at the Democratic National Convention, at the final presidential debate, and on Election Day. While making her concession speech to President-Elect Donald Trump and the nation on Wednesday, however, Clinton went with another color: purple.[3] This color, too, holds a tremendous amount of symbolism. Purple, along with white and gold, are the colors of the National Women's Party,[4] according to *The New York Times*. An early statement by the Democratic Party stated that purple symbolizes "loyalty, constancy to purpose, and unswerving steadfastness to a cause."[5]

---

[2] V. Friedman. 2016. On Election Day, the Hillary Clinton White Suit Effect. *The New York Times*. http://www.nytimes.com/2016/11/07/fashion/hillary-clinton-suffragists-white-clothing.html

[3] A. Romain. 2016. What Does Hillary Clinton's Purple Suit Mean? Her Concession Speech Outfit Was Symbolic. *Romper*. https://www.romper.com/p/what-does-hillary-clintons-purple-suit-mean-her-concession-speech-outfit-was-symbolic-22329

[4] V. Friedman. 2016. Why Hillary Wore White. *The New York Times*. http://www.nytimes.com/2016/07/30/fashion/hillary-clinton-democratic-national-convention.html

[5] A. LaCroix. The National Woman's Party and the Meaning Behind Their Purple, White, and Gold Textiles. National Woman's Party. http://nationalwomansparty.org/the-national-womans-party-and-the-meaning-behind-their-purple-white-and-gold-textiles/

To Better Understand the Impacts of Color

To better understand the impacts of color, there have been a number of studies conducted over the years.[6] Take a look at some of these interesting findings:

- Introducing blue streetlights in Glasgow, Scotland, and Nara, Japan, *decreased the number of crimes* in the areas with the new lights.
- Color *increases brand recognition by up to 80%*, according to a study at the University of Loyola, Baltimore, Maryland.
- An insurance company that began using color to highlight key information on their invoices began *receiving customer payments 14 days earlier*.
- An experiment showed that in a room with *red light, elapsed time was overestimated*, while in a *green or blue lit room, elapsed time was underestimated*.
- Workers *lifting black boxes thought that they were heavier* than the same boxes painted green.
- Silver cars are *least likely to be involved in an auto accident*, since they are most visible on the road and in low light.

---

[6] Brady Worldwide, Inc. www.bradyid.com

Chapter 42

Colors and Lighting for Parking Garages

The ceilings of parking garages should be painted or stained white to get the best reflection possible from lighting. With respect to lighting, consider LED because it is the most energy efficient, cost-effective lighting and produces a clean, white light. If you also paint or stain the walls white, it will enhance the effect of not only the crime prevention through environmental design (CPTED) principle of surveillance but also that of access control (due to visual sense of place) and maintenance, as related to the *broken windows theory*[1] of crime and disorder. The placement of lighting must be carefully considered in conjunction with video surveillance to avoid obscuring or making images undetectable due to glare and possible "hot spots" when using warm lighting sources.

---

[1] A.J. McKee. Broken Windows Theory. Britannica. http://www.britannica.com/topic/broken-windows-theory

Chapter 43

Street Lighting

Street lighting can have an effect on *perceived* personal safety and reduce the fear of becoming victimized in a particular environment. Street lighting is generally seen as the most important physical feature of an environment to affect *perceived* personal safety. The general consensus is that adequate street lighting can help reduce crime rates and also help to reduce the fear of crime.

Consideration again must be given to the environment that is addressed and its intended use. Over-lighting or too much light in a neighborhood may have a negative consequence on the surveillance principle of crime prevention through environmental design (CPTED) because residents may close their blinds or curtains to block out the offending, trespassing light, which will limit natural surveillance.

Chapter 44

"Hot Spots"

Since the 1980s, policing has shifted from a person-focused approach to include a location-based approach. Policing strategies that are concerned with the geographic distribution and explanation of crime include "hot spots" policing, community policing, problem-oriented policing, broken windows policing, third-party policing, and focused deterrence strategies. Hot spots policing focuses police efforts at crime prevention in a very small geographic area where crime is concentrated. Hot spots policing is grounded in both theory and research and has proven that crime concentrates at places more often than it concentrates in people.[1]

Hot spots should be eliminated. If they cannot be completely eliminated, develop a program, such as one of those mentioned above, to keep unauthorized users or unwanted individuals out of the area. Community policing programs, including the formulation of public-private sector partnerships[2] and the crime prevention through environmental design (CPTED) principle of territoriality, are useful to help fight disorder and crime and also to eliminate hot spots. Put criminals on notice that if illegal acts are committed in the area, they will be noticed and there will be consequences. Low fencing, gates, signage, different pavement textures, or other landscaping elements that visually show the transition between areas will indicate a sense of active "ownership" of the property. These are examples of territorial reinforcement.

Vacant lots are sometimes hot spots and are best monitored by citizens who take "ownership" of them. One example is a location in Richmond, Virginia, where there

---

[1] T. Kochel. Hot Spots Policing. Retrieved on May 1, 2017, from: http://www.oxfordbibliographies.com/view/document/obo-9780195396607/obo-9780195396607-0178.xml

[2] http://www.policechiefmagazine.org/building-partnerships-between-private-sector-security-and-public-sector-police-2/; Community Policing Consortium. 1994. *Understanding Community Policing: A Framework for Action*. Washington, DC: Bureau of Justice Assistance. http://www.ncjrs.gov/pdffiles/commp.pdf

is a community flower garden, and people who work in the garden monitor the space. Another option is for the city to share the property, giving the lot to Habitat for Humanity to build a structure within a given time frame, thus resulting in tax revenue.

Inspections from local government agencies can also result in the owners of vacant properties being held responsible for the upkeep of the properties or being made to pay fines for noncompliance.

Properties can be redesigned using CPTED principles to make them more crime resistant and reduce criminal opportunity from within the community.

There are some properties, such as Housing and Urban Development (HUD) properties, that may need a higher level of protection, such as additional lighting and video surveillance systems. Law enforcement support is also needed to address specific issues and to support a safe community.[3]

To Help Prevent Hot Spots

Locate open spaces and recreational areas in neighborhoods so they are visible (natural surveillance) from nearby homes as well as the street. Avoid landscaping that might create blind spots or hiding places. Make sure there is effective lighting. Design streets to discourage cut-through or high-speed traffic by using "traffic calming" measures. Owners and tenants should join or start a Neighborhood Watch in your neighborhood.[4,5]

In apartment buildings, ensure that interior hallways are well lit with a secure front door. Install good-quality deadbolt locks and provide door viewers (peepholes) on individual apartment exterior doors. Provide a secondary locking device to any sliding glass doors, windows on ground floor, and fire escapes. Provide common space in central locations to encourage tenant interaction. Join or start an Apartment Watch or Neighborhood Watch in your building.

For retail businesses, locate checkout counters near the front of the store, clearly visible from outside. Window signs should cover no more than 15% of the windows to provide clear visibility into and out of the store. Use shelving and displays no higher than 4 feet to help see who is in the store.[6] Avoid creating outdoor spaces that encourage loitering. Install mirrors at strategic locations as well as a security surveillance system.

[3] U.S. Department of Housing nd Urban Development. 2014. Vacant and Abandoned Properties: Turning Liabilities Into Assets. http://www.huduser.gov/portal/periodicals/em/winter14/highlight1.html

[4] L. Fennelly. 2017. *Effective Physical Security* (5th ed.). Oxford: Elsevier.

[5] National Crime Prevention Council. https://www.ncpc.org/resources/home-neighborhood-safety/

[6] https://www.ncpc.org/resources/home-neighborhood-safety/; Joliet Police Department. CPTED. http://tplha.org/prevention.pdf

Chapter 45

Managing Risk: CPTED Strategies for Single-Family Homes

Residential areas are the heart of the city, where people should feel most safe. While we may have multiple choices when it comes to walking through a certain part of town or using public transportation, we have fewer choices when it comes to the streets where we already live.

The principle here is "know thy neighbor." Promote Neighborhood Watch programs and design streets and homes to encourage interaction between neighbors.[1]

Natural Access Control

- Use walkways and landscaping to direct visitors to the proper entrance and away from private areas of individual homes.

Natural Surveillance

- Fully illuminate all doorways that open to the outside.
- Make sure the front door is at least partially visible from the street.

---

[1] Crime Prevention through Environmental Design, General Guidelines for Designing Safer Communities, City of Virginia Beach Municipal Center, January 20, 2000, updated in 2017. permission obtained to re-produce, https://www.vbgov.com/government/departments/planning/areaplans/Documents/Citywide/Cpted.pdf

- Install windows to provide visibility of the property.
- Provide appropriate illumination to sidewalks and all areas of the yard.
- Place the driveway to be visible from either the front or back door and at least one window.
- Properly select and install landscaping so that it allows unobstructed views of vulnerable doors and windows from the street and other properties.

Territorial Reinforcement

- Use front porches or stoops to create a transitional area between the street and the home.
- Define property lines and private areas with plantings, pavement treatments, or fences.
- Make the street address or house number clearly visible from the street and public areas.

Maintenance

- Keep trees and shrubs trimmed back from windows, doors, and walkways.
- A good rule to apply when visibility is an issue is keep shrubs trimmed to 3 feet in height and prune the lower branches of trees 7–8 feet to maintain clear visibility.
- Use exterior lighting at night, and keep it in working order.
- Keep litter and trash picked up and the yard neat at all times.
- The house and garage should be kept in good repair and locked at all times.

Chapter 46

Managing Risk: CPTED Strategies for Industrial Sites

In most industrial site designs, the most important issue is the safety of those who will be working or traveling to the sites.[1] Unfortunately, safety regarding crime is often given little consideration. After work hours, industrial areas are, for the most part, badly illuminated, seldom under any type of surveillance, and virtually deserted, which in itself can be a problem. Add to this isolation, blind alleys and expansive parking areas, and you have the potential for an extremely unsafe environment.

Natural Access Control

- Avoid dead-end driveways and design roadways to increase surveillance opportunities from passing traffic and patrols.
- Use easily securable site entrances.
- Install entrance controls to employee parking areas (fence, gate, and attendant).
- Assign parking by shifts, and appoint late-night workers with spots close to the building spaces.
- Plan storage yards for vehicular or visual access by patrol cars.
- Restrict access to roofs by way of dumpsters, loading docks, stacked items, ladders, and so on.
- Keep building entrances to a minimum, and monitor them.

---

[1] City of Oviedo, Florida. http://cityofoviedo.net/files/CPTED.pdf

- Use a separate, well-marked, monitored entrance for deliveries.
- Have the employee entrance close to the employee parking and workstations.
- Keep nighttime parking separate from service areas.
- Provide access to both the front and back of the site so that the grounds can be patrolled.
- Use separate docks for shipping and receiving.

Natural Surveillance

- Illuminate and define all entrances so that they are visible to the public and patrol vehicles.
- Make parking areas visible to patrol cars, pedestrians, parking attendants, and building personnel.
- Position parking attendants for maximum visibility of property.
- An open stair provides good visibility from entrances as well as the parking area.
- Design the reception areas to have a view of parking areas, especially the visitor's parking.
- Use walls only where necessary and, if used, make them high enough to prevent circumvention.
- Avoid creating hiding places in alleys, storage yards, loading docks, and so on.

Territorial Reinforcement

- Create a well-defined entrance or gateway with plantings, fences, gates, and so on.
- Limit deliveries to daylight hours only, if possible.
- Define vehicle entrances with different paving materials and signage.
- Separate visitor parking from employee parking and shipping and receiving areas.

Maintenance

- Keep all exterior areas neat and clean.
- Keep all plantings looking well managed and well maintained.

Chapter 47

Crime Prevention

The National Crime Prevention Institute (NCPI) definition of crime prevention provides some insight into a new focal point for law enforcement and security programs: "The anticipation, recognition, and appraisal of a crime risk, and the initiation of some action to remove or to reduce it."[1]

The crime-related aspects of law enforcement and security include at least six major functions. It is useful to examine each element individually to see how it relates to crime prevention:

1. Crime prevention in this limited context is the process of eliminating or reducing the opportunity to commit an offense, or the denial of access to crime targets.
2. Detection is the critical process of monitoring the activities and functions of the community to gather intelligence about the activities and associations of known offenders, and to identify and discover criminal activity that would have gone unnoticed. This process is fundamental to crime prevention and crime control. You cannot prevent it if you do not know about it.
3. Suppression is the act or method of restraining or controlling the activities of would-be or known offenders. A simple example of suppression is the monitoring and intense supervision of habitual juvenile offenders. Another example is the practice of active warrant service, particularly for repeat adult offenders. The object of these community control strategies is to prevent crime.
4. Investigation is the follow-up procedure for examining a criminal incident with the objective of solving the crime and resolving the problem. Contemporary case management procedures are limited to solving the crime and arresting the offender, instead of the traditional practice of following up on an offense

---

[1] M. Perry. 2010. National Crime Prevention Institute, The Basics of Physical Security Seminar.

to resolve the situation, to prevent it from happening again, or to bring the offender to justice. Contemporary case management systems focus on solvability factors that are valid for no more than 20% of all serious crimes that are solved, thus overlooking effective case resolution for 80% of the crimes that will not be solved. Case resolution and victim follow-up are good crime prevention.

5. Apprehension is the first step in the application of legal sanctions for accused offenders. Traditional police values call for the use of prevention and suppression of crime, using the arrest and the prosecution process only where punishment was required. That is, apprehension and prosecution were traditionally viewed as a final resort when other methods of crime control failed, not the primary solution.

6. Prosecution is the official presentation of fact to the court, with the intent of denying basic rights of freedom because of criminal activity. The courts are used where other social controls fail. Crime prevention can be enhanced by providing special support to the prosecution for habitual offenders who have proven themselves to be career offenders. Offenders do not have to be locked up to be incapacitated. All that has to be done is to effectively control them, either through close supervision or residential treatment programs. The effective control of repeat offenders is good crime prevention. Prosecution programs can assist in crime prevention.

Criminologists and public policy makers have perpetuated a limited definition and understanding of crime and criminal behavior. Many myths about the causes of crime exist because they are socially desirable. However, criminal behavior is pervasive throughout all levels of society, although it is popular to focus on common crime and common criminals. The concept of loss adds to the magnitude of crime and criminal behavior. It also adds to the reality that conventional reactive approaches to crime and loss are failing. Crime prevention through environmental design (CPTED) concepts integrate productivity and profit with security and loss prevention. The profit to a neighborhood is quality of life. A happy neighborhood does not tolerate, or experience, crime and loss problems. A well-run business has fewer losses. A good school has higher achievement levels and a lower incidence of disruptive behavior and criminal incidents. A downtown or shopping center that is successful in attracting customers makes greater profits and has fewer losses. Attention to crime and loss prevention will produce payoffs. Crime and loss prevention are inherent to human functions and activities, not just something that police or security officers do.

Chapter 48

CPTED Landscape Security Recommendations

An important element of crime prevention through environmental design (CPTED) that defines semiprivate and private space on property is landscape design.[1] It is recommended that the height of bushes be no higher than 3 feet. The Federal Emergency Management Agency (FEMA) recommends the height of bushes to be 18 inches and that tree branches should be trimmed to between 7 and 8 feet off of the ground to provide for natural surveillance. ASIS also recommends an 8-foot clearance height.[2] Hiding spots are eliminated so intruders can be detected. The landscaping of an area, if properly laid out, can be a deterrent and prevent criminal opportunity.

Landscape furniture should be vandal-resistant, and if benches are installed they need to be designed so that homeless individuals cannot sleep on them. Take into consideration exterior lighting, video surveillance, maintenance, barriers, security officers, entrances and exits to the property or building and appropriate signage.

Adequate lighting should be provided and walkways and entryways to buildings clearly visible for members of the community. Landscaping should be maintained to minimize obstacles for clear observability and places of concealment for potential assailants (Photo 48.1).

Sidewalks, streets, and parking lots must be clean (power washed) and free of graffiti. Ensure that there is proper signage and adequate lighting. There should be

---

[1] M. Perry. 2010. National Crime Prevention Institute, The Basics of Physical Security Seminar.
[2] M.E. Knoke and K.E. Peterson. 2015. *Physical Security Principles.* Alexandria, VA: ASIS, p. 214.

Photo 48.1   A house completely hidden with trees and bushes. (Photo taken by Marianna Perry, CPP.)

360° views of open areas. Consider creating a venue for after-school activities that encourage youth to take ownership of the space for socializing, such as small, secure shelter areas with cell phone chargers and Wi-Fi access.

Signage plays an important role in security, and there should be signage with information for those visiting or utilizing the area. Proper signage removes the excuses for unacceptable behavior, draws attention to the illegitimate activity, and legitimizes police involvement, thus making the violation of the information on the posted signs an excellent crime prevention tool.

There is a vast array of traffic calming devices, such as speed bumps and raised crosswalks. These areas should be painted yellow with proper signage posted.

Eliminate "hot spots" by planting thorny bushes (Barberry, Holly, etc.) in problem areas. Use boulders or bollards to control vehicular access. Consider adding community art or sculptures that not only control access but also reinforce the purpose by giving implied ownership to the artists. For natural access control, space should give some natural indication of where people are allowed and are not allowed. Do not depend just on locks, alarms, surveillance systems, and security officers, but make security part of the layout (Photos 48.2 and 48.3).

Perimeter fencing should be 7-feet tall with three strands of barbwire on the top for a total of 8 feet in height. We would not recommend this unless it was a large property and the perimeter was a significant distance from the business or

Photo 48.2 **Bollards to control vehicular access to building and also natural surveillance and proper landscape maintenance. (Photo taken by Marianna Perry, CPP.)**

Photo 48.3 **Bollards used to restrict vehicular access (e.g., from a car or truck bomb or intentional ramming) to a federal building as well as painted crosswalks for pedestrian safety. (Photo taken by Marianna Perry, CPP.)**

facility. Careful consideration to the type of fencing, the desired impact (boundary definition versus security), and the location of the facility (rural versus urban) must be taken into account and at least 10 feet of clear space should be allowed on both sides of the fence.

Landscape Security

Start burglar-proofing an area when designing and planting trees and bushes. Trees make great shade but can also lead burglars to upper stories where you are more apt to leave windows open or unlocked. Plant trees far enough away from houses or buildings so that they do not provide easy access to upper floors. This will also help prevent a tree from damaging the foundation of the house or building as it grows.

Think of the ground level, too. A tangle of shrubs near a door can create lurking places for thieves. Keep shrubs trimmed short, or plant perennials instead. Do not forget the back entry—many thieves look there first. If there is no convenient hiding place, thieves will generally look for an easier *target* in another location.[3]

For mailboxes, plant low-level vegetation around the base, and consider using a mixture of small rocks along the curb and at entryways.

Shrubbery, Trees, and Hedges

When picking out a potential target, thieves will often look for a property with thick shrubbery or tall hedges. A burglar will use the hedge for concealment as he or she looks in the windows for items of value to steal. Thick shrubbery also can become a hiding place for the burglar until the last person leaves the home or building. The goal is to have shrubbery trimmed down to a point where it is possible to see anyone near the premises. Some privacy may be lost, but on the other hand, you are giving a burglar fewer places to hide[4] (Photos 48.4 through 48.6).

Author Morgan Grove, who is also a researcher with the U.S. Forest Service (USFS), says that criminals tend to look for spaces where they can operate without being seen, or where if they are seen, they will not be reported. "The level maintenance of the yard is almost like a neighborhood watch sign saying, "We have eyes on the street and we will say something," Morgan Grove says, "There a physical fact, which is that People can see criminals, but this symbolic meaning that reinforces the social order that people will intervene on their own behalf and on the behalf of others."[5]

The "broken windows theory" suggests that criminals look for physical signs of neglect when scoping out targets. Research supports the "Cues to Care theory," meaning that visible maintenance of shared spaces presents "a sign of social capital and cohesion that might deter criminals."

---

[3] Better Homes and Gardens. Landscaping for Security. Retrieved on November 1, 2016, from: http://www.bhg.com/gardening/landscaping-projects/landscape-basics/landscaping-for-security/

[4] K. Raposo. 2012. Home Security Landscaping—Nature's Home Security System. Retrieved on November 1, 2016, from: http://simplisafe.com/blog/home-security-landscaping-natures-home-security-system#sthash.BqC3cPT7.dpuf

[5] http://thevillagefreepress.org/2016/04/13/one-possible-solution-to-maywoods-crime-problem-more-green-space-and-well-kept-laws/

Photo 48.4   Trees on each side of a house trimmed to 8 feet from the ground to allow for natural surveillance. (Photos taken by Marianna Perry.)

Photo 48.5   Overgrown bushes that are obstructing the natural surveillance of the apartment building. (Photo taken by Marianna Perry, CPP.)

Urban greenery[6] should play more of a role in a city's plans to reduce crime. A good first step would be increasing public attention to landscaping in high-crime areas and assisting residents in taking care of their own property. This will bring

---

[6] https://www.citylab.com/solutions/2016/04/vacant-lots-green-space-crime-research-statistics/476040/

Photo 48.6   Can you see the window obstructed by the vegetation? (Photo taken by Marianna Perry, CPP.)

more urgency to the maintenance of vegetation in public areas. A dead tree on the sidewalk is not just a dead tree anymore, it is an indication that no one cares about the area.[7]

Conclusion: We cannot emphasize enough the importance of landscape security and the importance of natural surveillance if no other reason than for the safety of your community.

[7] J. Spector. 2016. Another Reason to Love Urban Green Space: It Fights Crime. Retrieved November 2016, from: http://www.citylab.com/cityfixer/2016/04/vacant-lots-green-space-crime-research-statistics/476040/

Chapter 49

Design Out Crime

The Designing Out Crime Association (DOCA) is seeking to build upon the original principles of crime prevention through environmental design (CPTED) by defining our principles as[1]:

Reducing the possibility, probability, and harm from criminal and related events, and enhancing the quality of life through community safety; through the processes of planning and design of the environment; on a range of scales and types of place, from individual buildings and interiors to wider landscapes, neighborhoods, and cities; to produce designs that are "fit for purpose," contextually appropriate in all other respects and not "vulnerability led"; whilst achieving a balance between the efficiency of avoiding crime problems before construction and the adaptability of tackling them through subsequent management and maintenance.

---

[1] Reprinted from Designing Out Crime Association. About- DOCA. http://www.doca.org.uk/

Chapter 50

Block Watch in Canada: CPTED

Crime prevention through environmental design (CPTED) is a crime prevention approach based on a theory that the built environment influences the behavior of people. The proper design and effective use of the built environment can lead to a reduction in the incidence and fear of crime, thereby improving the quality of life. CPTED involves the design of the physical space relative to the needs of the users, the normal use of the space, and the predictable behavior of the users of the space. Crime decreases if the opportunity to commit the crime is reduced or eliminated. CPTED works by eliminating criminal opportunities in and around your property. This can result in properties becoming a less-appealing target.

Block Watch

See Figure 50.1.

A Neighbor Is Your Best Burglar Alarm

Block Watch is all about neighbors helping neighbors.[1] Households, apartments, or condominiums on a block form a communication chain aided by a map of names, telephone numbers, and addresses. Participants watch out for each other's homes

---

[1] CPTED. Toronto Police Service. http://www.torontopolice.on.ca/crimeprevention/environmental.pdf

Figure 50.1 An example of a sign that can be used for blockwatch/neighborhood watch.

and report suspicious activities to the police and each other. This communication is crucial in reducing the likelihood of residential crime.[2]

History

The Block Watch Program was initiated in Seattle, Washington, in 1974, with participating homes seeing a decrease in residential break-ins of between 48% and 62%. Surrey was the first municipality in British Columbia to start a Block Watch Program, which has now spread the length of the Lower Mainland and through several communities across the Province.[3]

Mission

Working together, building safer neighborhoods throughout your community.

---

[2] The Vancouver Police Department. Block Watch. http://vancouver.ca/police/community-poli cing/block-watch/

[3] Victoria Police Department. Block Watch. http://vicpd.ca/block-watch

How Does Neighborhood Watch Work

As part of the program, you learn the following:

- How to make your home less inviting as a target for thieves
- How to participate in an engraving program to mark your valuables under the operation ID program
- How to recognize and report suspicious activity to the police
- How to increase your personal safety
- How to prevent auto theft
- What is happening in community crime prevention through a Block Watch newsletter[4]

Top Eight Things You Need to Know about Crime Prevention and Neighborhood Watch

1. Ever wonder why one house is broken into and the one next door is not, or did they make it easy for them since a door was left unlocked?
2. People like to generally hide a key and it is within 25 feet of their front door.
3. Home intrusion alarms need a 100% test month to make sure it is working.
4. Sliding glass doors need secondary locking devices or a wooden stick in the track.
5. You are walking down the street, and you see four newspapers on the lawn. What does this tell you?
6. CPTED and landscape security are mentioned several times in this text.
7. Do you know your neighbors, check on them, say hello, and so on?
8. Finally, Neighborhood Watch is a serious program. One of its objectives is to be a good neighbor and be an extra set of eyes for your law enforcement authority. To reduce criminal opportunity, *do not* make it easy for these crooks—*be proactive.*

Purpose

- A commitment to communities to build safer neighborhoods by providing support, guidance, training, and resource materials to develop and operate Block Watch programs.

---

[4] http://www.rcmp-grc.gc.ca/en/client-and-partner-surveys-2016

Join a Block Watch

Joining or starting a Block Watch in your neighborhood takes just a couple minutes of your time. If your street does not have an active Block Watch, someone must volunteer to become the block captain and enlist the help of a co-captain. All captains and co-captains must be security cleared by the police. This merely involves the completion of a security clearance application form.

Four Steps to Starting a Block Watch

The following four steps are used when starting a Block Watch[5]:

1. Recruit and organize as many neighbors as possible.
2. Discuss community concerns and develop an action plan.
3. Hold regular meetings and train on relevant skills.
4. Implement a phone tree and take action steps.

Benefits of the Block Watch Program

These benefits include the following[6]:

■ Studies have shown that crime is reduced in active Block Watch neighborhoods.
■ Block Watch teams can develop a sense of community pride and connection with their neighbors.
■ Learn how to better protect the home, identify suspicious behavior, and more effectively report it.
■ Active Block Watch teams have direct access to a police officer for support and guidance in dealing with neighborhood crime issues and crime patterns.
■ You will be connected with your local community policing center for additional support in crime prevention in your neighborhood.
■ Receive recognizable Block Watch street signs and door and window decals to identify your block as one that reports suspicious activity to police.
■ Get connected to the Victoria Police Neighborhood Crime Alert Program and receive e-mails with postal code–specific crime alerts informing of important changes in crime trends in the neighborhood.

---

[5] http://www.covingtonwa.gov/block-watch-handbook.ashx.pdf
[6] Abbotsford Police Department. Block Watch. http://www.abbypd.ca/block-watch

Chapter 51

Designing Out Crime in the United Kingdom: Why Design Out Crime?

Introduction

Why design out crime? Crime in the United Kingdom has fallen over the last decade, but as society and technology have evolved, new crime challenges have emerged.[1] Changing behavior is of course one aspect of crime reduction, but design also has an important role to play in preventing crime and reducing criminal activity without compromising the enjoyment and usability of products, places, and services by legitimate users. So, central in designing out crime is being focused on those you are designing for, as well as those you are designing to thwart. If designers consider the ways in which the object, systems, or environments they are designing might be susceptible to crime—and do this early enough in the design process—they can prevent crime from occurring, or at least reduce the opportunities for offender behavior. This might mean, for example, product designers understanding more about how portable consumer electronics like mobile phones and MP3 players are attractive to thieves because they are small, valuable, and easy to re-sell. Interior designers working on bar and restaurant projects might need to think about how the layout of interior space and the furniture they specify can help prevent thefts of and from customers' bags, or how the design of bathrooms and toilets can help prevent illegal drug use. Similarly, designers of bicycles, cycling accessories, and

---

[1] Design Council. Case Study: Design Out Crime. http://www.designcouncil.org.uk/resources/case-study/design-out-crime. Permission obtained to reproduce, August 2017.

street furniture might need to understand how and when bicycle theft most often occurs.

Designing Out Crime

From the start, it is important to understand that designing out crime is not simply a case of designing better locks and bolts. For it to be most effective (and cost effective), crime prevention needs to be designed-in at the start of a project, where it is able to influence choices and behavior, not added on at the end.

Designers

Designers already use sophisticated techniques throughout the design process to fully understand people's latent and unmet needs, in order to create products, services, and spaces that are usable and desirable. In taking time to research users and customers at the beginning of the design process, designers will often find that what people say they do often does not reflect what they actually do in practice. In the same way, by researching abuser "needs" such as loopholes and weaknesses in systems, situations, and premises, designers can apply this creativity and innovation to developing sophisticated solutions that can prevent and ultimately preempt crime. When places, products, and services are developed with crime resistance in mind, designers can help to make it more difficult, more risky, or less attractive for offenders to commit crimes, and help to make it easier for people to stay safe and keep their belongings secure. This makes people and communities feel safer. The cost of crime brings with it a cost to individuals and businesses in three ways: costs incurred in anticipation of crime (the cost of security), costs incurred as a consequence of crime, and costs of responding to crime—for individuals the cost of crime can include time off work through injury, as well as the hidden costs of anxiety, stress, feelings of vulnerability, and reduced confidence. For businesses, this can lead to a fall in productivity or difficulty retaining or recruiting staff. And of course, crime has additional costs for local and national authorities in terms of police time and the cost to the National Health Services and other public services. It is difficult to calculate the cost of crime against businesses, but British Chambers of Commerce estimate that crime costs UK businesses £12.6 billion a year.

How Designing Out Crime May Differ from Other Design Briefs and Projects

Crime is a social issue—it involves individuals (both the victims of crime and people who commit crimes) as well as social systems including the police and the justice system. For designers, one of the hardest things to grasp when thinking about designed responses to crime is the complexity of the whole ecosystem. This complexity, in turn, means that the solutions to design out crime problems may turn out to be very different from what the designer or client may have imagined at the start. For example, the theft of prestige vehicles is often not the result of an opportunistic criminal act: frequently, this involves organized criminal gangs, using the vehicles as currency to fund other offenses such as the supply of drugs or firearms. This is why in design out crime projects particularly, it is crucial to undertake research, user observation, and stakeholder interviews at the start of the design process, and to engage in divergent, wide-ranging thinking and idea generation, which will enable designers to consider all the areas where a designed approach can help to reduce crime or lessen its impact. For designers, this is an opportunity to extend the reach and influence of the work they do.

On a purely commercial level, this may mean that in considering how to design crime out of a product or service, designers may identify new clients or new markets for their work. In-house designers and brand owners may see opportunities for brands to extend their reach or to differentiate themselves from competitors. For example, glassware manufacturer Arc International and UK glassware firm Utopia are both currently developing new, safer glasses for use in pubs and clubs. These separate projects aim to help reduce the estimated 87,000 violent incidents involving glass which occur each year across the United Kingdom. Both companies hope this early investment in "next-generation" pint glasses will improve market share. Designing out crime can also help designers and design agencies make their work responsive to broader social challenges. So, the approaches, tools, and methods that designers have always used are put to use to create products that are easy to use and that people want to own.

Chapter 52

CPTED in Canada

Crime prevention through environmental design (CPTED) is an approach to building and property planning and development that reduces opportunities for crime.[1] Communities, neighborhoods, individual homes, and other buildings, streets, and parks can all be made safer through the application of design principles that make it more difficult to carry out inappropriate or criminal activities.

CPTED can reduce crime and the fear of crime through the following[2]:

- Territoriality—fostering residents' interaction, vigilance, and control over their neighborhood
- Surveillance—maximizing the ability to spot suspicious people and activities
- Activity support—encouraging the intended use of public space by residents
- Hierarchy of space—identifying ownership by delineating private space from public space through real or symbolic boundaries
- Access control/target hardening—using physical barriers, security devices, and tamper-resistant materials to restrict entrance
- Environment—a design or location decision that takes into account the surrounding environment and minimizes the use of space by conflicting groups
- Image/Maintenance—ensuring that a building or area is clean, well maintained, and graffiti free

The North Vancouver RCMP offers CPTED evaluations for free to the citizens of North Vancouver. During an evaluation, a police officer trained in CPTED will attend the location in question to photograph and review the area. They will then

---

[1] http://www.popcenter.org/tools/cpted/PDFs/NCPC.pdf
[2] Design Centre for CPTED. http://www.designcentreforcpted.org/

compose a formal report with suggestions about how to change the environment of the location to reduce crime.[3]

Some key areas[4] for action were highlighted in the audits and confirmed in focus group discussions with the residents. These findings are consistent with police hot spots and service calls to the city.

Streets

1. *Trim trees and bushes*
2. *Clean up streets and yards*
3. *Improve lighting*
4. *Improvements to signage*

Alleys

1. Continue efforts to light the alleys of North Central. Auditors strongly recommended back alley lighting. Care would have to be given to install lights that could not easily be vandalized and that would not create shadows.
2. Trim trees and bushes. Overgrown bushes and trees need cutting back to open up alleys, improve sight lines, and reduce the number of hiding sites.
3. Clean up the alleys and yards. Maintenance issues to be addressed include cleaning up litter and graffiti in certain blocks.

Parks

1. Update parks and provide more activities. While the auditors felt that, overall, the parks were good, they wanted more attractions, especially updated play equipment, and activities for youth. This would attract more people, decreasing the sense of isolation and increasing the number of legitimate users.
2. Improve maintenance. Maintenance was described as mostly satisfactory. Overgrown bushes and trees need trimming, especially in Confederation, Parkdale, and Dewdney Pool Parks, around buildings and along parkways. The equipment in some parks needs to be fixed, and gang tags, graffiti, and litter cleaned up.
3. Improve lighting. Electrical lighting could be brighter.

---

[3] http://bc.rcmp-grc.gc.ca/viewpage.action?siteNodeId=50&languageId=1&contentId=4814
[4] North Central Crime Prevention through Environmental Design (CPTED) Final Report. http://www.regina.ca/opencms/export/sites/regina.ca/residents/social-grants-programs/.media/pdf/North_Central_CPTED_Project_Report.pdf

For more information, visit: North Central Crime Prevention through Environmental Design (CPTED) Final Report. http://www.regina.ca/opencms/export/sites/regina.ca/residents/social-grants-programs/.media/pdf/North_Central_CPTED_Project_Report.pdf

Chapter 53

Crime Prevention Ottawa Study and Recommendations for CPTED in Ottawa: January 19, 2009

Introduction

Crime prevention through environmental design (CPTED) is an important component of a comprehensive approach to crime prevention. CPTED entails understanding the relationship between physical design and levels of criminal activity and then manipulating design to reduce the incidence of crime.

In this report, we review the evidence on the ability of CPTED strategies to reduce crime and fear of crime, and review best practices concerning CPTED. We use key actor interviews to examine the need for strategic, coordinated CPTED in Ottawa and to assess the use of and support for CPTED programs.

Methodology

The study involved a literature review of CPTED research and in-person and telephone interviews with 24 key actors who were knowledgeable about CPTED use. The majority of those interviewed were from Ottawa.[1]

Findings

There is a growing body of evidence that CPTED can reduce crime and fear of crime.

CPTED has been successfully used in Ottawa, but its impact has been limited because the use of CPTED is not coordinated, is not adequately funded, is not mandated by legislation or regulation, and is not linked to a broader crime prevention strategy.

Recommendations

Our recommendations are based on the views of the key actors we interviewed and the lessons learned from the best practices review. Both of these sources gave very consistent direction about the best way to proceed. Ottawa can take a global leadership role by incorporating CPTED as a core part of a broad and comprehensive crime prevention strategy. To accomplish this, we recommend the following:

Crime Prevention Ottawa should begin the process of integrating CPTED into municipal planning by organizing a planning meeting for those with an interest in community safety and CPTED.

The goals of the meeting might include the following:

1. Familiarizing people with CPTED. Participants will have different levels of knowledge about CPTED and all should know the strengths and weaknesses of CPTED and understand its role as part of a comprehensive crime prevention strategy.
2. Developing an inventory of the CPTED-related activities now taking place in Ottawa.
3. Establishing a network of people who should be involved in increasing the use of CPTED in Ottawa.
4. Establishing the structure for a CPTED Working Group to move ahead with the next steps in the process.

---

[1] Crime Prevention Ottawa Study and Recommendations for CPTED in Ottawa—January 19, 2009. http://www.crimepreventionottawa.ca/uploads/files/initiative/final_report_jan_19.pdf

5. Crime Prevention Ottawa should convene and support the CPTED Working Group that will coordinate CPTED activities. This CPTED Working Group should have the responsibility of developing Terms of Reference, setting priorities, assigning tasks, monitoring activities and outcomes, and making recommendations concerning the resources required to implement CPTED recommendations. The Working Group should report back to the City Manager's office.

6. A municipal official should be given the task of facilitating the use of CPTED in Ottawa. This person would be responsible for moving the initiative through the political and administrative systems. The person could be a senior planner or other senior administrator who could champion the process and deal with barriers to change. This person would also be a key member of the CPTED Working Group and would likely work on CPTED along with his or her regular duties rather than as a full-time job.

7. Crime Prevention Ottawa should coordinate CPTED training for people involved in the planning process who have not yet received it. A less-intensive familiarization should be given to key decision-makers including politicians and senior city managers.

8. A public education campaign should be developed to familiarize the public with the benefits of CPTED. The Working Group should consider following several other jurisdictions that use terms such as Design Out Crime which may have more public appeal than the term *CPTED.*

9. A process must be developed that will give the public input into the use of CPTED. Members of groups such as neighborhood associations and women's organizations should have access to CPTED training and have the opportunity to participate in community crime audits and to review development plans. Alignment of some aspects of CPTED planning with the Neighborhood Planning Initiative would help to ensure public input.

10. The City of Ottawa and Crime Prevention Ottawa should work with other municipalities to encourage the provincial and federal governments to play a greater role in developing and supporting CPTED as part of a broad crime prevention strategy.

Recommendations Concerning New Development

CPTED should be integrated into existing planning and development programs. CPTED standards should be written into regulations and be part of the design process from the beginning. This would represent a significant change in the process and so could be implemented incrementally over time as guided by the CPTED Working Group. It is far more difficult to incorporate CPTED planning at a later stage of the design process when many key decisions have already been made. Planning programs such as Community Design Plans, the Downtown Ottawa

Urban Design Strategy, and the Neighborhood Planning Initiative should include CPTED design principles.

Recommendations Concerning Problems with Existing Facilities

1. The CPTED Working Group should develop a process to set priorities for safety audits of existing facilities, parks, or neighborhoods and ensure that these audits are coordinated.
2. The CPTED Working Group should also establish a mechanism that will ensure follow-up on audits to encourage the responsible parties to act on the recommendations. Requiring private owners to make changes to existing facilities can be difficult, so we recommend that a combination of regulations and incentives such as certification (which is used in Crime Free Multi-Housing) be used to deal with CPTED problems in existing construction.

Chapter 54

CPTED: Calgary Police Services

Crime prevention through environmental design (CPTED) is being used worldwide.[1] It enhances safety by influencing the physical design of our environment and encouraging positive social interaction. CPTED recognizes that our environment directly affects our behavior, because we constantly respond to what is around us. These responses help us to interact safely in our communities.

How Does CPTED Work?

An environment designed using CPTED principles reduces opportunities for criminal acts to take place and helps us to feel safer.[2] By doing so, it improves our quality of life. CPTED uses strategies that work together to create safer communities. It complements crime prevention strategies such as locks and bars, police, and security personnel.

Here Are a Few Examples

- Create a sense of guardianship to deter criminals by maintaining homes, buildings, parks, and community areas.

[1] Calgary Police Service. Crime Prevention through Environmental Design (CPTED). http://www.calgary.ca/cps/Pages/Community-programs-and-resources/Crime-prevention/Crime-Prevention-Through-Environmental-Design.aspx

[2] Retrieved on August 21, 2017, from: http://www.popcenter.org/tools/cpted/PDFs/NCPC.pdf

- Discourage criminals in public places and encourage community involvement by legitimate users, such as residents and visitors.
- Natural access control can guide how people use space by the placement of entrances, exits, fences, landscaping, lighting, and cameras.

CPTED tips to enhance security:

- Keep shrubs and trees trimmed from windows and doors to improve visibility
- Use lighting over entrances
- Use thorny plants along fence lines and around vulnerable windows
- Join Block Watch or Apartment Watch
- Avoid landscaping that might create blind spots or hiding places
- Ensure apartment hallways and parking areas are well lit
- Install good-quality deadbolts and peepholes on apartment doors

Chapter 55

CPTED: a.k.a. Design against Crime

It *is* possible to use the built, urban environment to improve quality of life and reduce opportunities for crime.[1] There are physical design features that encourage legitimate users, while at the same time discourage criminal behavior. Crime prevention through environmental design (CPTED) strategies use designs with a positive visual impact that offer protection, without a "fortress" appearance. When CPTED concepts are integrated into the construction process, they are cost effective and can work well with the overall design of the building.

In the book titled, *Design against Crime*, Barry Poyner describes an eight-step program set out by the British Home Office, Research Unit:

1. *Target hardening*
2. *Target removal*
3. *Removing the means to crime*
4. *Reducing the pay-off*
5. *Formal surveillance*
6. *Natural surveillance*
7. *Surveillance by employees*
8. *Environmental management*

---

[1] B. Poyner. 1983. *Design against Crime*. Oxford, UK: Butterworth-Heinemann, p. 8.

In *Crime Prevention through Environmental Design: Applications of Architectural Design and Space Management Concepts* (Crowe, 2000),[2] Crowe asserted, "the proper design and effective use of the built environment can lead to a reduction in the fear and incidence of crime, and an improvement in the quality of life."

The goal of CPTED is to reduce opportunities for crime to occur.

---

[2] T. D. Crowe, 2000. *Crime Prevention Through Environmental Design: Applications of Architectural Design and Space Management Concepts*, Boston: Butterworth-Heinemann.

Chapter 56

The Role of Police in Crime Prevention through Environmental Design[1]

Why Should Police Departments Be Involved in Crime Prevention through Environmental Design?

Police should be involved for a number of reasons:

- Police have ongoing current knowledge of criminal behavior, which manifests itself in crimes being committed. This knowledge arises in the "micro" sense (reporting of individual offences) and in the "macro" sense (through the collating of offenses to establish trends of criminal activity).
- Police personnel often are the only "public officers" attending consistently at locations where offenses are being committed, and who have the opportunity to recognize the need for new design and redesign of physical factors influencing the commission of offenses.
- Police departments have, over the years, been establishing specialist intelligence collecting and collating functions, procedures, and systems. These operate at both tactical and strategic levels. They have the capacity to identify trends of crime or other antisocial activity that could be deterred or prevented by crime prevention through environmental design (CPTED) techniques.

[1] Chief Superintendent Robert J. Potts, Officer in Charge Research and Development, South Australia Police Department—Adelaide and http://www.popcenter.org/tools/cpted/PDFs/NCPC.pdf

■ Police departments have been developing specialist crime prevention bureaus to supplement and support local crime prevention initiatives. Considerable expertise has been built up in these areas especially regarding personal safety, home and commercial security, and other anticrime measures, or until social programs can be devised, which reduce the motivation of people to commit such crimes, CPTED can help make our homes and streets safer (Geason and Wilson, 1989, pp. 9–10).[2]

---

[2] S. Geason and P. R. Wilson. 1988. *Crime Prevention: Theory and Practice*, Australian Institute of Criminology.

Chapter 57

Milan: Crime Prevention through Urban Design[1]

Main Findings

The value of the research is to have identified those factors in the urban environment that have an incidence on crime and fear of crime and to have grouped them in simply observable or measurable indicators. Indicators are physical, temporal, and social factors that contribute to make an environment potentially safe—or unsafe—in terms of real risk and in terms of perception. They are a useful technical tool that allows technicians and decision-makers to introduce concepts of safety in the planning, design, and rehabilitation of neighborhoods. Their role is to clarify the factors in the urban environment that have an implication on safety and present them in a structured and organized form.

The 12 indicators that have been considered in this report are as follows:

1. Main land use
2. Urban grid map
3. Urban forms and open spaces
4. Street frontage
5. Lighting
6. Day activities
7. Night activities
8. The hidden activities
9. Pedestrian flows

---

[1] Academic Research and Training, September 2014: A Case Study. http://costtu1203.eu/milan-crime-prevention-through-urban-design-academic-research-and-training/

10. Car traffic
11. Public transport
12. Decay

Through a mapping and scoring process, these indicators allow maps to be built up that assess the propensity to safety of a studied area. By propensity to safety is meant the potential of one space to be safe or unsafe according to some of its physical and social characteristics.

Emerging Issues

■ The system of indicators and maps is an important support for urban projects that are implemented by local authorities. It can be applied to correct existing situations or to prevent errors in new developments.

■ In existing areas, it allows the propensity to safety of a neighborhood to be evaluated and can be used, for instance, for locating playgrounds, community parks, transport stops, and so on. They also are a useful support for any crime prevention policy in an area, as they provide the necessary indications of where to intervene.

■ For new projects, the indicator system is useful to check whether the project is meeting the criteria for safe public places, for example, if the entrances are safe and overlooked, if spaces for activities are lacking, if public transport to home is safe, if the parks are well located, and so on. This allows situations of insecurity to be corrected or prevented.

Lessons Learned

■ Positive aspects
■ The tools work: they are appropriate methods to assess the situation of a built environment.
■ The teaching courses with students have been successful experiences, in one semester of intensive work the students were able to gain knowledge of crime prevention criteria and develop a project taking them into account.
■ Working with local authorities on crime prevention projects, the indicators prove also to be a very useful tool.
■ The indicators are a useful tool for assessing projects of future developments and can provide a guide for improving the projects or for assessing them before planning permission.
■ Negative aspects
■ The indicator method is quite costly (surveys); the mapping system is heavy and needs to be simplified with new cartographic methods and applications.

- The indicator method asks for a staff trained in this specific technique; this is not very easy to obtain.
- Like most crime prevention strategies, the method of the indicators encounters the resistance of architects to be applied to projects.
- The laboratory, which has been working for many years and accumulating a long and specific know-how, is a vulnerable structure and depends on the decisions at the management level of the university and has no guarantee of continuity.

Transferability

- The indicators mapping has the advantage to be highly transferable to other countries in Europe and the tools can be easily understood by architects and planners—maps are an international graphic language.
- The tools are close to those already used by architects and planners; thus, they are very easy to use for these professionals and are easy to transfer.
- With some training, these indicators can also be used by anthropologists and sociologists. For other disciplines, they are not easily understandable instruments; for decision-makers, they speak a language that is too analytical.

For information on the COST-Action TU 1203:
http://www.cost.eu/COST_Actions/tud/TU1203

Chapter 58

The Community Policing Consortium Project: Partnerships Involving Community Policing and CPTED

The Community Policing Consortium Project—a project initiated by the Bureau of Justice Assistance and continued by the Office of Community-Oriented Policing Services that involved the International Association of Chiefs of Police, the National Sheriffs' Association, the Police Executive Research Forum, the National Organization of Black Law Enforcement Executives, and the Police Foundation— recently underscored community partnerships and problem-solving processes as the two core components of community policing.[1]

Both crime prevention through environmental design (CPTED) and community policing rely on partnerships with community, government, educational, and social agencies in order to implement crime prevention strategies. Both programs also use the SARA problem-solving model as a key part of their approach. The Newport News Police Department, under the sponsorship of the

---

[1] Understanding Community Policing: A Framework for Action, 1994, U.S. Department of Justice, Bureau of Justice Assistance.

National Institute of Justice (NIJ) and the Police Executive Research Forum, created this four-step model[2]:

- Scanning—identify the problem.
- Analysis—study the problem and identify possible solutions.
- Response—implement a custom-designed response.
- Assessment—evaluate the action taken.

This problem-solving model provides an easy and understandable framework for developing the broad partnerships necessary for CPTED and community policing initiatives to succeed. Decisions regarding the use and management of the physical environment can have an even broader effect on security throughout a neighborhood. For example, environmental strategies that are designed to reduce crime and fear (such as closing drug houses and using traffic diversion and control to promote neighborhood cohesion) can also increase informal social control and enhance the quality of neighborhood life.[3]

In Hartford, Connecticut, police and community residents used a comprehensive CPTED/community policing strategy that gave back to residents control over their neighborhood (see "CPTED and Community Policing in Hartford"). Another example concerns enhancing security in a public housing development by reducing the number of families using a specific building entrance. This action increased residents' sense of responsibility for controlling who entered their building.

What Police and Residents Can Do

Thus, police agencies, community residents, and local officials all have roles to play in implementing a comprehensive CPTED/community policing strategy to promote public safety in private neighborhoods, business areas, and public housing.[4]

Police can:

- Conduct security surveys for residents and provide security improvements such as adequate lighting and locks.
- Conduct park patrols and patrols of other public spaces to eliminate crime and drug use.

[2] J. Eck and W. Spelman. 1987. Problem Solving: Problem-Oriented Policing in Newport News. Police Executive Research Forum (also reported in the NIJ Research in Brief, Problem-Oriented Policing, Spelman and Eck, January 1987).

[3] S. Greenberg et al. 1985. *Informal Citizen Action and Crime Prevention at the Neighborhood Level.* Washington, DC: U.S. Department of Justice.

[4] H. Goldstein. 1979. Improving policing: A problem-oriented approach. *Crime and Delinquency* 25: 236–258.

- Use their substations to inform residents of high-risk locations in the neighborhood.
- Work with urban planners and architects to review the designs and plans in order to enhance community security.
- Prepare educational materials for building owners and managers to deal with problem tenants and enhance the livability and security of rental units.

These materials are useful because they address not only the manner in which the physical environment is designed but also how the environment can be managed more effectively to enhance public safety.

Control traffic flow to reduce the use of streets by criminals and enhance neighborhood cohesion and resident interaction. Streets can be closed or traffic diverted to create residential enclaves that give residents greater control of their living environment. Residents can improve their neighborhoods by

- Engaging in cleanup programs to remove trash or graffiti
- Carrying out programs to improve the appearance, safety, and use of public spaces
- Conducting their own patrols to identify neighborhood problems
- Joining an organized Block Watch program
- Participating in specific crime prevention activities

Security in Parks

Parks can be refurbished, lighting installed, and opening and closing times scheduled to improve security. Adopt-a-park programs can be used to involve residents in cleaning up trash and litter and providing information to police about illegal activities being carried out in recreational areas. Recreational events can be scheduled to increase the community's informal social control of these places.

Building Regulations

Local governments can be encouraged to use building codes as well as inspection and enforcement powers to increase environmental security. The owners of deteriorated or abandoned buildings can be required to repair, secure, or demolish them. Provisions related to security can also be incorporated into the city building code. These provisions include target hardening tactics (e.g., locks, strengthening of doors, lighting, and closed-circuit television [CCTV]).

NIJ research in Hartford, Connecticut, provides a useful demonstration of a comprehensive CPTED/community policing approach to neighborhood crime prevention. This program successfully incorporated resident initiatives, CPTED (in the form of traffic diversion and the development of neighborhood enclaves), and community policing. CPTED strategies were also critical in helping residents gain more control over their neighborhood.

These included a focus on citizen patrols, increased lighting, greater control of juvenile activities, and the use of cleanup campaigns to enhance the quality of neighborhood life. These efforts influenced the residents' use of their neighborhood and the level of interaction and social control exercised by citizens in that setting.

Trends

One general trend has been for CPTED and community policing strategies to reinforce each other as they focus on comprehensive problem solving, the promotion of working relationships with the community, and the development of education and orientation programs.

Chapter 59

CPTED versus Traditional Security: Security Surveillance Systems (CCTV) and the Theory of Deterrence

Introduction

Over the years, much has been written (articles and books) on video surveillance systems (or closed-circuit television [CCTV]) because they are frequently used as one component in an overall security program.[1]

Security Surveillance Systems

The promise of video surveillance lies in the expectation of deterrence. Deterrence approaches, and of crime prevention strategies in particular, aim to put into place practices or conditions that "convince criminals to desist from criminal activities, delay their actions, or avoid a particular target" expectations—and some

---

[1] CCTV: Literature Review and Bibliography. Royal Canadian Mounted Police, Research and Evaluation Branch, Community and Aboriginal Policing Service Directorate, Wade Deisman, University of Ottawa, 2003, p. 10.

submerged assumptions about the cognitive processes, motivational impulses, and empirical experiences of potential offenders. To the extent that the efficacy of video surveillance as a deterrent tactic depends, at least in part, on the degree to which these expectations and assumptions hold true, so a reconstructive explication of the chain of expectations and assumptions is necessary.

The deterrent effect of video surveillance depends on the following:

1. A potential perpetrator enters a space monitored by video surveillance and is either already aware of the fact of monitoring or somehow became aware of the fact.
2. The potential perpetrator either (a) already holds the belief that a crime committed in a space monitored by video surveillance is more likely to be detected or (b) somehow comes to that conclusion once he or she observes the cameras in operation. The submerged assumption here is that a potential perpetrator is motivated to avoid detection.
3. The potential perpetrator either (a) already holds the belief that he or she is more likely to be identified if he or she commits a crime in a space monitored by CCTV or (b) comes to that conclusion once he or she observes the cameras in operation. The submerged assumption here is that the potential perpetrator is motivated to avoid identification.
4. The potential perpetrator either (a) already holds the belief that he or she is more likely to be apprehended if he or she commits a crime in a space monitored by CCTV or (b) comes to that conclusion once he or she observes the cameras in operation. The submerged assumption here is that the potential perpetrator is motivated to avoid apprehension.
5. The potential perpetrator engages in a calculation, in which he or she weighs the potential gains against the following motivations: (a) not to have his or her crime detected, (b) not to be identified, or (c) not to be apprehended.
6. The potential perpetrator concludes, as a result of this recalculation, that not having his or her crime detected, not being identified, not being apprehended, or any combination outweighs the potential gains associated with going ahead and committing the crime anyway.
7. The potential perpetrator, in the face of this conclusion, makes the decision not to commit a crime.
8. The potential perpetrator abides by this decision. The submerged assumption is that the potential perpetrator is actually in control of himself or herself to the degree that he or she is capable of obeying reason rather than impulse.

To the extent that the assumptions or expectations with respect to particular potential perpetrators are correct, we can expect the probabilities of crime to decline proportionally with video surveillance. In assessing the findings about the effects of video surveillance on crime, three caveats must be acknowledged. First, video surveillance systems are often only one part of a larger crime control or prevention strategy, making it impossible to determine whether observed changes in crime rates following installation are casually connected to, or even in any way a consequence of reduced levels of crime.

The UK Home Office review excludes studies that do not employ before and after measures and a control group to avert this conundrum. They found that there was no statistically significant effect in reducing crime. I have not followed this standard here. In one of the three study areas, however, the evidence was less positive (Welsh and Farrington, 2002).[2] The effects appeared to be more positive for theft of property as opposed to theft from vehicles. While the problem of conflation militates against the validity of causal inference, we need not dismiss the data derived from such cases *tout court*. After all, in its naturalistic setting, video surveillance will typically be employed in conjunction with a variety of other strategies. Second, we cannot forget that changes in crime rates may not be a reliable measure of changes in actual incidence. Third, as emphasized at the outset, there are methodological complications associated with comparing individual video surveillance systems, because each system is different and so are the procedures for monitoring.

That much said by way of qualification, the evidence about the effect of video surveillance on crime is mixed, conflicting, and sometimes quite contradictory. The only thing the literature does show, quite unambiguously, is that video surveillance systems do not have uniform effects across crime categories.

It follows that, when investigating questions about prevention, crime cannot be operationalized that distinguishes between crime types will be employed.

Solar-Powered Cameras

Eyetrax, Inc., a leader in the video surveillance industry, has a camera system that is 100% solar powered and transmits over cellular networks providing a 100% "wire-free" security camera solution. The charging system allows for autonomous operations all day and even all night.

The design of the solar-powered wireless camera system can be used in a variety of industries.[3] The remote cellar camera systems are new to the security market, and different industries are quickly discovering that they can use these camera systems to save money, decrease work time, increase communication, secure sensitive remote locations, and increase market share.

---

[2] B. C. Welsh and D. P. Farrington. 2002. *Crime Prevention Effects of Closed Circuit Television: A Systematic Review*, Home Office Research, Development and Statistics Directorate.

[3] Eye Trax. Solar Powered—4G Wireless—Motion Activated Camera Systems. Retrieved on June 30, 2017, from: https://www.eyetrax.net/solar-powered-motion-activated-cellular-camera-how-it-works

Property Crime

Some studies suggest that video surveillance is most effective in reducing property crime. Some reductions in the commission of certain types of property crime appear to be correlated with video surveillance coverage.

Chapter 60

CPTED versus Traditional Security: 15 Shopping Safety Tips

Many times, crimes of opportunity can be avoided by taking some practical and commonsense precautions. Crime prevention through environmental design (CPTED) and traditional security countermeasures can work together to keep people and places safe:

1. Use debit or credit cards instead of carrying cash. If the stores that you will visit do not take credit cards, consider obtaining traveler's checks, which, unlike cash, can be replaced if lost or stolen.
2. Carry purses with straps close to your body and away from aisles, especially when walking in the parking lot. If someone grabs your purse, let it go. Your safety is more important than your property. Carry minimal cash and valuables, preferably in your front pockets, and wear minimal jewelry.
3. When parking, roll up the windows, lock the vehicle, take the keys, and conceal valuables, preferably in the trunk.
4. During hours of darkness, park and walk in lighted areas when possible.
5. When returning to your vehicle, carry your keys in your hand and be ready to unlock the door and enter as quickly as possible. Wait to use your remote control to unlock the car door until you are close enough to look around and only press the unlock button once so only the driver's door is unlocked. As you approach your vehicle, scan the area, glance underneath the vehicle, and take a quick look inside before entering.

6. Return to your vehicle periodically to check on it. Reduce the number of items you are carrying and keeping track of. Put packages in the trunk or, if your vehicle does not have one, out of plain view (on the floorboard, under a blanket, clothes, etc.).

7. Move your car to another parking space after putting packages away. When possible, have purchases delivered instead of taking them with you; many businesses offer free delivery, especially during the holiday shopping season. Stay alert while loading items into or out of the vehicle or arranging packages. If someone approaches, and you feel threatened, get in and lock up until they leave the area; if they loiter, drive away.

8. Most malls and some stores have uniformed security officers both inside and outside for your safety. They work with the local police to keep the malls, stores, and parking lots safe. Ask for an escort to your car if you feel nervous. Return to the mall or store for assistance if you spot suspicious activity near your vehicle.

9. While out and about, be alert and stay aware of your surroundings. Notice what is going on around you. Avoid concentrating so hard on shopping or your cell phone that you fail to be aware of your surroundings.

10. Shop with friends or relatives if possible; there *is* safety in numbers. As you shop, be alert in crowded places. Among pickpockets' favorites are revolving doors, jammed aisles, elevators, and public transportation stops and vehicles, especially at rush hour. Carry your most expensive purchases closest to your body, and do not carry so much you lose the ability to react quickly.

11. Keep a close eye on your children while shopping. Teach your children to go to a store clerk or security officer if they ever get separated from you in a store or mall and be sure they know their first and last names so they can tell someone who they are. It is best to keep children under age 4 in a stroller. Children in shopping carts should be properly belted and seated in the child carrier area at all times. Never let your child stand in or push a shopping cart. If possible, leave your children with a babysitter while you are shopping. For holiday shopping, consider making arrangements with family or friends/neighbors, and take turns babysitting.

12. Visit ATMs only at well-lighted and populated locations—during daylight hours if possible. If anyone is loitering, or onlookers make you uncomfortable, go to another ATM. Stand so that those behind you cannot see your PIN as you enter it. Your PIN should *never* be written down on or carried with your ATM card. If the ATM appears to be tampered with, do not use it and report it to management.

13. If you have access to a cell phone, carry it with you. Remember that 9-1-1 works on a cell phone, even those that are not activated. Be prepared to give your location and stay on the line.

14. When shopping online, use only reputable companies and websites that have proper security features. Secure sites have an address that begins with

https:// (The "S" stands for "secure"). Be wary of pop-up ads that lead you to another website and ask for personal information, credit card numbers, or bank account numbers.

15. Promptly report suspicious persons, vehicles, and crimes to local law enforcement and store or mall security.

Chapter 61

After CPTED and COPS: Situational Crime Prevention and Situational CPTED

Crime prevention through environmental design (CPTED) and community-oriented policing services (COPS) have been around for years, and both have been implemented by thousands of communities and have proven to be very effective.

So, what is the next program after CPTED and COPS? After a degree of research and discussion, we feel that the next program is situational prevention. So, what is situational prevention? Situational prevention comprises opportunity-reducing measures that

1. Are directed at highly specific forms of crime.
2. Involve the management, design, or manipulation of the immediate environment in as systematic and permanent a way as possible.
3. Increase the effort and risks of crime and reduce the rewards as perceived by a wide range of offenders. A detailed classification of such measures includes the following:
   a. "Target hardening" with physical security
   b. More sophisticated forms of technology including intruder alarms, video surveillance, breathalyzers, and radar speed traps; the surveillance of specific locations provided by employees such as park-keepers, subway guards, and concierges; the use of vandal-resistant designs and materials in schools and other public facilities

  c. Block Watch, Neighborhood Watch, "defensible space," and other attempts to capitalize on the natural surveillance provided by members of the public; and some less easily categorized measures such as improved coordination of public transportation with pub closing times and the separation of rival soccer fans in different enclosures at the stadium (Clarke, 1997)[1]

Situational prevention is a proven concept to "increase the effort, increase the risks, reduce the rewards, reduce provocations and remove the excuses" when designing neighborhood prevention programs.

Twenty-Five Techniques of Situational Prevention

The following is adapted from information from R.V. Clarke.[2]

Increase the Effort

1. Target hardening
   a. Steering column locks and immobilizers
   b. Antirobbery screens
   c. Tamper-proof packaging
2. Control access to facilities
   a. Entry phones
   b. Electronic card access
   c. Baggage screening
3. Screen exits
   a. Ticket needed for exit
   b. Export documents
   c. Electronic merchandise tags
4. Deflect offenders
   a. Street closures
   b. Separate bathrooms for women
   c. Disperse pubs
5. Control tools/weapons
   a. "Smart" guns
   b. Disabling stolen cell phones
   c. Restrict spray paint sales to juveniles

---

[1] R. V. Clarke. 1997. *Situational Crime Prevention: Successful Case Studies, Second Edition*, School of Criminal Justice Rutgers University, Guiderland: Harrow and Heston.
[2] Retrieved on June 18, 2017, from: http://www.popcenter.org/library/25%20techniques%20grid.pdf The original author is Ronald V. Clarke.

Increase the Risks

6. Extend guardianship
   a. Take routine precautions: go out in group at night, leave signs of occupancy, carry phone, "Cocoon" Neighborhood Watch
7. Assist natural surveillance
   a. Improved street lighting
   b. Defensible space design
   c. Support whistle-blowers
8. Reduce anonymity
   a. Taxi driver IDs
   b. "How's my driving?" decals
   c. School uniforms
9. Utilize place managers
   a. CCTV for double-deck buses
   b. Two clerks for convenience stores
   c. Reward vigilance
10. Strengthen formal surveillance
    a. Red light cameras
    b. Burglar alarms
    c. Security guards

Reduce the Rewards

11. Conceal targets
    a. Off-street parking
    b. Gender-neutral phone directories
    c. Unmarked bullion trucks
12. Remove targets
    a. Removable car radio
    b. Women's refuges
    c. Prepaid cards for pay phones
13. Identify property
    a. Property marking
    b. Vehicle licensing and parts marking
    c. Cattle branding
14. Disrupt markets
    a. Monitor pawn shops
    b. Controls on classified ads
    c. License street vendors
15. Deny benefits
    a. Ink merchandise tags
    b. Graffiti cleaning
    c. Speed humps

Reduce Provocations

16. Reduce frustrations and stress
    a. Efficient queues and polite service
    b. Expanded seating
    c. Soothing music/muted lights
17. Avoid disputes
    a. Separate enclosures for rival soccer fans
    b. Reduce crowding in pubs
    c. Fixed cab fares
18. Reduce emotional arousal
    a. Controls on violent pornography
    b. Enforce good behavior on soccer field
    c. Prohibit racial slurs
19. Neutralize peer pressure
    a. "Idiots drink and drive"
    b. "It's OK to say No"
    c. Disperse troublemakers at school
20. Discourage imitation
    a. Rapid repair of vandalism
    b. V-chips in TVs
    c. Censor details of modus operandi

Remove Excuses

21. Set rules
    a. Rental agreements
    b. Harassment codes
    c. Hotel registration
22. Post instructions
    a. "No Parking"
    b. "Private Property"
    c. "Extinguish campfires"
23. Alert conscience
    a. Roadside speed display boards
    b. Signatures for customs declarations
    c. "Shoplifting is stealing"
24. Assist compliance
    a. Easy library checkout
    b. Public lavatories
    c. Litter bins
25. Control drugs and alcohol
    a. Breathalyzers in pubs
    b. Server intervention
    c. Alcohol-free events

Chapter 62

Deterrents: Physical Barriers

Physical barriers are used to control, impede, or deny access and to direct the flow of personnel through designated portals. Barrier system effectiveness is measured against specific standards and performances testing; specifically to reduce the number of entry and exit paths, facilitate effective use of protective force personnel, delay the adversary so the threat can be assessed, and protect personnel from hostile action and channel adversaries into preplanned neutralization zones.

A *deterrent* by definition is as follows[1]:

Definition of DETERRENT

1. serving to discourage, prevent, or inhibit: serving to deter
   a. The ads had a *deterrent* effect on youth smoking.
2. relating to deterrence
   b. A *deterrent* view of punishment

Synonyms: hindrance, impediment, balk, baulk, handicap, check

Adj. 1. Deterrent–tending to deter; "the deterrent effects of high prices"

Delay Action

We have had a debate for some time over the question of deterrents. What are they? Where can I find out more on the topic? What we have found out is that many people believe that more research is needed on the topic. Some people will say that having an armed security officer at the front of my bank is a deterrent. We

---

[1] "deterrent." *Merriam-Webster.* Retrieved September 2017, from: https://www.merriam-webster.com/dictionary/deterrent

asked a bank manager, "I see you have a security officer at your front door." "Yes." she replied. "How is that working out for you?" we asked. "Well, I can tell you that we are not having the problems other banks are having," she said. So, then we searched many security books and talked to authors of security books and asked them whether or not they state or list deterrents in their books. They all said no and then added, "We just assumed everyone knew or knows what deterrents are. Conduct some research on your own for more information."

Based on our research and discussions with authors and practitioners, the following is a list of deterrents that are used or recommended by security professionals.

Category A

- Security surveillance system used to prevent crime in private and public locations
- CPTED principles and concepts
- Defensible space principles and concepts
- Situational crime prevention principles and concepts
- Lighting that meets standards and design by increased visibility
- Biometrics and access control to specific areas
- CPTED design
- CPTED landscape principles
- Signage or visible security signs
- Padlocks (case harden) and door locks and peepholes
- Intrusion alarms and signage of alarm
- Security surveillance systems (CCTV)
- Security awareness programs
- Planters and thorny bushes
- Bollards or barricades closing down streets
- Barking dog, inside or outside
- Vehicle in driveway
- Area traffic and escape route available
- Policy and procedures, master plan
- Training programs

Category B

- Security officers armed and unarmed in private function (i.e., hotel doorman, bus drivers, tickets sellers or ticket takers, conductors)
- Police officers in uniform and armed security who may deduce that a crime is about to be committed and deter the incident in their presence

- Security officer patrolling the parking lots of hotels, hospitals, and retail locations, protecting corporate assets and customers
- Guardian angels patrolling streets, neighborhoods, and subways
- People in the area

Situational crime prevention incorporates other crime prevention and law enforcement strategies in an effort to focus on place-specific crime problems. Results and objectives are as follows:

- Reduce violent crime
- Reduce property crime
- Displace crime
- Eliminate threats and risk
- Reduce the likelihood of more incidents
- Eliminate vulnerabilities and protect assets
- Defensible space principles and concepts
- Situational crime prevention principles and concepts
- Lighting that meets standards and design by increased visibility
- Biometrics and access control to specific areas
- CPTED design
- CPTED landscape principles
- Signage or visible security signs
- Padlocks (case harden) and door locks and peepholes
- Intrusion alarms and signage of alarm
- Security surveillance systems (CCTV)
- Security awareness programs
- Planters and thorny bushes
- Bollards or barricades closing down streets
- Barking dog, inside or outside
- Vehicle in driveway
- Area traffic and escape route available
- Policy and procedures
- Training programs

Chapter 63

CPTED Assessments for K-12 Schools[1]

Introduction

Our nation's children are welcomed into their schools every day by their teachers and staff. Our educators are focused on educating their students in a safe and secure environment that allows their students to excel. However, safety has become a very complex issue in our schools. Deadly shootings at Columbine, Virginia Tech, and Sandy Hook, to name only a few, have significantly impacted our schools. School shootings are still a rare event, but an event that must be prepared for nevertheless. The sheer number of people who are affected by school safety is compelling: "As of fall 2010 approximately 75.9 million people were projected as enrolled in public and private schools at all levels including elementary, secondary, and postsecondary degree-granting. In addition, the number of professional, administrative, and support staff employed in educational institutions was projected at 5.4 million" (U.S. Department of Education 2010).[2]

Crime prevention through environmental design (CPTED) is a concept that was first introduced in the 1970s.

A CPTED assessment attempts to evaluate the physical setting of facility and maintenance factors that affect the safety and crime quotient capability of a particular school. Environmental factors such as the type of neighborhood, housing facilities, businesses, streets, and institutions surrounding the school affect the school's operation.

---

[1] Chapter is reproduced with permission from Linda Watson, MA, CPP, CSC, CHS-V.

[2] Buildings and Infrastructure Protection Series Primer to Design Safe Schools Projects in Case of Terrorist Attacks and School Shootings. FEMA–428/BIPS-07/.

Classrooms, security systems, lighting and color designs, accessibility, and quality of maintenance were all evaluated to determine their effect on the school climate, natural supervision, defensible space, and differentiated space. The survey items are to be rated as satisfactory (S), unsatisfactory (U), or not applicable (NA).

School CPTED Survey or Assessment

A thorough CPTED survey should address the following 30 points:

1. Visibility at entry to site
2. Vehicular access onto grounds
3. Off-site activity generator
4. Inadequate distance between school and neighbors
5. Easy-access hiding places
6. Area hidden by vegetation or landscaping
7. School adjacent to traffic hazard
8. Portion of building inaccessible to emergency vehicles
9. Secluded hangout area
10. Vegetation hides part of the building
11. Site not visible from street
12. No barrier between parking and lawn
13. Gravel in parking area
14. Dangerous vehicular circulation
15. Enclosed courtyard conceals vandals
16. High parapet hides vandals
17. Trees located where visibility is required
18. Pedestrian-vehicle conflict
19. Structure provides hideout
20. Building walls subject to bouncing balls
21. Parts of bus shelter not visible
22. Mechanical equipment accessible
23. Stacked materials and downspouts provide roof access
24. Recessed entry obscures intruders
25. Portions of building not visible from vehicle areas
26. Walkway roof eases access to building roof
27. Recess hides vandals
28. Skylight proves easy access
29. Mechanical screen conceals vandals
30. Access throughout the complex

CPTED Risk Assessment

Conducting a CPTED assessment or survey of a school starts with the physical security exterior areas described in the above security survey. Additionally, it is important to interview the stakeholders who work in the school. These stakeholders are the eyes and ears of the school, and they can identify the problems that exist within their school. Using an all-hazards approach will cover many of the natural events that are possible: fire, hurricane, tornado, earthquake, flood, or severe wind. Add in man-made events such as chemicals, hazardous substances, and biological catastrophes, and you can see many of the threats to be considered. These events are more likely to occur than a school shooting or a terrorist attack. With the all-hazards approach, you prepare for all possible events versus "just" a school shooting or terrorist attack. An all-hazards approach is the approach that best serves every school, large or small, public or private. A security assessment is a process of identifying the security risks that a school may be exposed to and how you will respond to them. When identifying risks, you must decide if it is too costly to protect or replace an item. If that is the case, then you may choose to protect the existing item, but know if a loss occurs it will not be replaced. This is the basis of a security assessment: mitigation, preparedness, and response. Every school is unique and there is no one security assessment that fits every school. By speaking with the stakeholders, you get to learn about the community and how the school fits into that community. As you identify the threats, you can then evaluate and rate the level of the threats to the school as a whole. Use a scale starting with very low (1) through very high (10). By rating the threats, you are assessing the likelihood or credibility of a threat. These threats are evaluated on the type of loss or damage that would result from an event. This subject has been successfully covered in great detail in the book *Crime Prevention through Environmental Design* (3rd ed.) by Timothy D. Crowe, revised by Lawrence Fennelly.

Much has been written on the methodologies of how to conduct and evaluate security assessments for school systems. There are many useful tools located on the U.S. Department of Education and American Clearinghouse on Educational Facilities websites. It is important to emphasize how essential the physical security assessment is as the basis of all other security work. An assessment encourages you to evaluate the potential for internal threats within a school, and when evaluating these internal threats, it is wise to look at the vulnerabilities within the school and evaluate "how" the school would be attacked. When you look at the security assessments from this perspective, your individual stakeholders can contribute regarding where they think an attack might be launched from. The internal threats may be a jilted lover or a recently fired employee who feels "wronged." These potential threats are very dangerous because the "actor" (the person who acts) has intimate knowledge of the campus and the unique culture within the educational institution. These actors know all the rules of getting into and out of the campus buildings and where there are vulnerabilities they can exploit because they are a known face at a dorm or classroom complex. When you look back at past violent school events, we can see many patterns emerging within the events themselves. Lessons learned from past school shootings at Columbine, Virginia Tech, and Sandy Hook teach us how to improve our communications with students, visitors, staff, and faculty during an emerging critical event on campus. Unfortunately, the active shooters can also study the past attacks and may have learned from the mistakes of the past as well.

Many times, after a tragic event on a school campus, people who have taught the student or were acquainted with the faculty member responsible for the attack say they noticed odd things prior to the event but did not think to report them to authorities. Having an independent reporting system in place that is widely advertised gives concerned persons the ability to report their observations without the fear of reprisals. In his book, *The Gift of Fear*, Gavin de Becker discusses in great detail the cues that are usually present before an incident (pre-incident cues) but are often ignored by coworkers or faculty and staff. Many times, after an event, when the media is interviewing persons who knew the actor, a pattern of odd or unusual behavior emerges. However, many of these persons only know the actor in the context of school or work. They do not have the opportunity to compare notes with other parties who also know the actor in a different venue.

Tragedies

After the Columbine, Virginia Tech, and Sandy Hook tragedies, we have learned that having a critical incident team (CIT) in place and ready to evaluate a potential at-risk student, faculty member, or employee is very important. These teams focus on a holistic approach to evaluating the at-risk individual. The CIT can be composed of many different professionals: commonly there will be administrative, human resources, mental health, legal, and law enforcement members. This diversity gives the team the opportunity to evaluate an at-risk person from their "specialty" and report back to their CIT peers with their findings. In the past, communication was an issue if a student went before the student review board for a violation of some student infraction. Many times, the student review board did not pass their findings onto law enforcement or the mental health counselors. The advantage of a CIT is that they now have the ability to follow up on the student and make cross-department notes with other CIT peers. They are immediately getting involved and holistically evaluating the potential risks that are exhibited by an at-risk student. In some past tragedies, family members have told the interviewing authorities that they were unaware of any issues involving their loved ones at school prior to the tragic event. With a CIT in place, they can get the family involved in evaluating and discussing their plans for how the student should proceed since the last known issue that has been brought to their attention. Family members often say in hindsight that given the opportunity to get involved with their loved one they would have done whatever would have been helpful to defuse the situation and avoid the tragic event that occurred. A review of many of the recent tragic events that have occurred at educational institutions reveals that many times there appears to have been a mental health issue that is only brought to the community's attention after the incident. Children who have been bullied or attacked on social media after school have nowhere to hide now. Prior to smartphones and current technology, when a child got off the bus at the end of the day, the child had a break from school until the next day. Now a child can connect 24/7 with his or her peers, which can cause the child to feel that there is no escape from the harassment or bullying. Despite established rules designed to protect at-risk students from cyberbullying, many times the student does not disengage from social media when school ends. The impact of being bullied or picked on can become enormous, forcing a student to withdraw from the school environment. Some students become isolated and may not have adequate parental supervision or a trusted adult who can help them engage in a healthy dialog with their peers. Some students react to bullying by acting out with violence.

Natural Surveillance

Natural surveillance can be employed in CPTED in schools[3]:

- Position restrooms to be observable from nearby offices or reception areas.
- Install and use good lighting at all exterior doors, common areas, and hallways.
- Keep dumpsters visible and avoid creating blind spots or hiding places, or place them in secured, locked corrals or garages.
- Design windows and exterior doors so that they are visible from the street or by neighboring buildings.
- Install windows into all facades.
- Place parking as to be visible from windows.
- Keep shrubbery under 3 feet in height for visibility.
- Prune the lower branches of large trees to at least 7–8 feet off the ground.
- Do not obstruct views from windows.
- Design interior windows and doors to have visibility into the hallway.

Traditional security is typically a hardened target with locks, lighting, securing doors and windows, and law enforcement/security officers on patrol. CPTED takes security a bit further.

---

[3] CPTED Durham Guide to Creating a Safer Community, Durham City and County CPTED Private Sector Taskforce.

CPTED Strategies

The following suggests a series of general design strategies that can be applied in any situation to improve natural access control, natural surveillance, and territorial behavior:

- Provide a clear border definition of controlled space.
- Provide a clearly marked transition from public to semipublic to private space.
- Locate gathering areas in places with natural surveillance and access control and away from the view of potential offenders.
- Place safe activities in unsafe locations and unsafe activities safe locations.
- Provide natural barriers to conflicting activities.
- Improve the scheduling of space to provide for effective and critical intensity of uses.
- Design space to increase the perception of natural surveillance.
- CPTED involves design of physical space in the context of the needs of bona fide users of the space (physical, social, and psychological needs), the normal and expected (or intended) use of the space (the activity or absence of activity planned for the space), and the predictable behavior of both bona fide users and offenders. Therefore, in the CPTED approach, a design is
  - Proper if it recognizes the designated use of the space, defines the crime
  - Problem incidental to and the solution compatible with the designated use, and incorporates the crime prevention strategies that enhance (or at least do not impair) the effective use of the space. CPTED draws not only on physical and urban design but also on contemporary thinking in behavioral and social science, law enforcement, and community organization.
- The emphasis on design and use deviates from the traditional target-hardening approach to crime prevention. Traditional target hardening focuses predominantly on denying access to a crime target through physical or artificial barrier techniques (such as locks, alarms, fences, and gates).
- Target hardening often leads to constraints on use, access, and enjoyment of the hardened environment.

Chapter 64

Part 1—CPTED and the Homeless: The Problem of Homeless Encampments

Homeless encampments are only one aspect of the larger set of problems related to homelessness, street life, and public disorder.[1] The term "transient" is often used to refer to this small group. Further, it addresses only the particular harms created by homeless encampments, not the issues commonly associated with homeless people. These related problems, each of which requires separate analysis, include:

- Chronic public intoxication
- Panhandling
- Loitering
- Trespassing
- Shoplifting
- Drug dealing
- Mental illness
- Disorder at day laborer sites

---

[1] Reprinted from S. Chamard. 2010. Homeless Encampments. Guide No. 56. Center for Problem-Oriented Policing. http://www.popcenter.org/problems/homeless_encampments

A discussion of the broad economic and social conditions that give rise to homelessness and to homeless encampments is beyond the scope of this paper.

The Philosophical Debate on Chronic Homelessness

Dealing with homeless people living in encampments can be fraught with moral danger. Few people would argue that the police should do what they can to reduce burglary or car theft. Yet there are many strong and organized advocates of the chronically homeless. Some believe chronic homelessness is a lifestyle choice and, as such, should be protected by law. Others claim it is a consequence of social-economic factors, such as high unemployment and the lack of affordable housing, or that the chronically homeless are victims of abusive childhoods, addiction, or mental illness. In any event, they oppose criminalizing what they perceive to be a status beyond a homeless person's control. Still others object to the "criminalization of homelessness" because it violates fundamental constitutional rights, in particular those codified in the First, Fourth, Eighth, and Fourteenth Amendments.

On the other hand, problems associated with transients and their encampments can often lead business owners and residents to demand the police use traditional, and perhaps somewhat punitive, law enforcement methods to solve them.

It is important to be aware of the fundamental differences in people's beliefs about chronic homelessness (put simply, the homeless are victims who need society's help to recover versus the behaviors of homeless people drain public resources and damage the community) because how the problem is defined determines what is considered to be an "effective strategy."[2]

General Description of the Problem— What Are Homeless Encampments?

The term "homeless" refers to someone who is usually poor and frequently on the move from one temporary dwelling situation to another. Many slang words are used to describe such a person: transient, squatter, hobo, bum, vagrant, and vagabond. Homeless encampments take a variety of forms: tent cities; groups living under freeway overpasses; and groups sleeping in parks, in skid rows (urban areas with concentrations of poverty and dilapidated buildings), in subway tunnels, on sidewalks, etc. One person setting up shelter in such a location does not constitute an encampment. Studies show homeless encampments vary in size. Some, particularly those in the woods, can be fairly small with only a few campers. Those under freeway overpasses and in urban vacant lots and parks may be larger, with some

---

[2] http://www.popcenter.org/problems/homeless_encampments/

reportedly having 100 or more people. Shelters in homeless encampments range from lean-tos made of cardboard, to tents, to more elaborate structures—in one case including French doors, a skylight, and a picture window. Obviously, the more established the encampment, the better constructed the "housing" is likely to be.

Some encampments, particularly those in the woods, ... can be fairly small with only a few campers.

Who Lives in Homeless Encampments?

To understand who lives in homeless encampments, it is useful to begin with the entire population of homeless people and whittle it down.

The behavior in question is known as "sleeping rough" in the United Kingdom.

It is important to realize that although people living in homeless encampments are homeless, most homeless people do not live in homeless encampments. The U.S. Department of Housing and Urban Development (HUD) classifies homeless people in two broad categories: sheltered and unsheltered. A "sheltered" homeless person lives in an emergency shelter or transitional housing. This includes domestic violence shelters; residential programs for homeless or runaway youth; or a hotel, motel, or apartment paid for with a voucher provided by a governmental or private agency because the person is homeless. An unsheltered homeless person lives in "a place not meant for human habitation, such as cars, parks, sidewalks, abandoned buildings, or on the street." About 44 percent of homeless people are unsheltered. Unsheltered homeless are usually single men, who, unlike homeless families, are less likely to live in emergency shelter, transitional housing, or permanent supportive housing.

Another categorization of homelessness is whether the status is temporary (due to an eviction, prolonged unemployment, job layoff, or domestic violence) or chronic. The federal definition of chronically homeless is an "unaccompanied homeless individual with a disabling condition who has either been continuously homeless for a year or more or has had at least four episodes of homelessness in the past three years" (U.S. Department of Housing and Urban Development, 2009: 15).[3] About 18 percent of the total homeless population (unsheltered and sheltered in emergency shelter) is considered chronically homeless, and, of those, two-thirds are unsheltered. In other words, an estimated 12 percent of the United States' homeless population, or close to 83,000 people, is unsheltered and chronically homeless.

This relatively small group of homeless people may end up in homeless encampments because they have exhausted all resources available to them or their conditions (e.g., drug use, alcoholism, criminal record) hinder them from using them (shelters, for example). Others may have chosen the lifestyle because it frees

---

[3] *The 2008 Annual Homeless Assessment Report to Congress.* U.S. Department of Housing and Urban Development, Office of Community Planning and Development: July, 2009.

them from competing in a consumerist society, or because it is better than previous living arrangements. However, most residents of homeless encampments say they would prefer to live in a more conventional way with their own room and a job.

Compared with the general population, people in homeless encampments are more likely to be male, older, and a minority. A significant number of transients living in encampments are addicted to drugs or alcohol, and a sizable portion are also mentally ill ("dually diagnosed").

Panhandling is one way homeless encampment dwellers make money, but more work at odd short-term jobs, such as street vending and day labor. Collecting cans or bottles is also common. Relatively few receive public benefits. A very small number engage in prostitution. The relationship between crime and transients will be discussed later.

Harms Caused by Homeless Encampments

Problems associated with homeless encampments fall into three categories: impact on the homeless population, impact on the environment, and impact on the larger community.

Impact on the Homeless Population

Unhealthy Encampment Conditions

Conditions in homeless encampments can be dangerous to health. Garbage attracts rodents and other vermin. Food cannot be stored, and dishes cannot be washed properly, facilitating the spread of food-borne diseases. Depending on a camp's location, some residents might use portable toilets or public facilities, but most are likely to use an outdoor location. Poor hygiene contributes to dental and skin problems. Other environmental hazards, such as batteries and fuels, are used for heating and cooking.

Most people who live in homeless encampments lack health insurance, but they frequently have chronic physical and mental health conditions that require ongoing medical attention. Barriers to seeking routine medical care lead many to the emergency room for non-emergency care. There is some indication that tuberculosis and sexually transmitted diseases are of special concern. Many transients living in encampments report addiction to drugs or alcohol.

Victimization of the Chronically Homeless

Not much is known about victimization among this population because they are not included in large-scale household-based surveys, such as the National Crime

Victimization Survey. Official data, such as the National Incident-Based Reporting System and the Uniform Crime Reports, typically do not include victims' housing status. Further, specific information on victimization of chronically homeless people who live in homeless encampments is based on case studies of particular jurisdictions or is anecdotal.

However, smaller studies paint a troubling picture. The chronically homeless report high rates of child and sexual abuse that occurred before they became homeless. Further, once homeless, the population continues to be victimized at a rate about twice that of the general population. Chronically homeless people are also more likely than the general population to be victims of crime against the person than property crime. These patterns are particularly true for chronically homeless women; one British study found that 95 percent of chronically homeless women had been victimized compared with 75 percent of men.

Chronically homeless people are victimized by the public and by their peers. Violence against the homeless committed by non-homeless offenders appears to be increasing even while violent crimes are generally decreasing. Many of these incidents are beatings. Over the nine-year period from 1999 to 2007 in the United States, 217 homeless people were killed by those who were not homeless.

Despite the notion that homeless encampments are safe havens for those living an otherwise rough or unconventional life, these camps can be venues for serious violent crime. In November 2008, five people in a Long Beach, California, encampment were shot to death, and one man was fatally stabbed at a homeless camp in Tucson, Arizona. A homeless encampment in a wooded area off a freeway in Orlando, Florida, was the site of three homicides in the 10 months between October 2006 and August 2007. In Sacramento, California, in September 2008, two men were murdered within hours of each other in a "well-established homeless camp" near some light-rail tracks. Other research found that the incidence of victimization by strangers was lower for the homeless population (16 percent) than for the general population (which ranges from 28 percent to 89 percent depending on the type of violent crime).

Impact on the Environment

In addition to concerns about the hazardous materials mentioned above, which potentially harm both the transients and the surrounding environment, inadequate human waste disposal at large encampments along rivers can pose a hazard to the water supply of nearby communities. Another hazard linked to homeless encampments is fire. Residents of homeless encampments turn to wood stoves and camp fires for heat and cooking. If left unattended (typically by intoxicated transients), these fires can become out of control and burn down camp structures and injure people. Larger fires can spread to more populated areas and damage buildings and infrastructure. More significantly for the environment, these fires may kill animals and vegetation and destroy their habitats. Although most wildfires are started by people, there are no data on how many of those are started specifically by transients.

Wilderness areas are further damaged through abusive camping practices, such as cutting down trees and leaving garbage on site.

Impact on the Larger Community

Criminal Activity by the Chronically Homeless

Numerous studies have pointed to a strong relationship between homelessness and criminality. Yet contrary to popular opinion, the typical chronically homeless person is not a hardened violent felon, but someone with a disproportionately high arrest rate for crimes such as public intoxication, petty theft, and trespassing. The longer someone is unsheltered and chronically homeless, the more involved he or she becomes in criminal behavior, largely due to the increased use of "non-institutionalized survival strategies," such as panhandling, street peddling, and theft. Chronically homeless people who are mentally ill are arrested more than those who are not mentally ill.

Many researchers have argued that the high rates of arrest and low-level offending by the chronically homeless are results of the "criminalization of homelessness." Laws against lying down or sleeping in public, public excretion and urination, public intoxication, and the like, make it difficult for the street homeless to carry out routine behaviors in public places. Some police observers report that being homeless subjects people to more strict enforcement for activities that are dealt with more leniently if the person can show proof of address.

Even if transients are not hard-core violent offenders, evidence from police case studies shows areas adjacent to transient encampments have higher levels of petty and serious crime unrelated to "routine behaviors," such as drug dealing and usage, disturbance, theft, prowling, burglary, panhandling, fighting, vandalism, armed robbery, rape, and aggravated assault. Stolen property, weapons, and wanted felons have been found in homeless encampments.

Threats to Business Viability

Urban homeless encampments have a more immediate impact on the nearby community because of proximity. Many chronically homeless behaviors, such as sleeping on the streets, panhandling, public excretion or urination, and public intoxication, are threatening or undesirable. In some urban settings, police rate transients and their behaviors as a bigger problem than drugs, car burglaries, public fighting, cruising, or noise. Entertainment districts are particularly vulnerable to transient behavior because of the availability of people with disposable income, park benches, unattended public restrooms, and lax enforcement of laws governing street behavior. The presence of transients creates an environment of lawlessness. During the day, transients sitting in front of businesses can scare away customers.

Illegitimate Use of Public Space

Regular citizens may not use public parks and other facilities because they fear the spaces are controlled by transients. Often the homeless are victimized at night, prompting them to sleep only during daylight hours in parks and other public places. Thus, the park may be laden with individuals sleeping on benches or in picnic shelters during the park's busiest hours. This condition only exacerbates the conflict with legitimate park users. Further, due to the homeless taking over and sometimes vandalizing park barbeques, sinks, and faucets designed for regular park visitors to use, officials may remove these amenities thereby penalizing everyone. In Madison, Wisconsin, a group of 30–40 men (not all of whom were homeless) took over a lakeside park shelter, moving in furniture and other personal belongings. They drank there during the day and slept there at night. Nearby residents reported car break-ins, firewood thefts, and attempted burglaries. Legitimate park users reported aggressive panhandling. Use of this park by permit-holders was considerably lower compared with other area parks.

Factors Contributing to Homeless Encampments

Encampments are usually located close to goods and services that transients need: food, alcohol, employment (or crime) opportunities, and shelter (in case of inclement weather). Services geared toward this population obviously contribute to a concentration of transients in certain areas. Although soup kitchens attract the chronically homeless, food pantries are less popular with transients because they often lack facilities to cook the items pantries distribute. Social service providers and day labor sites attract some transients. Liquor stores and drug markets attract others. Homes and businesses are targets for theft or burglary, but also for short-term work for those so inclined.

Because many transients do not have their own vehicles, encampments, even in wooded areas, are likely to be located by pedestrian access points (such as trails), or close to public transportation facilities and railroad tracks.

Transients look for overgrown brush to help hide their encampment from public view, providing privacy and the opportunity to establish the camp before it is discovered and dealt with by the authorities.

People in homeless encampments benefit from food and clothing provided by church groups, missions, and social services agencies, but such charity is not always combined with efforts to facilitate transition from the streets. In some respects, this enables encampment residents to stay where they are.

Chapter 65

Part 2—CPTED and the Homeless: The Response to Homeless Encampments

The following responses, drawn from a variety of research studies and police reports, provide a foundation of ideas for addressing the problem of homelessness.[1] It is critical that you tailor responses to local circumstances and that you can justify each response based on reliable analysis. In most cases, an effective strategy involves implementing several different responses. Law enforcement responses alone are seldom effective in reducing or solving the problem. Do not limit yourself to considering only what the police can do; give careful thought to others in your community who share responsibility for the problem and can help police better respond to it. The responsibility of responding, in some cases, may need to shift toward those who can implement more effective responses.

General Principles for an Effective Strategy

Enlisting Community Support to Address the Problem

Because of the intense public debate in many cities about how to deal with homelessness, it is a very good idea to involve homeless advocacy groups early in your planning process. Otherwise, you risk being derailed later by legal challenges.

---

[1] Reprinted from S. Chamard. 2010. Homeless Encampments. Guide No. 56. Center for Problem-Oriented Policing. http://www.popcenter.org/problems/homeless_encampments

Other stakeholders, particularly those who may be making demands for police action, such as residents, business owners, politicians, and city officials, should be involved in negotiating what is acceptable in public spaces. Dismantling homeless encampments or altering their environmental features to discourage living there can easily be perceived as cruel by some if they do not understand how the overall effort will improve the lives of both transients and the larger community. Notwithstanding your efforts, it is unlikely that all will agree with the following strategies of eradicating homeless encampments:

- Educating the community about homelessness
- Educating police officers about homelessness
- Helping with your community's long-range homelessness plan
- Promoting the "Housing First" model
- Lobbying for more resources for mental health and substance abuse
- Regulating structured camping facilities
- Changing the physical environment
- Clear-cutting overgrown brush
- Deploying water sprinklers
- Encouraging private property owners to secure vacant lots and buildings

Photo 65.1   Example of signage posted in a former encampment. (From Anchorage Responsible Beverage Retailers Association [ARBRA].)

- Removing or altering street furniture
- Restricting public feeding of transients
- Diverting donations from the public
- Installing more public toilets
- Opening a day resource center
- Working with land use enforcement officers
- Shutting down homeless encampments (Photo 65.1)
- Retrieving shopping carts
- Developing a departmental policy within the police department
- Creating a specialized unit
- Contacting homeless people
- Enforcing "sidewalk behavior" ordinances
- Enforcing ordinances against panhandling
- Doing "bum" sweeps
- Creating safe zones
- Increasing the capacity of local shelters

Crime prevention through environmental design (CPTED) strategies are an important component of eradicating homeless encampments. For more information on homeless encampments, see the Center for Problem-Oriented Policing, Guide 56, Homeless Encampments.

Chapter 66

Violent Behavior and Music: Is There a Relationship?

Many people think that classical music is perfect background music to relax and soothe, but it can also be used as a "bug spray" for crowd control for people you do not want hanging around your property.[1] It was proven to be a successful deterrent to crowds of young people who had been congregating in the parking lot of a 7-Eleven in the mid-1980s. Since that time, many other stores have continued to use that technique. For example in 2001, the police in West Palm Beach, Florida, played loud Mozart and Beethoven on a crime-ridden street corner and crime was reduced. In 2010, the transit authority in Portland, Oregon, began playing classical music at light-rail stops and calls to police stopped. The Port Authority Bus Terminal in New York is one of many public spaces across the United States that uses classical music to help control vagrancy and to drive the homeless away.[2]

Given the amount of time people spend listening to music, it is not surprising that a significant amount of research has been done to determine whether or not music can provoke violent behavior. Do aggressive music lyrics cause individuals to

---

[1] A. Midgette. 2012. Blasting Mozart to drive criminals away. *The Washington Post*. Retrieved on January 31, 2017, from: https://www.washingtonpost.com/lifestyle/style/blasting-mozart-to-drive-criminals-away/2011/10/11/gIQAgDqPEQ_story.html?utm_term=.8147b15f1cf9

[2] A. Midgette. 2012. Blasting Mozart to drive criminals away. *The Washington Post*. Retrieved on January 31, 2017, from: https://www.washingtonpost.com/lifestyle/style/blasting-mozart-to-drive-criminals-away/2011/10/11/gIQAgDqPEQ_story.html?utm_term=.8147b15f1cf9

act violently?[3] This is closely related to the research that was conducted by Anderson et al. (2003)[4] about whether or not young people are influenced by media violence. The researchers randomly assigned young people to watch either a short violent or a short nonviolent music video and then observed how they interacted with other people after this to see if there was a correlation between an individual watching the violent music video and acting violent, or watching the nonviolent music video and not acting violent. After each participant watched a music video for approximately 15 minutes, both physical and verbal aggression toward others was assessed using a 10-point scale: with 1 showing nonviolent behaviors and 10 showing a lot of violent behaviors. The results showed that exposure to media violence had a statistically significant association with aggression and violence among young people. This research demonstrates that exposure to media violence increases the likelihood that a young person will exhibit aggressive behavior and have aggressive thoughts for a period of time.[5]

An activist group, the Parents Music Resource Center (PMRC),[6] was founded in 1985 by the "Washington Wives" (Tipper Gore, Susan Baker, Pam Howar, Nancy Thurmond, and Sally Nevius) to protest against the "multiple evils in society to be rooted in popular music." The group appeared before the U.S. Senate to propose measures that would require record labels to "rate" them similar to the way movies are rated. The PMRC wanted advisory labels on albums that contained lyrics referencing sex, the occult, violence, drugs, and alcohol. PMRC made a playlist of what they determined to be the most offensive music. Included on this list were music by Madonna, Prince, Venom,[7] and Mercyful Fate, and their music was used as an example of how music albums should be rated. The PMRC wanted content-based ratings: "X" for profane or sexually explicit lyrics, "O" for occult references, "D/A" for lyrics about drugs and alcohol, and "V" for violent content.[8]

This prompted the Senate's Committee on Commerce to hold a *Record Labeling Hearing* on the "Contents of Music and the Lyrics of Records." The hearing was called the "Porn-Rock Hearing" because Frank Zappa, John Denver, and Twisted

---

[3] E. Tropcano. 2006. Does rap or rock music provoke violent behavior? *Journal of Undergraduate Psychological Research*. Retrieved on January 31, 2017, from: http://citeseerx.ist.psu.edu/viewdoc/download?doi=10.1.1.578.2378&rep=rep1&type=pdf

[4] C.A. Anderson et al. 2003. The influence of media violence on youth. *Psychological Science in the Public Interest* 4(3): 81–110.

[5] E. Anderson. 1998. The social ecology of youth violence. *Crime and Justice* 24: 65–104. Retrieved on January 31, 2017, from: http://www.journals.uchicago.edu/doi/abs/10.1086/449278 and http://doi.org/10.1086/449278

[6] Parents Music Resource Center. Retrieved on January 31, 2017, from: http://www.nndb.com/org/374/000128987/

[7] Parents Music Resources Center. https://en.wikipedia.org/wiki/parents_music_resources_center#the_fifty_fifteen

[8] Record Labeling Hearing before the Committee on Commerce, Science, and Transportation United States Senate. Retrieved on January 31, 2017, from: http://www.joesapt.net/superlink/shrg99-529/

Sister's Dee Snider protested the proposed measures because they were concerned that the labels might influence retailers not to carry their albums.[9] They were correct because after this hearing, Walmart refused to sell albums with advisory labels.

Even before the 1985 Senate hearing, Stanley Gortikov, then president of the Record Industry Association of America (RIAA), met with 19 record labels, and they all agreed to include parental advisory stickers on their albums. Eventually, the labels of albums with specific content stated the following: "Parental Advisory: Explicit Lyrics."[10]

In 2015, Tipper Gore stated, "All of the artists and record companies who still use the advisory label should be applauded for helping parents and kids have these conversations about lyrics around their own values."[11]

In 2015, Tipper Gore's statement on the PMRC was, "In this era of social media and online access, it seems quaint to think that parents can have control over what their children see and hear," she says. "But, I think this … is a universal language that crosses generations, race, religion, sex and more. Never has there been more need for communication and understanding on these issues as there is today."[12]

Continued research is being conducted at the University of Oxford on the Psychology of Music, which is concerned with "understanding the psychological processes involved in listening to music, playing music and composing and improvising music, using empirical, theoretical and computational methods." Experiments were done by interdisciplinary researchers on "music perception and cognition, computer modelling of human musical capacities, the social psychology of music, emotion and meaning in music, psychological processes in music therapy, the developmental psychology of music, music and consciousness, music and embodiment and the neuroscience of music."[13]

A study published in the May 2003 issue of the *Journal of Personality and Social Psychology* (Vol. 84, No. 5) investigated precursors to aggression rather than aggressive behavior itself and indicates "a relationship between violent song lyrics and increased aggressive thoughts and feelings of hostility. Humorous, violent

[9] Record Labeling Hearing before the Committee on Commerce, Science, and Transportation United States Senate. Retrieved on January 31, 2017, from: http://www.joesapt.net/superlink/shrg99-529/index.html

[10] K. Grow. 2015. Tipper Gore reflects on PMRC 30 years later. *RollingStone*. Retrieved on January 31, 2017, from: http://www.rollingstone.com/music/news/tipper-gore-reflects-on-pmrc-30-years-later-20150914

[11] K. Grow. 2015. Tipper Gore reflects on PMRC 30 years later. *RollingStone*. Retrieved on January 31, 2017, from: http://www.rollingstone.com/music/news/tipper-gore-reflects-on-pmrc-30-years-later-20150914

[12] K. Grow. 2015. Tipper Gore reflects on PMRC 30 years later. *RollingStone*. Retrieved on January 31, 2017, from: http://www.rollingstone.com/music/news/tipper-gore-reflects-on-pmrc-30-years-later-20150914

[13] Psychology of Music. University of Oxford. Retrieved on January 1, 2017, from: http://www.music.ox.ac.uk/research/disciplines/psychology-of-music/

songs also increased aggression levels, relative to humorous nonviolent songs."[14] Lead author Craig Anderson of Iowa State University stated that this study was the "first clean demonstration of violent lyric effects." The findings of the research were confirmed even with different genders, personality differences, as well as their reactions to the different artists and musical styles.[15]

Everyone agrees that more research is needed, but studies have confirmed that repeated exposure to violent lyrics may contribute to the development of an aggressive personality and lead to the creation of a more hostile social environment. Songs with violent lyrics increase aggression-related thoughts and emotions, and this effect is directly related to the violence in the lyrics.

"The violent-song increases in aggressive thoughts and feelings have implications for real world violence," according to Craig A. Anderson. "One major conclusion from this and other research on violent entertainment media is that content matters," said Anderson. "This message is important for all consumers, but especially for parents of children and adolescents."[16]

Music has always had effects on human emotion.[17] Music can make anyone feel anything.

---

[14] C. Anderson, N.L. Carnagey, and J. Eubanks. 2003. Exposure to violent media: The effects of songs with violent lyrics on aggressive thoughts and feelings. *Journal of Personality and Social Psychology* 84(5): 960–971. http://www.apa.org/pubs/journals/releases/psp-845960.pdf

[15] APA. 2003. Violent song lyrics may lead to violent behavior. *Monitor on Psychology* 34(7). Retrieved on January 31, 2017, from: http://www.apa.org/monitor/julaug03/violent.aspx

[16] APA. 2003. Violent song lyrics may lead to violent behavior. *Monitor on Psychology* 34(7). Retrieved on January 31, 2017, from: http://www.apa.org/monitor/julaug03/violent.aspx

[17] Retrieved April 2017. https://psuc53.wordpress.com/2012/03/11/the-psychological-effects-of-heavy-metal-music-2/

Chapter 67

CPTED in Australia

Introduction

We selected this fact sheet of information on CPTED which came out in July 2015 in Australia. It must be noted that crime prevention through environmental design (CPTED) in Australia and New Zealand is huge, and as you read this material, we think you will agree, we are all on the same track with CPTED.[1]

This information is intended for use by developers, land owners, and land administrators, and applies to all urban land. It is designed to create awareness of CPTED. Developers can contact the city council for general advice. Development concept formation of CPTED principles must be factored in at development concept formation. Development applications will need to clearly demonstrate on plan and in writing that CPTED principles are satisfactorily addressed.

Australia–What Is Crime Prevention through Environmental Design (CPTED)?

Traditionally, the community has relied upon the police and the justice system to prevent and reduce the incidence of crime.[2] This is often reactive and ineffective. Criminals make rational choices about their targets, and generally

---

[1] Crime Prevention through Environmental Design (CPTED) Fact Sheet. Retrieved on January 29, 2017, from: http://www.wollongong.nsw.gov.au/factsheets/Crime%20Prevention%20through%20Environmental%20Design%20(CPTED).pdf

[2] Crime Prevention through Environmental Design: Guidelines for Queensland. Part B: Implementation Guide. Retrieved on September 12, 2017, from: http://www.police.qld.gov.au/programs/cscp/safetypublic/documents/CPTEDPartB.pdf

- The greater the risk of being seen, challenged or caught, the less likely they are to commit a crime.
- The greater the effort required, the less likely they are to commit a crime.
- The lesser the actual or perceived reward, the less likely they are to commit a crime. We can design and manage the environment to ensure that
- There is more chance of being seen, challenged or caught.
- Greater effort is required on the part on the part of the criminal.
- The actual or perceived rewards are less.
- Opportunities for criminal activity are minimized.

Chapter 68

CPTED in Denmark

A leading figure in the movement, architect John Allpass, was responsible for designing the first housing area in Denmark where creating safety and security was implicit in the design.[1] Five miles out of Copenhagen, the Sibelius estate is still considered a model of the Designing Out Crime philosophy, shaped around

- Creating a social space where the natural surveillance of the people within it prevents crime
- Increasing people's attachment to an area
- Encouraging people to use common areas with seating, foyers, and lobbies that invite social contact
- Providing facilities for adults and young people in particular
- Avoiding alleyways, hiding places, and blind spots, and only using locks, cameras, and physical barriers as a last resort

---

[1] S. Laville. 2002. Designing out crime in Scandinavia: 'Cities cannot be completely safe and completely exciting at the same time'. *The Guardian*. https://www.theguardian.com/cities/2014/jun/24/designing-out-crime-scandinavia-copenhagen-cities-safe-exciting

Chapter 69

Predictable Routes: Brisbane, Australia

Predictable routes are a safety concern as they enable potential attackers to easily identify the route taken by users.[1] These include pedestrian paths, stairwells, underpasses, and corridors. This is particularly problematic where the route ends up close to an entrapment spot. Entrapment spots are small, confined spaces close to or adjacent to publicly accessible places. They are usually shielded on three sides by barriers such as walls or vegetation, and provide for easy concealment. The following principles should be taken into account in development design to minimize predictable routes and entrapment locations:

- Eliminate predictable routes and potential entrapment locations from design wherever possible.
- Provide adequate sight lines and lighting where there is no alternative to predictable routes.
- Provide adequate distance between any potential concealment or entrapment locations to allow users adequate reaction time.
- Ensure that predictable routes have good casual surveillance and provide for alternative access arrangements.
- Identify alternative routes by effective signage, which are preferably well lit, and frequently used pathways.

---

[1] Crime Prevention through Environmental Design (CPTED) Planning Scheme Policy. Brisbane City Plan 2000—Volume 2. https://www.brisbane.qld.gov.au/sites/default/files/Appendix2_CrimePrevention_PSP.pdf

Crime Prevention through Environmental Design Planning Scheme

Risks associated with predictable routes such as underpasses can be alleviated with generous path width, use of surveillance technology, and the presentation of excellent levels of lighting, light-colored walls, and signage.

Chapter 70

New South Wales, Australia: CPTED Recommendations

Development Requirements

Developments accessible to the public shall incorporate the following[1]:

- Vandal-resistant lights.
- Securing all flammable and other materials which may be used in vandalism.
- Graffiti-resistant paint on external surfaces.
- Materials which are hardy and not easily removable from the building. (Where materials are likely to be removed from a building, they should be easily replaceable).
- Avoidance of solid fences and blank walls which attract graffiti. (Where solid, blank surfaces are provided, consideration should be given to the use of screen landscaping or creepers, murals, vandal-resistant paint and other means to discourage graffiti.)
- Locating elements which may be vandalized, e.g., appropriately designed external seating in areas of high natural surveillance or in inaccessible locations.

---

[1] Kempsey DCP. 2013. Chapter B15—Crime Prevention through Environmental Design (CPTED). Retrieved January 2017, from: https://www.kempsey.nsw.gov.au/development/kdcp/pubs/b15-crime-prevention-through-environmental-design-cpted.pdf

■ Toughened glass, screens, and other measures in windows which are provided at ground floor level to deter break and enters.
■ Landscaping/vegetation shall enhance safety by maximizing the visibility of cars.
■ Paths between buildings and car parks should be well lit and obvious to ensure safe pedestrian access.
■ Lighting utilized in car parks should be in accordance with relevant Australian Standards.
■ Car parks[2] should be sited to permit maximum opportunities for surveillance from both users of the current development and passersby.
■ Private spaces such as courtyards, stairwells, and parking bays should be clearly identified to reduce use by undesirable users.
■ Strategies may include the use of pavers, varied textured paths, fencing, log barriers, landscaping, and others.
■ Private spaces should be clearly distinguished from public areas.
■ Accommodation units should be designed to allow people within the units to observe and monitor communal areas within the development and the street area, e.g., car parks, swimming pool areas, gardens, etc.
■ Lighting[3] should be provided within the site. Areas requiring lighting should include driveways, property entrances, parking areas, footpaths, communal service areas (e.g., rubbish bin bays, letterboxes, clotheslines), lobbies, and stairwells.
■ Lighting in communal areas and areas accessible by the public should be illuminated in hours of darkness or should have motion sensors.
■ Safe walkways and pathways should be sufficiently well lit at all times to avoid use of unsafe routes (e.g., underpasses).
■ Good sight lines and signage to assist people along paths. Where possible pathways to be overlooked from residential properties.
■ Paths should be located near activity generators and areas with natural surveillance.
■ Walkways and pathways, including walkways provided between allotments and subdivisions, should be designed and located such that they do not become potential assault sites.
■ Walkways and pathways should be designed to have at least one clearly marked "exit" sign to an area of traffic (vehicular, pedestrian or residential) every 50 meters.

---

[2] NSW Car Park Guidelines for Crime Prevention: For use in publicly owned car parks in NSW. Retrieved from http://www.crimeprevention.nsw.gov.au/Documents/car_park_guidelines.pdf
[3] *CPTED and Access Control Measures to Prevent Stealing from Motor Vehicles. Handbook for Local Government.* Australian Government. Australian Institute of Criminology. Attorney General & Justice. Retrieved from http://www.crimeprevention.nsw.gov.au/Documents/zzzArchive/steal_from_motor_vehicle_cpted_handbook.pdf

Chapter 71

CPTED Best Practices: Policy Objectives

The objectives of crime prevention through environmental design (CPTED) Best Practices policy are as follows[1]:

- To ensure that issues of community safety and crime prevention are adequately considered in land use, development, and redevelopment activities
- To aid the integration of safety and security measures in the development assessment process for all private and public projects
- To be a consideration in the development of a security master plan

As we look at this section, we realize it is too short; however, we feel the whole book belongs in your best practices policy. We therefore suggest that what applies in this book should be in your best practices policy.

---

[1] Crime Prevention through Environmental Design (CPTED) Planning Scheme Policy. Brisbane City Plan 2000—Volume 2. https://www.brisbane.qld.gov.au/sites/default/files/Appendix2_CrimePrevention_PSP.pdf (Modified January 2017.)

Chapter 72

International CPTED Association (ICA) Conference: Calgary, Canada

The familiar terms and concepts we use in crime prevention through environmental design (CPTED) evolved from initial theorizing via practical application.[1] They have rarely been explicitly scrutinized as tools for thinking, action, and communication.

All the core concepts of CPTED overlap such as where does defensibility end and territoriality begin? It is the same for defense and access control. All of them fail to distinguish between nature of action and qualities of place, for example, defense and defensibility or surveillance and surveillability. Target hardening has particular limitations: what exactly is the target to be protected, the house or the TV set inside it?

This situation arose from the way CPTED evolved, through a gradual and haphazard accumulation of theory, research, and practice, combined with schools and generations approaches rather than systematic progress and consolidation. The upshot is that both the professional discipline of CPTED and the applied academic research that supports it are held back from making the progress and the practical contribution that they are potentially capable of delivering.

---

[1] Sharpening up CPTED. Design Against Crime Research Center Content. Excerpt presented by Paul Ekblom at the 2015 International CPTED Conference. University of the Arts London Central Saint Martins. Retrieved from http://www.cpted.net/resources/Documents/ICAConf/2015/Ekblom_ICACalgary2015.compressed.pdf

The situation is exacerbated by confusion within and between security and mainstream situational crime prevention. Knowledge is tangled and difficult to retrieve and transfer. As a result, this confusion

- Limits the scope of the problems we can tackle
- Allows objectives to drift
- Reduces the quality of interventions
- Disadvantages CPTED in the wider planning/development process
- Hinders the importation of fresh perspectives from other fields of research and practice

How can we sharpen up CPTED to overcome these limitations and help realize its potential? We have to deconstruct the familiar CPTED concepts and build deeper foundations. My suggestion is to start with environmental primitives like containment, movement, and resistance to force, that relate to the properties, structures, and features of built environments and human activity (and do an equivalent process with more generic security and crime prevention). Then the task will be to reconstruct the familiar CPTED concepts like territoriality on these fundamentals. Ultimately, CPTED needs a controlled vocabulary with sharpened concepts. Designers must combine discipline and rigor with exploration and creativity while covering material, informational, and social dimensions. After all, it is the people stuff in particular that makes or breaks CPTED.

Chapter 73

CPTED: Designing Out Crime (DOC) and Secured by Design (SBD)—United Kingdom

Background

The key ingredient to cost-effective and sustainable environments is to "design out" opportunities for crime within the built environment, during the conception and preplanning stages of the build.[1] This is achieved by using the CPTED process of man-made and natural structures to inhibit crime by influencing both conscious and subconscious behavior. The object of environmental design recommendations is to create safe and secure environments that will present a less attractive target for the criminal. This must be the aim of all involved in the development process, as this is the most effective means of achieving safety and security. Adopting CPTED principles provides a platform from which safe, secure, controlled environments and communities are built. The above processes can and have been used to great effect during regeneration of deprived and high-crime areas.

The above CPTED principles when used through design of a physical and social environment, achieve an environment that is conducive to overall security and the well-being of the users of that community. CPTED is an approach to

---

[1] UK Security Consortium International Ltd., C3 Birdineye Farm, Framfield Road, Uckfield East, Sussex; Design Council. 2015. Design Out Crime. Case Study. http://www.designcouncil.org.uk/resources/case-study/design-out-crime. Permission obtained to reproduce.

crime reduction and comes from criminological theories and practical application for reducing crime opportunity and fear of crime within the built environment.

How Does It Work?

It works by changing the features of the environment and the attitudes of the users in such a way as to influence the incidence of crime. CPTED involves seven core components: access control, surveillance, defensible space, territory, target hardening, image, and activity support. Target hardening processes (both internal and external designs) will be subtle, provide clear delineation between private and public space, deter offenders, and encourage people to take ownership through aesthetically pleasing environments. CPTED is about identifying environmental designs that will not assist the offender but will protect the user.

Where Is It Used?

■ Everywhere! For example: personal home security to schools, shopping malls, stadiums, businesses, railways, ports, residential, major developments and regeneration project, to landscaping, road, parks, urban and recreational areas. The key objective for new developments should be that they create safe and accessible environments where crime and disorder or the fear of crime and disorder does not undermine quality of life or community cohesion. Furthermore, to demonstrate how crime prevention measures have been considered in the design of the proposal, and how the design reflects the attributes of safe, sustainable places. Good environmental design can make a major contribution to deterring the most determined of criminals. Incorporating sensible security measures during the design and building process reduces the level of crime, fear of crime and anti-social behavior. This is the most highly cost-effective and balanced means of achieving safety and security and must be the aim of all involved in the development process.

Security Consortium International Ltd. (SCI) Will Deliver

■ A timely and professional specialist security design service at pre- and post-application stages.
■ Provide workable, innovative, highly effective environmental designs and security solutions for developers who have to fulfil the design parameters, restrictions, and development ethos of the client while ensuring a balanced approach to a required level of security compliance.

- Liaising and negotiating with key stakeholders to identify potential design issues and the possible crime impact implications from surrounding infrastructure.
- Working with on-site project managers during the development process to ensure security and design compliance and effective crime reduction and prevention strategies.

Chapter 74

Through-Roads and Cul-De-Sacs: United Kingdom

There are advantages in some road layout patterns over others, especially where the pattern frustrates the searching behavior of the criminal and his or her need to escape. While it is accepted that through-routes will be included within development layouts, the designer must ensure that the security of the development is not compromised by excessive permeability, for instance, by allowing the criminal legitimate access to the rear or side boundaries of dwellings, or by providing too many or unnecessary segregated footpaths. Overlooking of the street from the dwellings and a high level of street activity are desirable but are no guarantee of lower crime, which evidence proves is achieved through the control and limitation of permeability.[1]

The Design Council's/CABE's Case Study 6 of 2012 states that: "Permeability can be achieved in a scheme without creating separate movement paths" and notes that "paths and pavements run as part of the street to the front of dwellings. This reinforces movement in the right places to keep streets animated and does not open up rear access to properties."[2]

A review of available research in this area concluded that: "Neighborhood permeability ... is one of the community level design features most reliably linked to crime rates, and the connections operate consistently in the same direction across studies: more permeability, more crime. Several studies across several decades' link

---

[1] Secured by Design HOMES 2016 v1; February 2016. Official Police Security Initiative. Retrieved from http://www.securedbydesign.com/wp-content/uploads/2017/06/Secured_by_Design_Homes_2016_V2.pdf
[2] Design Council. Creating Save Places To Live Through Design. Residential Design and Crime Project. Retrieved from https://www.designcouncil.org.uk/sites/default/files/asset/document/creating-safe-places-to-live.pdf

neighborhood property crime rates with permeability versus inaccessibility of neighborhood layout.[3] Neighborhoods with smaller streets or more one-way streets, or fewer entrance streets or with more turnings have lower property crime rates ..."[4]

Cul-De-Sacs

Cul-de-sacs that are short in length and not linked by footpaths can be very safe environments in which residents benefit from lower crime.[5] Research shows that features that generate crime within cul-de-sacs invariably incorporate one or more of the following undesirable features:

- Backing onto open land, railway lines, canal towpaths, etc.
- Are very deep (long)
- Linked to one another by footpaths

If any of the above features are present in a development, additional security measures may be required. Footpaths linking cul-de-sacs to one another can be particularly problematic, and in such cases the layout may need to be reconsidered (particularly in higher crime areas).

---

[3] C. Bevis and J.G.B. Nutter. 1977. *Changing Street Layouts to Reduce Residential Burglary, Paper Presented at the Annual Meeting of the American Society of Criminology, Atlanta, Georgia,* Minneapolis: Minnesota Crime Prevention Center.

[4] R.E. Bechtel. 2002. *CPTED: Yes, No, Maybe, Unknowable and all of the Above by Taylor, R.B. in the Handbook of Environmental Psychology.* New York, NY: John Wiley and Sons (cited by Professor Ted Kitchen, Sheffield Hallam University, 2007).

[5] As Easy As Riding A Bike. Secured By Design - ACPO's blanket recommendation against permeability. February 2016. Retrieved from https://aseasyasridingabike.wordpress. com/2015/02/23/secured-by-design/

Chapter 75

Seating Next to a Footpath: United Kingdom

Before placing any seating (or structure capable of being used for seating) next to a footpath, always consider the context in terms of the physical and social environment. Seating can be a valuable amenity or a focus for antisocial behavior. In some parts of the country there may not be a problem, in others seating may have to be provided only after careful consideration. On the same footpath, seating at one point may be a focus for trouble, whereas at a different point on the same footpath, perhaps with better natural surveillance, it may be trouble-free. Where existing seating appears to be a problem, relocation is often an option worth exploring. The following specific points should be considered:

Who is most likely to be using the footpath?

- For example, is it likely to be used by elderly people?
- Can it be made more or less attractive to certain groups of users by the way it is designed?
- Is the footpath required simply as a means for traveling from one place to another without stopping?
- Is it the intention to encourage stopping and social interaction at particular points along the footpath?
- Would seating encourage or attract inappropriate loiterers such as drinkers or drug users?
- Is vandal-resistant seating necessary?

Should seating be placed right next to the path or set at the back of the verge (care should be taken to avoid creating a climbing aid)?

Where seating is necessary and inappropriate loitering is a problem, consider the use of single seats or stools set several meters apart to deter congregation. In some locations, the use of leaning bars might be more appropriate than seats. Creating space between pedestrians and inappropriate loiterers can help reduce the fear associated with having to walk past and thus promote legitimate use of the route.

Chapter 76

CPTED Tactics and Strategies: United Kingdom

Crime in the United Kingdom has fallen over the last decade, but as society and technology have evolved, new crime challenges have emerged.[1] Changing behavior is of course one aspect of crime reduction, but design also has an important role to play in preventing crime and reducing criminal activity without compromising the enjoyment and usability of products, places and services by legitimate users. So central in designing out crime remains being focused on those you are designing for, as well as those you are designing to thwart. If designers consider the ways in which the object, systems or environments they are designing might be susceptible to crime—and do this early enough in the design process—they can prevent crime from occurring, or at least reduce the opportunities for offender behavior. This might mean, for example, product designers understanding more about how portable consumer electronics like mobile phones, and MP3 players are attractive to thieves because they are small, valuable and easy to re-sell. Interior designers working on bar and restaurant projects might need to think about how the layout of interior space and the furniture they specify can help prevent thefts of and from customers' bags, or how the design of bathrooms and toilets can help prevent illegal drug use. Similarly, designers of bicycles, cycling accessories and street furniture might need to understand how and when bicycle theft most often occurs.

---

[1] Design Out Crime: A designer's guide. Retrieved from https://www.designcouncil.org.uk/sites/default/files/asset/document/designersGuide_digital_0_0.pdf

Designing Out Crime from the Start

It is important to understand that designing out crime is not simply a case of designing better locks and bolts. For it to be most effective (and cost effective), crime prevention needs to be designed-in at the start of a project, where it is able to influence choices and behavior, not added on at the end.

Designers already use sophisticated techniques throughout the design process to fully understand people's latent and unmet needs, in order to create products, services and spaces that are use able and desirable. In taking time to research users and customers at the beginning of the design process, designers will often find that what people say they do often does not reflect what they actually do in practice. In the same way, by researching abuser "needs" such as loopholes and weaknesses in systems, situations, premises, designers can apply this creativity and innovation to developing sophisticated solutions that can prevent and ultimately pre-empt crime. When places, products and services are developed with crime resistance in mind, designers can help to make it more difficult, more risky or less attractive for offenders to commit crimes, and help to make it easier for people to stay safe and keep their belongings secure. This makes people and communities feel safer.

The Cost of Crime

Crime brings with it a cost to individuals and businesses in three ways—cost incurred in anticipation of crime (the cost of security)—costs incurred as a consequence of crime—the cost of responding to crime. For individuals the cost of crime can include time off work through injury, as well as the hidden costs of anxiety, stress, feelings of vulnerability and reduced confidence. For businesses this can lead to a fall in productivity or difficulty retaining or recruiting staff. And of course crime has additional costs for local and national authorities in terms of police time and the cost to the NHS and other public services.

Example: Preventing Access to Alleyways in Terraced Housing

Introducing gates at both ends of alleyways behind rows of terraced housing, or at the street end of an alleyway in between terraced buildings, has been successful in reducing burglaries and helping to make residents feel safer. A study of alley-gating in Liverpool conducted by the University of Huddersfield found that residents in gated areas experienced less crime and less antisocial behavior, and felt safer in their homes than residents living in non-gated areas. Burglary in some areas of

Liverpool has reduced by 37% since the introduction of the gates. Gating alleyways and providing keys for residents only can also prevent other crimes and antisocial behavior, including: drug-taking/drug dealing and drug-related litter, graffiti and criminal damage, prostitution, arson attempts, dog mess, fly tipping of rubbish and abandoned vehicles.

Chapter 77

CPTED Management Strategies: France and Italy

The objective is to ensure that the project provides for the way in which the surveillance of the spaces will be made possible.[1] Urban design choices on surveillance effectiveness of the space must be made in such a way that facilitates the implementation of the measures listed in the following text. These measures must address the following:

- The clarity of the properties and their boundaries: a clear definition of space and real estate provides a basis for identifying the responsibilities and the competences of the stakeholders in charge of surveillance.
- The visibility of the spaces: the design of the space impacts on the capacity to "see and be seen" with regard to both the human and technical surveillance modes.
- The accessibility of the space for those in charge of surveillance: surveillance capacities are dependent on it. If access to an area is not physically possible, clear sight lines can improve the quality of visual surveillance from outside the site.

---

[1] C. Cardia. 2010. *Planning Urban Design and Management for Crime Prevention. Handbook.* Politecnico Di Milano–DiAP, IAU île-de-France Institut d'aménagement et d'urbanisme de la région Île-de-France; http://www.veilig-ontwerp-beheer.nl/publicaties/handbook-planning-urban-design-and-managemnet-for-crime-prevention#

Consider surveillance tasks during the first stages of the project. The involvement of those stakeholders responsible for surveillance at the conception of the project will make it possible to consider the feasibility of their tasks, their modes of operation, and the constraints. This involvement can result in a preliminary draft of a partnership agreement actionable from the earliest stage of the project, for example, an agreement enabling the police to enter the site.

With regard to the technical systems, it is possible to plan for the conditions under which a technical surveillance system may be implemented, by deciding on the routing of the electrical network at the initial onset of the project. It is also possible to plan ahead for a future decision to install such a system by either keeping open the possibility of a link to an existing electrical network, or of the installation of a completely new system.

Basic Strategies for Target Hardening

Identification of High-Risk Spaces and Potential Targets of Crime

A safety audit, part of the whole process of the project, can highlight which spaces are high risk or specific targets of crime.

Providing for Specific Measures of Protection and Surveillance

A safety plan of action aimed to protect these critical spaces and services can include both human and technical measures (i.e., formal surveillance as well as access control, for instance).

Physical Target Hardening

There are different ways of achieving target hardening, including different systems of physical security reinforcement, such as perimeter fencing, walls, strong exterior doors, deadbolt locks, secure basement windows, bars, adequate lighting, and alarm systems (one of the most diffused methods of protection). It has to be considered that target hardening is costly and that it is impossible to harden everything. In light of this consideration, target hardening should be used as a selective measure, primarily to deter, deny, detect, or delay a criminal attack.

The Specific Issue of "Access Control"

Control of access to high-risk places must be studied in detail. Different questions referring to the uses of the space must be dealt with: Why do we want to control access? Who is allowed to come into the place? How will it be achieved? For instance, a residential area can be designed with access control to allow only residents to come in. But, mailboxes and trash cans must be reachable by the appropriate services. This accessibility must be agreed with the manager. It also can be planned into the design (through the design of the entrances of buildings, see section on design strategies). A project can also be planned so as to keep open all public spaces; however, it should be planned for the possibility of closing some of them in the future, if the need should arise, so as to deal with new situations (for instance, providing the possibility to raise a physical barrier [fence, wall] between two type of spaces for the purpose of making the boundaries clean and clear).

Chapter 78

Natural Access Control Using "Hostile" Vegetation

Crime prevention through environmental design (CPTED) is a multidisciplinary approach to deterring criminal behavior by making changes in the environment to prevent or deter crime. Natural access control is one of the concepts of first-generation CPTED and can be emphasized with natural strategies for behavior management utilizing vegetation. By altering the physical design of an area, behavior can be controlled so crime and the fear of crime are reduced. Vegetation (plants or bushes) with thorns or spines can be used for natural access control and at the same time provide protection—especially for ground-level windows. There are numerous types of plants and bushes that can be used in any climate or environment. Defensive landscaping blends in with homes or commercial buildings and can also help protect against intruders. These natural barriers can keep potential criminals away from windows or vulnerable areas. Defensive barriers, such as walls, moats, and fences have been used for centuries, but plants can also help with security because defensive vegetation capitalizes on the thorns and spines of plants or bushes and at the same time, they also have an aesthetic appeal with flowers or colorful berries.[1]

Architect Oscar Newman wrote the book *Creating Defensible Space*[2] in 1972 because he was concerned about neighborhood safety and crime prevention.

---

[1] B.L. Grant. Defensive Shrubs for Landscaping: Tips for Using Shrubs with Thorns. Retrieved on September 29, 2017, from: https://www.gardeningknowhow.com/ornamental/shrubs/shgen/using-defensive-shrubs.htm

[2] O. Newman. 1996. *Creating Defensible Space*. U.S. Department of Housing and Urban Development. Retrieved on September 29, 2017, from: https://www.huduser.gov/publications/pdf/def.pdf

Another basic principle of CPTED includes natural surveillance, which can be attributed to Jane Jacobs' ideas about the "positive power of eyes on the street," which she described in her 1961 book, *The Death and Life of Great American Cities*.[3] Any bushes or plants should be kept to a height of no more than 3 feet so as not to interfere with natural surveillance.[4] Using vegetation for natural access control is a cost-efficient approach to crime prevention when used as a tool for problem-solving, and not as an independent intervention.[5]

CPTED strategies are not only used for crime prevention, but instead are intended to help improve the overall quality of life for everyone who lives, works, or plays in a particular area of the community. If crime prevention was the only goal, bars on ground floor windows may be more effective than defensive vegetation. The issue with bars on the windows is that it gives the area a "fortress" or "prison" appearance. Ornamental vegetation with thorns or spines is a deterrence and will keep intruders away from vulnerable areas, improve the appearance of the area, and also provide natural access control.

The following are some of the common plants and shrubs that are used for CPTED strategies:

Yucca[6]

- Sword-shaped and pointed leaves 1–3 feet long with sharp, brown tips
- Covered in numerous tiny marginal teeth
- Showy and white flowers

Japanese Barberry[7]

- Spiny, broad-rounded, deciduous shrub
- Obovate green leaves (variably sized to 1 1/4 inches long)
- Turn attractive shades of orange, yellow, and red in fall

---

[3] J. Ryan. 2014. What Is CPTED and How Can It Help Your Community? Retrieved on September 29, 2017, from: https://www.bjatraining.org/media/blog/what-cpted-and-how-can-it-help-your-community

[4] The 30 Plants That Can Help Protect Your Home against Burglary. *The Telegraph*. Retrieved on July 29, 2017, from: http://www.telegraph.co.uk/news/newstopics/howaboutthat/9108641/The-30-plants-that-can-help-protect-your-home-against-burglary.html

[5] J. Ryan. 2014. What Is CPTED and How Can It Help Your Community? Retrieved on September 29, 2017, from: https://www.bjatraining.org/media/blog/what-cpted-and-how-can-it-help-your-community

[6] Yucca. Retrieved on September 29, 2017, from: http://www.bio.brandeis.edu/fieldbio/Survival/Pages/yucca.html

[7] *Berberis thunbergii f. atropurpurea* 'Atropurpurea Nana'. Retrieved on September 2017, from: http://www.missouribotanicalgarden.org/PlantFinder/PlantFinderDetails.aspx?kempcode=b700

Bougainvillea[8]

- Thorny, evergreen summer bloomers
- Orange, yellow, crimson, or purple flowers are actually modified leaves called bracts and the bracts surround the actual flowers that are tiny and white

Longleaf Mahonia[9]

- Woodland groundcover, low barrier planting
- Mass of stiff, leathery ferns
- Produces clusters of yellow flowers

Creeping Juniper[10]

- Also known as "Blue Rug"
- Thorny stem and foliage

Common Holly[11]

- Evergreen shrub
- Dark green spiked leaves
- Large red berries on female plants only

Giant Rhubarb[12]

- Giant rhubarb-like leaves on erect stems
- Abrasive foliage

---

[8] T. Spengler. Bougainvillea Care—How to Grow a Bougainvillea in the Garden. Retrieved on September 29, 2017, from: https://www.gardeningknowhow.com/ornamental/vines/bougainvillea/bougainvillea-garden-care.htm

[9] Longleaf Mahonia. Retrieved on September 29, 2017, from: http://www.monrovia.com/plant-catalog/plants/4338/longleaf-mahonia/

[10] The 30 Plants That Can Help Protect Your Home against Burglary. Retrieved on July 29, 2017, from: http://www.telegraph.co.uk/news/newstopics/howaboutthat/9108641/The-30-plants-that-can-help-protect-your-home-against-burglary.html

[11] The 30 Plants That Can Help Protect Your Home against Burglary. *The Telegraph.* Retrieved on July 29, 2017, from: http://www.telegraph.co.uk/news/newstopics/howaboutthat/9108641/The-30-plants-that-can-help-protect-your-home-against-burglary.html

[12] The 30 Plants That Can Help Protect Your Home against Burglary. *The Telegraph.* Retrieved on July 29, 2017, from: http://www.telegraph.co.uk/news/newstopics/howaboutthat/9108641/The-30-plants-that-can-help-protect-your-home-against-burglary.html

Shrub Rose[13]

- Excellent ground cover, pale pink flowers
- Very thorny stem

Purple Berberis[14]

- Rich purple foliage
- Thorny stem

Blackthorn[15]

- Spiny shrub
- Dense growth, suitable for hedges
- White flowers with bluish-black fruit

Fuschia-Flowered Gooseberry[16]

- Fruit bush
- Spiny, produces greenish to greenish-pink flowers in clusters of two or three

The above list is not all inclusive of the types of plants that may be used to incorporate CPTED strategies into landscaping. When choosing plants for a particular area, base those decisions on specific site conditions such as sun exposure, soil type, maintenance, and the location of utilities.

---

[13] The 30 Plants That Can Help Protect Your Home against Burglary. *The Telegraph*. Retrieved on July 29, 2017, from: http://www.telegraph.co.uk/news/newstopics/howaboutthat/9108641/The-30-plants-that-can-help-protect-your-home-against-burglary.html

[14] The 30 Plants That Can Help Protect Your Home against Burglary. *The Telegraph*. Retrieved on July 29, 2017, from: http://www.telegraph.co.uk/news/newstopics/howaboutthat/9108641/The-30-plants-that-can-help-protect-your-home-against-burglary.html

[15] The 30 Plants That Can Help Protect Your Home against Burglary. *The Telegraph*. Retrieved on July 29, 2017, from: http://www.telegraph.co.uk/news/newstopics/howaboutthat/9108641/The-30-plants-that-can-help-protect-your-home-against-burglary.html

[16] The 30 Plants That Can Help Protect Your Home against Burglary. *The Telegraph*. Retrieved on July 29, 2017, from: http://www.telegraph.co.uk/news/newstopics/howaboutthat/9108641/The-30-plants-that-can-help-protect-your-home-against-burglary.html

Chapter 79

Access and Pedestrian Walkways: Malaysia

- Width of the road must comply with existing guidelines adopted by the local authority.
- Road network must be interconnected and has clear hierarchy. Dedicated pedestrian walkway is to be separated from motorized lanes.
- Ensure that new and existing roads have connectivity so that there is no separation between old and new areas.
- Ensure that the hierarchy and design of the road is suitable to the type of development and speed limit allowed.
- Pedestrian walkway is not encouraged to be connected to the dead-end road.
- Provide lighting in dark areas along the street and pedestrian walkway at the appropriate distance and height.
- Maintenance of access and pedestrian walkway should be performed regularly and constantly so as to be in good and clean condition to raise public confidence that the said area is well maintained and safe to use.
- The provision of through road that passes through residential area to the surrounding area is not allowed.
- Access roads should be limited and controlled (not exceeding two access points) for each development as per the Planning Guidelines on Gated Community and Guarded Neighborhood for details.
- Provide connected pedestrian walkways in residential areas, neighborhood centers, business area, and areas of public concentration for the comfort of the pedestrians.
- Ensure pedestrian walkways are provided on both sides of the road, especially in areas of public concentration.

- Provide pedestrian walkways that can be visible directly from nearby premises and are not obstructed by any structure.
- Avoid space that is concealed, hidden, and that can increase the potential for crime on the pedestrian walkways.
- Provide pedestrian walkways that can obtain optimal natural lighting during the day but are comfortable to the users through the provision of appropriate shade and landscaping elements.
- Bicycle lanes should be separated from vehicle lanes (available next to the pedestrian walkway but has a separate lane).
- Avoid design of a telecommunication service system that encourages criminals to commit crime. For example, telecommunication poles with steps.[1]

---

[1] Crime Prevention Through Environmental Design (CPTED) Implementation Guide. Department of Town and Country Planning, Ministry of Housing and Local Government, MalaysiaReka Bentuk, Bandar Selamat, Panduan Pelaksanaan. August 2012. Retrieved from http://www.townplan.gov.my/download/Penerbitan/NKRA/GP_CPTED%20Eng%20 Version_2nd.pdf

Chapter 80

Bicycle Paths: Australia

Bicycle paths are major benefits for any community, which can rely on bicycles for public transport, as any reduction in automobile use reduces the negative impacts of the city on local and global environmental problems.[1] As Burswood Lakes is to be a transit-orientated development (TOD), it is critical that convenient access for cyclists be provided.

To maximize use of cycle paths, it is essential that they provide a safe environment for cyclists of all ages, with adequate and safe facilities along the routes and at destinations.

Safe Routes

- Ensure that bicycle routes are selected both for convenience and security (i.e., routes with vehicle and pedestrian traffic during the day and evening, with as few empty spaces and underground crossings as possible).
- Ensure that routes are well lit and well maintained, with clear signage.
- Avoid tall bushes, dense shrubbery, and dense clusters of trees immediately adjacent to routes and at predictable stopping points such as road crossings.
- The rule of thumb is low planting (maximum height 600 mm) and high-branching trees (2 meters) to open sightlines. These are particularly recommended within a distance of 15 meters from bicycle stop signs or road junctions.

---

[1] Sarkissian Associates Planners Pty Ltd, 207 Boundary Street, West End Queensland 4101. Phone: (07) 3844 9818; Fax: (07) 3846 2719; Email: sarkissian@pacific.net.au

Signage

Clearly sign and light entrances to routes passing through relatively isolated areas and provide clearly signed alternative nighttime routes. As the identification of safe nighttime routes will differ in each location because of the contextual nature of crime, it will be necessary to use crime risk assessment procedures to determine specifically which routes need particular attention.

Bicycle Parking Areas

1. Ensure that bicycle parking areas are well lit and located where they can be informally surveyed from streets and buildings.
2. Provide bicycle parking and locking facilities in accordance with AS2890.3.[2] Rails (stands) are not secure facilities for long-stay users. Rails are only suitable for short stay users.

Illustrated CPTED Guidelines

All arrangements with respect to bicycle parking at the train station need to be resolved in consultation with police crime prevention specialists and the appropriate rail authority.

---

[2] White Paper. New Bicycle Parking Requirements. 3 steps to Design Compliant Layouts, Select Compliant Products and Avoid Costly Mistakes. Jon Rutledge. Contributor. February 2016. Referenced from http://cora.com.au/assets/downloads/AS2890.3-WhitePaper.pdf

Chapter 81

Bus Stops, Trains, Trolleys, and Taxi Stands

CPTED Principles Related to Bus Stop Provision

Safety at bus stops, rail stations, and taxi ranks is an important issue in crime prevention through environmental design (CPTED) principles related to bus stop provision.[1] These transport access points have been criticized due to their locations away from major activity areas such as shops, and the subsequent lack of opportunities for natural surveillance. Some stations have developed a deteriorated appearance and have become sites for graffiti. Bus stops are also a common gathering point for young people who may in some cases be perceived as a threat by women and older people waiting for public transport.

While site-specific interventions require crime risk assessments to be carried out, some basic principles can guide redesign and redevelopment of existing facilities and inform new planning and design. Because it is important to encourage use of the Burswood train station, careful attention to CPTED issues in its redevelopment is strongly recommended. *For this work, a crime risk assessment will be required.*

Five Ways to Improve Transit Passenger Security

How can transit agencies improve passenger security, especially in an era when declining funding means that night service is continually being cut back?

---

[1] Sarkissian Associates Planners Pty Ltd, 207 Boundary Street, West End Queensland 4101. Phone: (07) 3844 9818; Fax: (07) 3846 2719; Email: sarkissian@pacific.net.au

1. Install Security Cameras on Transit Vehicles and Stations
2. Improve Lighting at Stops and Stations
3. Initiate a Request Stop Program
4. Employ CPTED (Crime Prevention Through Environmental Design) Concept and Principles
5. Make Real Time Schedule Information Available on Phones (C. MacKechnie)[2]

Strategy: CPTED for Subways

Strategy crime prevention through environmental design (CPTED) is used to build a subway environment that deters the opportunity for crime to occur.[3]

Strategy

CPTED is used to build a subway environment that deters the opportunity for crime.

Crime Problem Addressed

The use of CPTED in subway construction will help deter and control all types of crime and help create an environment that is clean, well-lighted, and safe.

Key Components

CPTED is action to design the physical environment in ways that reduce or remove identifiable crime risks. Because of the cost of subway construction, it is vital to incorporate CPTED into the original design. A security design group should include architects, security and police, and the subway authority. Other cities where CPTED was a design component of the subway can provide input. CPTED design principles should address visibility, access control, lighting, security hardware, landscaping, resistance to vandalism, and maintenance.

Key Participants

Incorporating CPTED subway construction requires participation from security and police, architects, builders, and the subway authority.

---

[2] C. MacKechnie. How Much Does a Bus Cost to Purchase and Operate. https://www.thoughtco. com/ways-to-improve-security-2798820 (Updated August 4, 2016.)

[3] C. MacKechnie. How Much Does a Bus Cost to Purchase and Operate? Thought Co. Art, Music and Recreation. Cars and Motorcycles. Referenced from https://www.thoughtco.com/ bus-cost-to-purchase-and-operate-2798845 (Updated July 10, 2017.)

Potential Obstacles

It may be difficult to interest and organize the variety of individuals and professions necessary to incorporate CPTED into subway design. Many see CPTED as having high up-front costs. CPTED works best with new construction. CPTED for existing facilities is more complicated and costly.

Signs of Success

The Washington, DC, subway opened in the early 1970s. Because of the fear of crime, CPTED became one of the more important design components of the system. It was designed to discourage crime by providing excellent visibility, good lighting, and vandal-resistant materials. The subway has had fewer than five murders and averages about 100 robberies per year, many of which take place around bus stops and not in the subway (Washington Metro Crime Prevention Unit, 1993).[4]

Applying the Strategy

CPTED changes implemented by the New York Transit Authority have substantially increased the overall perception of security by passengers. Unfortunately, because the changes modified existing construction, they were very expensive. As the Washington subway continues to grow, CPTED remains a primary design requirement to keep passengers safe.

China Train Stations

China has over 5500 railway stations for passenger use along its 77,000 miles (124,000 kilometers) long rail lines.[5]

The early built China train stations are usually located in the center of the city or town, operating nonbullet trains and some also operating a few bullet ones. The newly built railway stations are generally located far from the city center and specialize in high-speed trains, such as Beijing South, Shanghai Hongqiao, and Xian North; but they mostly can be reached by subway.

A train station in China usually consists of one or two squares and a terminal building, inside which ticket offices, waiting rooms, boarding gates, platforms and

---

[4] National Crime Prevention Council. Strategy: CPTED for Subways. Referenced from http://archive.ncpc.org/topics/home-and-neighborhood-safety/strategies/strategy-cpted-for-subways.html
[5] China: How to Travel by Train in China. TripAdvisor. https://www.tripadvisor.com/Travel-g294211-c148494/China:How.To.Travel.By.Train.In.China.html

some affiliated facilities like toilets, hot drinking water, restaurants, and bilingual direction boards are provided.

Bicycle Guidelines

- Bikes ride for free with any paying transit riders!
- Please remember you are responsible for the loading and unloading of your bicycle.
- Remove all loose items not attached to your bike (e.g., bags on handlebars, lights, helmets, etc.).
- For extra security, lock your wheel to the frame of your bike before the bus arrives. *DO NOT* lock your bicycle to the bus rack.
- Each bus can accommodate two bicycles in the rack on the front of the bus. Wait for the next bus if the bike rack is full.
- Exit the bus through the front door and let the operator know you will be removing your bicycle from the rack.
- Rapid Express routes have lower-storage compartments for bikes.
- One bicycle is allowed per Trolley car during peak travel times, and two are allowed at all other times.

Design—Accessibility

Transit buses used to be mainly *high-floor* vehicles. However, they are now increasingly of *low-floor* design and optionally also "kneel" *air suspension* and have electrically or hydraulically extended under-floor ramps to provide level access for *wheelchair* users and people with *baby carriages*. Prior to more general use of such technology, these wheelchair users could only use specialist *paratransit* mobility buses.[6]

Accessible vehicles also have wider entrances and interior gangways and space for wheelchairs. Interior fittings and *destination displays* may also be designed to be usable by the *visually impaired*. Coaches generally use *wheelchair lifts* instead of low-floor designs. In some countries, vehicles are required to have these features by *disability discrimination laws*.

Configuration

Buses were initially configured with an engine in the front and an entrance at the rear. With the transition to one-man operation, many manufacturers moved to mid- or rear-engine designs, with a single door at the front or multiple doors. The move to the low-floor design has all but eliminated the mid-engine design, although some

---

[6] Bus. https://en.wikipedia.org/wiki/Bus

coaches still have mid-mounted engines. Front-engine buses still persist for niche markets such as American school buses, some minibuses, and buses in less developed countries, which may be derived from truck chassis, rather than purpose-built bus designs. Most buses have two axles; articulated buses have three.

Bus Stops

Accepted CPTED industry strategies are described as follows.[7]

- Natural surveillance. This strategy involves reducing crime by decreasing target opportunities in a space/area by placing physical features, activities, and people to maximize visibility.
- Natural access control. Channeling people into, alongside, or out of spaces/areas and deterring entry elsewhere along the boundary are the concepts of this principle (through the judicial placement of entrances, exits, fencing, landscaping, and lighting). This concept denies access to crime targets and creates a perception of risk for adversaries.
- Territoriality. Territoriality notifies users and nonusers of the boundaries of a space/area or facility. It creates a psychological deterrent to crime by notifying users of the space/area/facility that they are being watched and that the community is the space/area/facility for purposeful activities.
- Activity support. By encouraging authorized activities in public spaces, the community and transit system ridership understand its intended use. Criminal acts are discouraged, and an increase in safety and security of the transit system, its operations, facilities, ridership, and people are realized.
- Maintenance/Image. Care and upkeep demonstrate expression of ownership for the intended purpose of the area. A lack of care indicates loss of control of a space or area and can be a sign of tolerance for disorder. Establishing care and maintenance standards and continuing the service preserve the intended use of the space/area. CPTED maintenance and care standards also safeguard the best interests of the community and transit agency where they serve.

---

[7] American Public Transportation Association. 2010. Crime Prevention through Environmental Design (CPTED) for Transit Facilities. APTA Standards Development Program: Recommended Practice. http://www.apta.com/resources/standards/Documents/APTA-SS-SIS-RP-007-10.pdf

Chapter 82

The Role of Planning and Design Professionals: South Africa and Nigeria

When aligning local government functions with crime prevention objectives, officials involved with urban design, town planning, and architecture could be responsible for a number of activities.[1] These include the following:

- Developing and implementing design and urban planning guidelines aimed at reducing crime
- Designing retrospective improvements to physical environments in support of crime prevention
- Ensuring that building regulations are compatible with the principles of CPTED
- Promoting performance zoning in support of crime prevention and applying a flexible approach to zoning standards, for example, reducing large areas of vacant land by identifying appropriate land uses
- Ensuring context-specific design and management of the built environment to reduce crime
- Contributing to the planning and implementation of integrated crime prevention strategies, especially with regard to aspects related to the physical environment
- Assisting with the development of appropriate by-laws

---

[1] Introduction to Crime Prevention through Environmental Design (CPTED). http://www. cpted.co.za/cpted_summary.pdf

230

Planning, designing, and managing safer environments need not necessitate additional activities, effort, or resources. It may merely require emphasizing particular aspects of the conventional functions of officials and professionals such as architects, urban planners, and designers.

Conclusion

Environmental design is about more than the physical spaces—at its core lies community development in the broadest sense.[2] The key to the success of any intervention that involves the planning and design of the physical environment lies in the extent to which the people using these environments are involved in the process.

Factors Affecting Architectural Design for Crime in Nigeria: Role of the Architect

It has been acknowledged by researchers and practitioners of crime prevention that design is an important tool that could be used to prevent crime and reduce fear of crime while increasing sense of community.[3] However, the architect faces several challenges in the attempt to address crime prevention issues in his design. This paper assessed the factors that hinder architects in Nigeria from addressing issues of crime prevention holistically in their designs. Survey research method was adopted for the study. 132 questionnaires were administered to architects in Akwa Ibom and Cross River States of Nigeria. 87 properly filled and returned questionnaires were used for the study. Percentages and mean score analysis and ranking method were used as the analysis tools. Interviews were also carried out with key architects with 12 to 37 years of practice experience. The result revealed the major hindrances to architectural design for crime prevention to include lack of documented examples and no crime prevention requirements in planning and building regulations in Nigeria among others. These factors are knowledge related. This suggests that knowledge has a significant and positive effect on architectural design for crime prevention as it helps architects to take good and informed design decisions. It notes that documented examples have three major functions, namely, knowledge sharing, knowledge transfer and knowledge preservation. The paper concluded that these

---

[2] Introduction to Crime Prevention through Environmental Design (CPTED). Conclusion. Referenced from http://www.cpted.co.za/cpted_summary.pdf

[3] Reproduced from R.E. Olagunju, S.O. Ebong, S.N. Zubairu. 2017. Factors affecting architectural design for crime prevention in Nigeria. *Journal of Sustainable Architecture and Civil Engineering* 18(1). http://dx.doi.org/10.5755/j01.sace.18.1.17348. Revision February 28, 2017.

factors affect the ability of architects to design against crime because architectural design is knowledge dependent and knowledge driven. It recommended that physical security concepts and crime prevention through environmental design should be made part of formal architectural education training and/or professional continuing development program in Nigeria.

Chapter 83

CPTED and Defensible Space: Ottawa

Fences, locks, and surveillance have long been used to protect people and property.[1] Researchers and practitioners have built upon these practices by trying to understand the relationship between physical design and levels of criminal activity, and then by manipulating design to reduce the incidence of crime. This type of crime prevention is called crime prevention through environmental design (CPTED), and it focuses on the design of buildings and another infrastructure and on their geographical placement. CPTED is based on the view that the built environment affects crime. Crime is not randomly distributed but is concentrated in some locations. There are many reasons why some places have higher crime rates than other places; one reason is the built environment.

CPTED involves understanding the relationship between physical design and levels of criminal activity, and then manipulating design to reduce the incidence of crime. There is a growing body of evidence that suggests that CPTED can reduce crime and fear of crime.

CPTED is based on rational choice theory, which claims that crime is the result of deliberate choices made by offenders based on their calculation of the risks and rewards involved with these choices. Rational choice theory does not focus on the individual's background, but rather on the situational factors involved in deciding whether or not to commit a crime. The essence of CPTED and other types of situational crime prevention is the idea that criminals will be deterred if

---

[1] PRA Inc., Research and Consulting. Prevention by Design in Ottawa: Toward a Strategic Approach to Crime Prevention Through Environmental Design. Final Report. January 2009. Referenced from http://www.crimepreventionottawa.ca/uploads/files/initiative/final_report_jan_19.pdf

the environment can be changed to increase the perceived risk, increase the effort, or reduce the rewards of committing an offense.

There is a growing body of evidence that suggests that CPTED can reduce crime and fear of crime and describes evaluation research that has been done on several CPTED programs (Secured by Design and Graffiti Clean Up Programs) and tactics (street closures, public housing renewal, closed-circuit television, street lighting, convenience store ordinances, and target hardening).

Crime-Free Multi-Housing

One area where CPTED has been successfully applied to existing buildings is the Crime Free Multi-Housing program run by the Ottawa Police Service.[2] The program is aimed at reducing crime in rental housing. One component of the program is a CPTED inspection, and owners must meet a minimum standard in order to receive certification. Many of Ottawa's largest housing companies participate in the program, so it has been an effective way of encouraging the use of CPTED.

Community Involvement

One issue that was mentioned by several respondents is the need to involve the community in CPTED audits and find ways of getting the results back to the community. There have been efforts to do this. The Women's Initiatives for Safer Environments (WISE)[3] has built community consultation into their process, and they try to use their audits to build community capacity. The police have also worked closely with community groups on several projects. However, as with other processes involving CPTED, this would be more effective if there were policies that would encourage and facilitate this consultation where appropriate.

The Ottawa 20/20 plan calls for a new approach to city-building. The plan states that:

> Preventative thinking is the foundation of the City's approach to managing growth and providing services. At the macro-scale, the OP [Official Plan] will help prevent some of the fiscal, environmental and social problems that have arisen due to past development trends. At the level of specific services, preventative measures will help reduce the need for intervention and reduce the suffering experienced by citizens. Prevention is much more cost-effective than remediation or intervention

---

[2] North Central Community Association. Crime Free Multi Housing. Referenced from http://www.nccaregina.ca/crime-free-multi-housing/
[3] WISE IFSE. http://www.wiseottawa.ca/about.us

and can contribute to maintaining the high quality of services in the current climate of budget restraint. (City of Ottawa, 2003, p. 17)[4]

Preventing crime and improving public safety are so important that CPTED should be a core component of Ottawa's future planning. Decisions made today about the design of new neighborhoods, buildings, parks, and other facilities will have an impact on the safety of the citizens of Ottawa for many decades to come. CPTED is a proven method of crime prevention that should be a key building block in Ottawa's crime reduction and community safety strategy.

Ottawa can take a global leadership role by incorporating CPTED as a core part of a broad and comprehensive crime prevention strategy.

---

[4] Ottawa 20/20 – Human Services Plan. Priority on People. May 2003. City of Ottawa. Referenced from http://ottawa.ca/cs/groups/content/@webottawa/documents/pdf/mdaw/mdc4/~edisp/cap078814.pdf

Chapter 84

CPTED Foundations and Fundamentals: Risk, Risk Analysis and Assessments, and the Basis for Proper Planning[1]

Wise men say, and not without reason, that whoever wished to foresee the future might consult the past.

Niccolo Machiavelli (1469–1527)

Learn from yesterday, live for today, hope for tomorrow. The important thing is not to stop questioning.

Albert Einstein (1879–1955)

San Bernardino, Calif.—Gunfire erupted inside an elementary school classroom in San Bernardino, Calif., on Monday, leaving two adults and one student dead in what the authorities said was an apparent murder-suicide. The shooter, whom the police identified as Cedric Anderson, 53, walked into the classroom and without speaking opened fire on his wife, Karen Elaine Smith. Ms. Smith, 53, was the lead teacher in the class of 15 students with special needs, who ranged from first to fourth graders. (The New York Times, April 10, 2017)

---

[1] Chapter is reproduced with permission from J. Kelly Stewart, MBA, CHS-IV.

Headline news stories like this are becoming too prevalent in our educational institutions. It is with this backdrop and what has occurred to date, that we must endeavor to be more vigilant and knowledgeable about the foundations and fundamentals of security awareness and assessment. It is an essential preamble to return "Back to Basics." Therefore, understanding the definition of risk and the process of a thorough and comprehensive risk analysis and assessment is indispensable for developing the foundation of a security master plan or comprehensive blueprint for any level of educational institution—whether it be K-12 or higher education. In many instances our institutions have neglected this aspect due to several compromising variables—budgetary, regulations, compliance, quick fixes, policy and procedures, and so on.

What is emblematic in every one of these instances is the lack of focus on risk analysis and assessment. It is the disregard and neglect in being aware of our surroundings and comprehending the operational aspects of the educational institution. These crucial aspects set into motion the necessity to establish a thorough risk analysis and assessment process that can be the basis for proper security master planning and will ultimately assist in the development of subsequent and critical plans—Communication, Crisis Management, Active Shooter Training, a Workplace Violence Plan, and so on. What is tantamount, therefore, is an understanding and awareness of the environment in which the educational institution resides. Considering that the student body, teachers, and administrative staff are the life-blood of our educational institutions, it is critically important that this understanding of risk, the process of risk analysis and assessment, and the eventual planning are done meticulously. It goes to the very essence of not only protecting our greatest assets—our students, faculty, and staff—but also to our culture's future.

Critical Thinking

So, how does one conduct a risk analysis and a CPTED assessment in this environment? There are numerous ways in which to conduct this process and, depending on your situation, every way is done differently. Potentially, every one of these approaches could be correct. It simply depends. However, it has been my experience that nothing can be left to chance. The order of things has to follow a logical, detailed, and systematic process. A venerable and esteemed colleague of mine, Thomas Norman, in his book, *Risk Analysis and Security Countermeasures Selection*, said it best:

> Critical thinking is to thinking as economics is to money management. Critical thinking applies a scientific process to the act of thinking that helps result in far superior conclusions and helps the thinker to support his/her conclusions with rational and defend-able arguments.
> Critical thinking helps assure that personal weaknesses, prejudices, or personal agendas are not forwarded as part of the conclusions.

Critical thinking is important because it enables one to think about a problem more completely and to consider many factors that may not be intuitively apparent.[2]

Common Language

This needs to be the first step in the risk analysis and assessment process. Next, it must be understood that before one can commence, a level playing field must be established. This points directly to nomenclature, teamwork, and setting expectations. One has only to point to the U.S. Department of Homeland Security (DHS) and its program reviewing critical infrastructures—educational institutions being one area. Their initial step in identifying risks was to create a framework and guideline in order to have a clear and relevant comprehension of terms.

To support IRM (Integrated Risk Management) for the department, the DHS Risk Lexicon:

- Promulgates a common language to ease and improve communications for DHS and its partners.
- Facilitates the clear exchange of structured and unstructured data, essential to interoperability amongst risk practitioners.
- Garners credibility and grows relationships by providing consistency and clear understanding with regard to the usage of terms by the risk community across DHS and its components.[3]

Terms are important as they can literally define how one is to proceed with the task at hand. This is why it is necessary to ensure, especially within an educational environment, that the definition of risk is well defined early in the process. Bear in mind that each elementary, secondary, high school, and higher institution of learning have completely varying degrees of how to define risk and what that means to their particular environment, which must be taken into account prior to any type of process beginning. For our purposes in this paper, risk and risk assessment will be defined and based on the "process of managing uncertainty of exposures that affect a school district's assets and financial statements using the five steps: identification, analysis, control, financing and administration," as stated by Stacey Corluccio, CSRM the Academic Director of Risk Management Programs at the National Alliance for Insurance Education and Research until October 2015.[4] Security practitioners should further their scope by including best

---

[2] T.L. Norman. *Risk Analysis and Security Countermeasure Selection* (2nd ed.). Boca Raton, FL: CRC Press, p. 71.

[3] U.S. Department of Homeland Security. http://www.dhs.gov/dhs-risk-lexicon

[4] Effective School Risk Management. What Is It and Whose Job Is It? Administrator Resources by Stacy Corluccio, CSRM. November 23, 2014. Referenced from http://www.seenmagazine.us/Articles/Article-Detail/articleid/4383/effective-school-risk-management

practices as well as established standards and guidelines, such as those put forth by *ISO 31000:2009 Risk Management—Principles and Guidelines* and *ANSI/ASIS International/RIMS Risk Assessment Standard.*[5] Both documents serve as excellent guides to defining risk, establishing a risk assessment process, and forming a risk analysis and assessment program that meets the set objectives of the institution (ISO International Organization for Standardization).

Teamwork

Our next building block in the process must be the formation of an effective team and who will be assisting in the risk analysis and assessment process. This often brings up the dubious question as to who is responsible for risk within the institution. The simple answer is everyone. Everyone has their part to play within this process: "The whole is greater than the sum of its parts."[6] In order to complete a thorough and comprehensive review and assessment, it is a necessity that a team mindset is undertaken because each person has his or her own particular expertise. Total effectiveness of the team, each interacting with one another, is different or greater than their effectiveness when acting in isolation from one another. Therefore, that combined knowledge and experience should be able to identify assets, assign value, and prioritize level of importance so that the team can create a well thought out risk mitigation plan in the process.

It will further serve to address the unfortunately common aspects that have developed in schools today such as child abuse, bullying and cyberbullying, and bus safety, to name a few. Within this team, roles and responsibilities will be established so that everyone understands their personal accountability to the team.

The Process

Characterization and Identification

The process of risk analysis and assessment is quite simple, yet complex. It needs to be thorough in the sense that the process should cover the operational, cyber, and physical attributes of security and the institution as a whole. It is vital to understand

---

[5] ISO (the International Organization for Standardization) is a worldwide federation of national standards bodies. The American National Standards Institute (ANSI) is a private nonprofit organization that oversees the development of voluntary consensus standards for products, services, processes, systems, and personnel in the United States. The Risk and Insurance Management Society, Inc. (RIMS) is a professional association dedicated to advancing the practice of risk management. http://www.asisonline.org/standards:Guidelines/Standards/published/Documents/RA_ExecSummary.pdf

[6] Quote by Aristotle.

the assets at risk, determine their criticality to the mission of the institution, and determine the possible consequences if those assets are conceded. "The most important part of risk management within schools is risk identification. Whether risks are human in nature, or are related to property or liability, they must be identified first. Why? An exposure and/or risk must be identified before it can be effectively analyzed, controlled, or financed."[7] Realizing the importance of *context* is imperative. However, prior to entering into this area, practitioners need to identify all assets and categorize them by people, property, technology, reputation, business processes, and dependencies and infrastructure. One would think, why would an educational institution dive into such things? Whether it is K-12 or a higher institution of learning, both entities have these aspects associated with them. To neglect these areas exposes the institution to risk.

During risk analysis and assessment, context proves to be the undeniable piece of the puzzle that allows for clarity and obtaining the correct information necessary to establish the foundation in making the appropriate decision to mitigate risk. Of importance is interpreting the necessary components of context—environmental, property, organizational, and security. Each of these areas needs an in-depth examination and comprehension. Doing this will necessitate applicable assignment of value, criticality of the asset, and its eventual prioritization.

Threats, Hazards, and Consequences

Knowing threats and hazards that affect educational institution assets assists in determining the level of protection to be administered to mitigate risk. This examination is an all-hazards approach and should not be in silos as is often the case. The Federal Emergency Management Agency (FEMA) has a great example of an all-hazards approach (as shown in Table 84.1).[8]

To be clear, we have to understand all aspect of threats and their respective definitions. In the cyber world an insider threat is a malicious threat to an institution that comes from people within the institution, such as employees, former employees, contractors, or business associates, who have inside information concerning the organization's security practices, data, and computer systems. However, threat is also the capability and intention of an adversary to undertake actions that are detrimental to an institution's interest. Threat is a function of the adversary only. The owner or user of the asset cannot typically control it. However, the adversary's intention to exploit his or her capability may be encouraged by someone in collusion with an asset or discouraged by an institution's countermeasure.

---

[7] Effective School Risk Management. What Is It and Whose Job Is It? Administrator Resources by Stacy Corluccio, CSRM. November 23, 2014. Referenced from http://www.seenmagazine.us/Articles/Article-Detail/articleid/4383/effective-school-risk-management

[8] http://www.ready.gov/risk-assessment

Table 84.1 The Federal Emergency Management Agency (FEMA) All-Hazards Approach Example

Hazards	Assets	Impacts and Consequences
• Fire • Explosion	• People • Property including buildings, critical infrastructure	• Casualties • Property damage
• Natural hazards • Hazardous materials spill or release	• Supply chain • Systems/equipment	• Business interruption • Loss of customers
• Terrorism • Workplace violence • Pandemic disease • Utility outage • Cyber attack	• Information technology • Institutional operations • Reputation/confidence • Regulatory obligations • Environment	• Financial loss • Environmental contamination • Loss of confidence • Fines and penalties • Lawsuits

Examination, Control, and Countermeasures

Based on the information gathered, an examination of vulnerabilities, weaknesses in an assets or countermeasures that can be exploited by adversaries or competitors to cause damage, must be performed. This analysis will assist in determining level of vulnerability as well as level of risk, enabling the practitioner to potentially reduce the risk by control or countermeasure. Some pertinent questions to consider by an educational assessment team are as follows: (1) What is vulnerable? (2) Why is it vulnerable? (3) What makes it vulnerable? (4) Is the vulnerability easily exercised? (5) Can the vulnerability be mitigated? Recognize that vulnerability is defined as any weakness that can be exploited by an aggressor to make the asset susceptible to damage. The assessment piece is an in-depth analysis of a building's functions, systems, and site characteristics. The assessment identifies building weaknesses and the lack of redundancy that can increase potential damage resulting from man-made or natural disasters.

By completing this stage, we are able to apply cyber, operational, and physical security controls and countermeasures that will provide the basis for selection or implementation of a proper and effective security design.

Communication, Collaboration, and Consultation

Consistent and regular review of controls and countermeasures should take place during all stages of the risk analysis and assessment process. Communication strategies should be developed during the context stage so that a stakeholder's perception of risk is addressed, as well as ensuring mutual decisions to improve performance of security measures to mitigate risk to the institution.

Conclusion

What can we conclude about the risk analysis and assessment process when we speak about schools? Risk analysis and assessment drives decision-making. To ensure that that decision-making is sound, logical, and detailed, a systematic process should be developed and implemented so that all assets are identified, evaluated, and put into a realistic priority so that effective controls and countermeasures can be designed. We can further determine that risk management is based on specific business objectives and is objective focused, whether it is K-12 or a higher institution of learning. Risk assessment is defined in terms of institutional objectives. Risk management supports decision-making, and is therefore, proactive. Plus, it protects and creates value. Its process consistency and effectiveness depends on clear governance structure.

We have an opportunity with the higher institutions of learning, to see how they can enrich and change the landscape of risk analysis and assessment within school safety and security through their research and development efforts. Much work has been performed for the DHS, through grants, to think of better ways to protect our critical infrastructure. Some of those solutions have trickled down to K-12 and to some institutions of higher learning, but it has not been consistent.

How often in our industry do we not capitalize on examining our enterprise and delivering the full measure of our findings? How often do we as practitioners neglect the value that we can actually present due to political expediency? For security leaders as well as practitioners dealing and identifying the "risk" problem for administrators and their respective institutions can be a complicated and a complex task.[9] However, in today's economy it is essential that security leaders know and understand what can compromise the success of their educational institution in order to formulate a concise and comprehensive security strategy. Necessity dictates that direction is given to analyzing a situation then having the fortitude to assist leadership in making a determination as to whether or not any potentially associated risk is acceptable to the institution. Comprehensive risk analysis and assessment are the keys to ensuring the safety and security of our schools and educational institutions.

Our pursuit should be to advise and assist schools in removing inefficiencies and informing them on whether or not to accept risk based on cultivating a unified security strategy and master plan that is endorsed through a comprehensive risk, threat, and vulnerability assessment program that is flexible, scalable, and innovative.

---

[9] J.K. Stewart. 2016. Turning Point for Comprehensive Risk Assessment. http://www.linkedin. com/pulse/turning-point-comprehensive-risk-assessment-j-kelly-stewart

Chapter 85

CPTED Tips to Enhance Security: Calgary Police Service, Crime Prevention Unit, Canada

Crime prevention through environmental design (CPTED) enhances safety by influencing the physical design of our environment and encouraging positive social interaction.[1] CPTED recognizes that our environment directly affects our behavior, whether or not we are aware of it, because we constantly respond to what is around us. These responses help us to interact safely in our communities. An environment designed using CPTED principles reduces opportunities for criminal acts to take place and helps us to feel safer. By doing so, it improves our quality of life. CPTED uses many different strategies that work together to create safer communities. It complements crime prevention strategies such as locks and bars, police, and security personnel and, ultimately, increases our freedom to use our communities. The following sections list CPTED features for houses,[2] apartments,[3] neighborhoods,[4] and businesses.

---

[1] Calgary Police Service. Crime Prevention through Environmental Design. http://www.calgary.ca/cps/Documents/CPTED-brochure.pdf?noredirect=1

[2] http://www.commissionaires.ca/en/national/services/individual/securing-your-home

[3] Calgary Condo Security 9 Tips to Safe Condo Living. March 10, 2012 by Cody Battershill. Referenced from http://bestcalgaryhomes.com/calgary-condo-guide-condo-security

[4] City of Portland, Office of Neighorhood Involvement Crime Prevention Program. 2015. Good Neighbor Agreements. Referenced from https://www.portlandoregon.gov/oni/article/413126

Houses

- Use walkways and landscaping to direct visitors to the main entrance and away from private areas.
- Keep shrubs and trees trimmed from windows and doors to improve visibility.
- Use lighting over entrances.
- Use thorny plants along fence lines and around vulnerable windows.
- Join Block Watch.

Apartments

- Ensure hallways and parking areas are well lit.
- Install good quality deadbolts and peepholes on unit doors.
- Provide common spaces in central locations to encourage tenant interaction.
- Join or start Apartment Watch in your building.

Neighborhoods

- Locate open spaces and recreational areas so they are visible from nearby homes and streets.
- Avoid landscaping that might create blind spots or hiding places.
- Make sure there is appropriate lighting.
- Design streets to discourage cut-through or high-speed traffic using traffic calming measures.
- Join Block Parent and Block Watch.

Businesses

- Place checkout counters near the front of the store, clearly visible from outside.
- Window signs should cover no more than 15% of windows to provide clear visibility into and out of the store.
- Use shelving and displays no higher than 5 feet to help see who is in the store.
- Avoid creating outdoor spaces that encourage loitering and provide increased security.
- Install cost-effective lighting in parking lots.

Chapter 86

Situational Crime Prevention Theory and CPTED

Situational crime prevention comprises opportunity-reduction measures aimed at[1]

1. Specific forms of crime that
2. Involves the manipulation or management of the environment in a permanent way and
3. Makes crime more difficult, risky, less rewarding, and less excusable to a wide range of offenders

The crime prevention through environmental design (CPTED) strategies may be viewed in a context of "situational crime prevention" and with consideration of the criminal "rational choice."

Goals toward preventing crime *opportunity*:

- Increasing the risk potential for detection or capture during a criminal act
- Increasing the effort required for a successful criminal act
- Reducing the reward of any criminal act
- Removing the excuses for unauthorized persons, actions, and so on

---

[1] Department of Criminal Justice Services Virginia. Lesson plan course name: Understanding CPTED in Conducting Business and Home Security Surveys. 2015. Rick Arrington. Permission obtained to re-produce. Referenced from https://www.dcjs.virginia.gov/training-events/application-cpted-school-security-surveys

A suitable or soft target can be

- A person
- An object
- A place

Situational crime prevention focuses on

- Crime theories
- Crime, not criminality
- Events, not dispositions
- Near, not distant, causes of crime
- How crime occurs, not why it happens
- Situational and opportunity factors

Reduce the Rewards

An important part of situational crime prevention focuses on decreasing the benefits crime offers.[2] Offenders are constantly seeking benefits from their acts, be it material for thieves, sexual for sexual offenders, intoxication, excitement, revenge, or peer approval. Five strategies are employed to reduce such rewards. The first, concealing targets, involves hiding the potential gains, by hiding jewelry and closing curtains at home to prevent people from getting a peek of the inside, as well as parking one's expensive car in the garage rather than leaving it in the street. Although concealing targets is helpful, some go to the extent of removing them—to prevent robberies of bus drivers for instance, exact fare regulations and safes were introduced in the buses. Registering property identification, done through vehicle licensing and property marking, for instance, also reduce thieves' incentives. Another technique used is the disruption of markets of stolen or illegal goods. Monitoring street vendors and pawn shops is done in the view of reducing the influence of the benefits gained through the sales of illegally obtained products. Finally, a last technique is the simple denial of benefits. Road humps deny the benefits of speeding. Ink tags, used in resale, follow a similar objective: if tampered with, they release irremovable ink on the clothing, denying to the shoplifters the opportunity of wearing or selling the stolen article.

Loss control, loss prevention, and crime prevention are primarily about increasing the efforts or hardening the target.

Before a security assessment or survey is started, a few questions covering all environments will help identify specific problems. Using CPTED knowledge with the four methods of opportunity reduction, we are ready to begin the physical survey.

---

[2] Situational Crime Prevention. http://criminology.wikia.com/wiki/Situational_Crime_Prevention

Conducting Security Assessments of the Physical Environment

Security Assessments

An assessment is the process of evaluating a site for security vulnerabilities, and making recommendations to address said vulnerabilities. The goal is to remove or reduce the potential vulnerability.

Overview of Target-Hardening Devices and Measures

- Portals
- High-security locks
- Electronic access control
- Lighting and its pitfalls
- Cameras and alarms as prevention deterrents

The focus of the security assessment is fourfold:

1. Information gathering and overview of a site
2. Identification of vulnerabilities
3. Analysis of the facility functions and requirements, and development of solutions
4. Recommendations of the best possible solution

Step One

The first step should be an interview regarding the facility in order to identify the following:

1. Potential attackers (burglars, terrorists, robbers, etc.)
2. Potential threats received
3. Potential methodologies that might be employed
4. Limitations, due to policies, laws, and functions in what may be recommended as a solution

Step Two

The next step is a detailed walk-through where additional questions may be asked and answered and where most physical structure vulnerabilities may be observed.

Step Three

Identify possible solutions to correct vulnerabilities.

Step Four

Finally, the assessor will select the best solution for the final recommendations. *Completing a written report* is an essential part of the security assessment.

1. It protects the practitioner.
2. It provides a historic document for the customer.
3. It emphasizes issues and solutions.

Using target-hardening knowledge (locks, alarms, lights, etc.) in conjunction with CPTED and situational crime prevention will create a comprehensive security survey.

Recommendations should be based upon your experience, proven methods, and devices and training. The recommendations utilize your knowledge of

- Criminal activity (you have knowledge)
- Rational choice by the criminal of a victim
- Proven principles of CPTED and target hardening

This will briefly identify common treatments with devices to harden a target and some applications in business and residential settings where they may be useful or enhanced.

Chapter 87

Situational Crime Displacement

Situational displacement is defined as follows:

> Crime displacement is the relocation of crime from one place, time, target, offense, or tactic to another as a result of some crime prevention initiative.[1]

Crime displacement seldom happens because individuals do not know how to properly make it work. However, law enforcement's crackdown on crime in hot spot areas will cause crime displacement to move to other areas.

Examples of displacement include the following:

1. Park a police cruiser in front of a location that is a hot spot.
2. Plaster the lobby of a building with signs that read, "See Something Say Something, call the Police."
3. Basically, be creative.

---

[1] Rob T. Guerette. Analyzing Crime Displacement and Diffusion. Tool Guide No. 10, 2009. Referenced from http://www.popcenter.org/tools/displacement/print/

Chapter 88

First-, Second-, and Third-Generation CPTED

Introduction

Over the years, crime prevention through environmental design (CPTED) has grown beyond what the founders ever could have imagined. To describe three generations is a bit complicated, because so much is written about them and this book has limited space. However, we attempt to discuss them as well as provide a case study on the worst piece of property on which we ever conducted an assessment.

First Generation of CPTED

First-generation CPTED is 50 years of strategies and concepts whose main purpose is to reduce crime or discourage crime or design out crime. Originally, we had three strategies: natural access control, natural surveillance, and territoriality. As time has progressed, four more have been introduced: maintenance/image, activity program support, target hardening, and geographical juxtaposition (wider environment—the community). (See item 11.)

Natural Surveillance

- Clear windows
- Law enforcement
- Delineated boundaries

Natural Access Control

- Security awareness
- Reporting and reactive
- Reducing the number of entrances and access

Territoriality Reinforcement

- Sphere of influence
- Physical design
- Maintenance

Management/Image

- Positive and negative indicators
- Perception of space
- Behavioral effects

Activity Program Support

- Space to reduce crime
- Increasing the level of human activity in a particular space
- Additional eyes on the street

Target Hardening

- Securing of property
- Installation of physical security devices
- Use of security officers or law enforcement

Geographical Juxtaposition (Wider Environment)

- Land use
- Vacant or derelict sites
- Lack of pedestrian movement

Description of the First Generation of CPTED

The first generation focuses on twelve strategies and concepts that will reduce and discourage criminal opportunity:

- Define boundaries
- Clear lines of sight
- Determine users of space
- Establish urban zones prone to criminal activity
- Improve street lighting
- Add security surveillance systems (closed-circuit television [CCTV])
- Digitally administrated makes the offender visible to others (digital sign)
- Ensure proper maintenance of space signifies a sense of ownership that is influential in reducing fear of crime
- Spatial design
- Reinforcing positive behavior within the physical space through the use of physical attributes
- Public and private spaces
- Acceptable patterns of usage[1]

Second Generation of CPTED

Second-generation CPTED focuses on the concepts and strategies that will aid in the possibility of removing the reasons that crimes occur as well as the living environment and the structure of the family. The four principles are, briefly,

- Ecological threshold
- Community culture
- Community cohesion
- Connectivity (Saville and Cleveland, 1998)[2]

Third Generation of CPTED

Third-generation CPTED focuses on designing a green environment based on both security and physical measures to ensure that urban space is safe. It also looks at security as a global issue with geo-political and social-cultural divisions.

Third-generation CPTED[3] envisions a green sustainable approach to enhance the living standards of urbanites and improve the image of the city as user friendly,

---

[1] United Nations Interregional Crime and Justice Research Institute (UNICRI). Improving Urban Security through Environmental Design Joint UNICRI - MIT Senseable City Lab Report. Referenced from http://www.unicri.it/news/article/1104-2_urban_security
[2] Saville, G. and Cleveland, G. 1998. Second generation CPTED: An Antidote to the Social Y2K Virus of Urban Design, Paper presented to the 3rd International CPTED Association conference, Washington DC, December 14–16.
[3] From UNICRI, New Energy for Urban Security Improving Urban Security through Green Environmental Design.

safe, and secure. It also aims to create a sense of belonging and membership to a greater community of soliciting a citizens' engagement and participation in improving the conditions of urban living. It focuses on three main methodological branches. They suggest to the urban policy-makers an approach to be adopted when planning the security policies of the respective cities:

1. Anticipate the dynamics of the city
2. Collaborate on improving standards of living
3. Sense and actuate the city

The green environment design must also lead to a safer and more secure environment. The city's budget has to be managed in a way to achieve multiple results through more intelligent and efficient policies.

Chapter 89

Partnerships: Key to CPTED and Community Policing

Collaborative Partnerships with Government Agencies and the Community

To form a partnership,[1]

- Identify key agencies or businesses that should be in the partnership.
- Identify a purpose for the partnership.
- Decide on a plan of action and the future of the partnership and who to connect with, such as law enforcement, local government officials, community leaders, housing complex residents, housing complex management and the facilities manager, community members, local school officials, neighborhood business owners, and faith-based organizations and houses of worship.
- Identify challenges and identify a planning team.
- Share best practices, identify a planning team, and initiate a meeting to identify the stakeholders.
- Build on resources and skills.

---

[1] B. Geller and L. Belsky. *A Policymaker's Guide to Building Our Way Out of Crime.* The Transformative Power of Police-Community Developer Partnership. U.S. Department of Justice. Office of Community Oriented Policing Services. Foreword by Bill Bratton and Paul Grogan. Referenced from https://ric-zai-inc.com/Publications/cops-w0519-pub.pdf

School Districts

Partnerships are not only utilized for crime and other community problems, they are also effective for the following:

Emergency management in schools:

■ Identify a planning team and initiate a meeting to identify the stakeholders in the process within your jurisdiction, institution, or school district.
■ Invite those identified stakeholders to an initial meeting to describe the intent of the process (i.e., to produce a plan) and ask their help in beginning the information-gathering process about emergencies, disasters, and other potential issues within the community or school district.

Identify the stakeholders/partners in a school-based incident:

■ School officials
■ School staff
■ Students and their parents
■ Law enforcement
■ Fire department
■ Emergency medical services
■ Local government officials
■ Utility companies
■ Mental and public health providers
■ Hospitals
■ Faith-based organizations and houses of worship
■ Community leaders
■ Local businesses

Federal and State Partners in a School-Based Incident

State Resources

■ Governor
■ State Homeland Security Advisor
■ State Emergency Management Agency Director
■ National Guard

Federal Resources

■ Secretary of Homeland Security
■ FEMA Administrator

- Attorney General
- Secretary of Defense
- Secretary of State
- Director of National Intelligence

What Types of School-Based Incidents Need Partnerships?

- Active shooter/active assailant or mass shooter
- Bullying
- Trespasser or intruder
- Weapons
- Workplace violence
- Terrorism
- Hostage situation
- Fire
- Bomb threat
- Medical emergency
- Rape or sexual assault
- Suicide
- Kidnapping
- Bus or vehicle accident
- Weather emergency

Chemical/Biological/Nuclear Incidents

A community response is to *be prepared*. Conduct vulnerability and threat assessments. Organize your partners *before* an incident occurs. Prepare, plan, and train together with your partners on tabletop and with full-scale exercises. With your partners, anticipate challenges and develop possible solutions.

Effective community partnerships require:

1. Planning
2. Communication
3. Ongoing maintenance

Conclusion

Whether it is a neighborhood, an apartment complex, or a school district, the concept and the action to be taken are still the same.

Chapter 90

Using Crime Prevention through Environmental Design in Problem Solving

Diane Zahn: Conference—October 2017, Houston, Texas—QR-Code

Scan the QR-code that follows to read a file titled, "Using Crime Prevention through Environmental Design in Problem Solving" by Diane Zahn.[1]

---

[1] QR-Code prepared by Rick Draper. http://www.popcenter.org/tools/cpted

Chapter 91

Access and Wayfinding for Physically and Mentally Challenged Individuals

The building requirements for the physically and mentally handicapped generally improve accessibility and wayfinding, but rarely consider the risk of victimization that may be created by the use of out-of-the-way doors, hallways, or elevators.

Review Process

The work of builders, designers, and planners has long been affected by codes that govern nearly every aspect of a structure, except for security. Historically, a few jurisdictions enacted security ordinances, but most of these related to windows, doors, and locking devices. It is now becoming more common to find a local law or procedure calling for a full security or crime prevention review of plans before they are finalized. Nevertheless, it is still generally true that more attention is placed on aesthetics, drainage, fire safety, curb cuts, and parking access than on gaining an understanding of how a building or structure will affect the area in terms of security. A crime prevention through environmental design (CPTED) review process must be established within communities and organizations to ensure that good planning is being conducted.

The manner in which physical space is designed or used has a direct bearing on crime or security incidents. The clear relationship between the physical environment and crime is now understood to be a cross-cultural phenomenon, as recent international conferences on CPTED have disclosed the universal nature of human and environment relations. That is, despite political and cultural differences, people basically respond the same way to what they see and experience in the environment. Some places make people feel safe and secure, while others make people feel vulnerable. Criminals or other undesirables pick up on the same cues. They look at the environmental setting and at how people are behaving. This tells them whether they can control the situation or run the risk of being controlled.

Someone has to question design, development, and event planning decisions. Do you think that anyone from the police department, or fire department for that matter, was given the opportunity to ask the builder of a major hotel in Kansas City whether they had extra steel reinforcing rods leftover when they built the cross bridge that fell and resulted in many deaths and injuries? No! Major planning mistakes were made because no one asked the right questions.

Chapter 92

Facilities Managers: How Secure Is Your Security Operation?

A former surgical resident impersonated a physician and gained access to restricted areas to observe surgical procedures and participate in patient rounds at Brigham and Women's Hospital in Boston, Massachusetts.[1] Cheryl Wang, who was previously dismissed from a residency program in New York City, wandered into operating rooms in official Brigham scrubs she was thought to have obtained from a previous visit. Although Brigham staff is required to scan their identification badges to enter operation rooms, Wang slipped into the surgical suites by walking in behind other employees who were holding the door open for each other. Following the security breach, the hospital says it has strengthened its policy for allowing observers into its operating rooms. Physicians now are required to verify that a doctor-in-training is in good standing with his or her educational institution. The hospital also plans to educate staff about the dangers of "tailgating," or letting people follow staff into restricted areas without scanning an ID card. Electronic card access and surveillance cameras are considered security best practices, but hospital security experts are considering other safeguards, including turnstiles, security officers, and biometric systems.

We have always felt that if someone looked professional, greeted others, and gave the impression that they "fit in," they could gain access practically anywhere. We

---

[1] The Intruder in the Brigham OR–How Did She Get There? Retrieved on February 8, 2017 from: https://www.bostonglobe.com/metro/2017/02/04/dressed-scrubs-she-roamed-hospital-but-she-wasn-supposed-there/3OkuPYs4PklE3MGdeLirhM/story.html

frequently get to test our theory because some organizations want penetration testing conducted to determine whether or not their access control policies and procedures are effective. We were doing such an exercise at a country club in California at 3:00 p.m. on a Sunday afternoon. As we drove up to the guard house, the security officer on duty waved as he let us in. Another time while doing an assessment at a school, the facilities manager took us to the third floor of the administration building, pointed to different offices, and said, "This is the president's area, the VP's office is over there, the Controller is there, and my office is at the other end. This is a secure area, so you don't have to worry about this part of the building." When we came back to the building later that night, we took the elevator to the second floor, walked down the hall to the freight elevator, and pushed the third-floor button. We were not really surprised when the elevator door opened and we were in the "secure area." We went into the facility manager's unlocked office and left a note on his desk: "So, How Secure Is Your Security Operation?"

Chapter 93

What Is Meant by "Urban Safety"?

Research and experience in the field has shown that when citizens ask for increased safety, they are referring not only to criminal behavior, but to a number of factors that make the urban environment unsafe; these range from the real risk, to fear and uneasiness.[1]

Five main components can be identified:

1. The real risk of becoming the victim of intimidation, aggression, or other acts of violence (whether it is with intent to rob or gratuitous violence)
2. Anti-social behavior due to the breaking of the traditional codes of civil conduct (spitting, urinating in public, aggressive begging, etc)
3. The lack of up-keeping of the area: maintenance of parks and public spaces, cleanliness, presence of police on the streets, doormen, repair of street furniture
4. The feeling of not being safe, as opposed to the real danger, which is often connected to factors such as squalor, lack of easy routes, lack of vitality, poor street lighting, etc.
5. Fear and all factors along with it: fear considered as a subjective feeling, not necessarily linked to risk, but related to wider factors often far away from the specific site which one is afraid of

---

[1] This handbook, *Planning Urban Design and Management for Crime Prevention*, is one of the outputs of the Action SAFEPOLIS with funding from the European Commission—Directorate-General Justice, Freedom and Security (Contract JLS/2006/AGIS/208). http://designforsecurity.org/downloads/Designing_Out_Crime.pdf. Permission was obtained to reproduce.

Three Approaches to Urban Safety

The policies, which are used today to guarantee environmental safety, stem from three main approaches.

The first approach deals with security, mainly in terms of law enforcement through the use of rules and police ("law and order"). Laws regulate people's actions, and police forces watch that laws are respected.

The second approach concentrates its efforts on the prevention of crime in social terms. It acts to reduce the conditions of disadvantage and poverty which are often factors generating criminal/antisocial behavior: unemployment, lack of family, mental problems, isolation.

A third approach concerns environmental prevention and is aimed at "preventing crime from happening". It deals with all those factors in the environment which can somehow affect a criminal act to take place. In the past, these three approaches were considered as conflicting. Today the opposed positions finally seem to have been overcome. Recent experience shows that the integration of the three approaches is necessary to produce a cumulative effect and to obtain long-term results.

Chapter 94

Recommendations for Urban Decay: A Case Study at the XYZ Courts

XYZ Courts, located on Fagel Street, is a family setting of 250 units. The area consists of a playground that borders Grand Avenue with Fagel Street on the right and Ben Franklin Street on the left, with train tracks on the opposite end of the property. The tenants and visitors are the most critical assets. Mostly families live at this complex. The main problem is drug dealers—this is the worst of all the complexes we have ever, ever visited—and the second problem is deterioration and disorder.

Controlling Physical Deterioration and Disorder

Physical deterioration, wear and tear, and large-scale accumulations of graffiti and trash routinely occur in many older, urban neighborhoods. If, however, people or agencies do not do anything for a significant period about such deterioration or accumulations, residents and store personnel working in the neighborhood feel increasingly vulnerable.

Feeling more concerned for their personnel safety, residents and store personnel participate less in the maintenance of order in public places. They are less likely to stop teens or adults who are "messing around," "being rowdy," or "hassling people."

Recommendations are as follows:

1. Remove all tenants who are involved in dealing drugs.
2. Because of the major drug problem, we recommend that during the construction of the complex the basketball courts be taken down and not replaced—because of the drug transactions, it has turned into a hot spot.
3. The complex needs to do everything possible to move the location of the homeless shelter that is adjacent to its property, because they are warning the drug dealers when the police arrive via cell-phones given to them by the dealers.
4. XYZ Courts should have a substation manned by local police at this location.
5. Area lighting should be LED lights and 5-foot candles evenly distributed.
6. In addition, lights were on during the day and need to be shut off.
7. The security surveillance system (closed-circuit television [CCTV] monitoring system) located in the building at the rear complex needs to be relocated to the facilities manager's office.
8. The security surveillance is in need of an additional 24 cameras mounted in vandal-proof housing units.
9. Remove all wireless CCTV units since they are not working.
10. The manager of the complex needs to be trained by the vender on how to use the system and its recording devices.
11. Secure the back end of the complex with existing hardware by closing and locking the gate.
12. The broken window theory applies here. I would estimate about 1,000 pieces of trash are scattered around the complex and the grounds. Trash pickup needs to be relocated; 250 units produce a lot of trash. Provide additional barrels around the property.

Chapter 95

Security for Commercial Properties: Deterring Crime through Design

Consider crime prevention through environmental design (CPTED) when designing commercial properties.[1]

Windows and Doors

Use a burglar-resistant material that meets Underwriters Laboratories (UL) 972 standards. These materials look like safety glass but will not shatter easily, even after repeated blows. They include laminated, tempered, wired-glass, plastic acrylics, polycarbonate sheets, and glass with a security film on the inside. Install folding security gates or roll-down security shutters inside office windows and doors. Where motion detectors are installed to open or unlock exit doors from the inside when a person approaches the door, set the detectors far enough back from the door so a person outside the door cannot slip something between the door and the frame to create motion on the inside and open the door. Install single-cylinder deadbolt locks above the lever arms of doors that are opened with level arms on the inside to prevent them from being opened by a special tool that is inserted in the gap between

---

[1] *Deterring Crime through Design: CPTED Concepts and Measures for Land Development (A Guide for Architects, Designers, Developers, Urban Planners, and Problem Solvers)*. SDPD Crime Prevention. August 27, 2015. Retrieved from https://www.sandiego.gov/sites/default/files/legacy/police/pdf/crimeprevention/DeterringCrimeThroughDesign.pdf

the bottom of the door and the floor. Another advantage of a deadbolt is that it will keep the door locked if the burglar breaks off the lever arm on the outside. Either apply tint or install a reflective film on ground-level windows to prevent someone from seeing in during the day, especially if there are computers or other valuable equipment inside. If the office is lighted at night by janitors, shutters or blinds will need to be used because reflective materials will not be effective.

Intrusion Detection (Burglar) Alarms

Install an alarm system and have it monitored 24/7. Use multiple sensors or dual sensors to reduce false alarms. Provide a wireless backup that can send an alarm signal with a cellular dialer if the telephone line is cut.

Trash Enclosures and Dumpsters

Keep trash enclosures locked except when the containers in it are being filled or emptied. Dumpsters should have locking lids with an open space through which material can be put in but not taken out. This is to prevent scavenging.

Secure Utilities

Install external circuit breakers and telephone connections in sturdy boxes with shielded padlocks or locate them on the interior of the building, if possible.

Parking Structures

In parking garages and parking lots, install simple swing-arm gates at the entrances and exits. A security officer in a booth may operate the gate upon exit, but drivers may take a ticket to enter the garage. Provide a separate, secure parking area for employee's vehicles.

Provide employees with individual access cards, fobs, or keypad codes to open the gates to enter and leave. Provide visitor parking in a separate, open area.

Barriers

Install fences or other barriers to prevent misuse of public facilities or areas (e.g., bathing in fountains, camping overnight under bridges, or violating protected open spaces). Design benches with armrests to discourage sleeping and skateboarding.

Roofs

Install locking covers to shroud ladders. Secure hatches, skylights, ventilation shafts, air conditioning and heating ducts, and other rooftop entrances on the inside with grills or grates. Alarm those that cannot be secured. Install a motion detector that would activate an alarm if someone is on the roof.

Elevators and Stairways in Mixed-Use Buildings

If separate elevators are not provided, install access card, fob, or keypad code readers at the elevators so residents can only go to their floors, parking garage level, and the lobby. (Residents' access would mean being programmed for this.) Install a telephone system in the lobby for visitors to use to call for elevator access to a residential floor, and for residents to use to visit a resident on another floor.

Elevators and Stairway Controls in Multi-Floor Office Buildings

If access to office floors needs to be controlled, install card, fob, or code readers at the elevators so employees can only go to their office floors, parking garage levels, and the lobby. If visitor access to the office floors is to be controlled, install a telephone system in the lobby for visitors to use to call for elevator access to an office floor. Host employees could be called to escort visitors in the building.

Lock stairwell doors to the office floors and parking levels on the stairwell side and install an access card, fob, or code reader to enable employees to enter their floor and parking level from the stairwell. (Photo 95.1)

Because stairwell reentry is necessary in a fire emergency, provisions must be made to release the locks when a fire alarm is activated.

Signage

Install signs that do the following:

- Prohibit trespassing, loitering, soliciting, scavenging, consumption of alcoholic beverages, and so on
- Direct visitors to the building or development office.
- Designate visitor parking spaces, and warn that public parking is prohibited and unauthorized vehicles will be towed
- State the hours that activities are prohibited (e.g., no visitors after 10:00 p.m.)
- Inform persons of camera surveillance

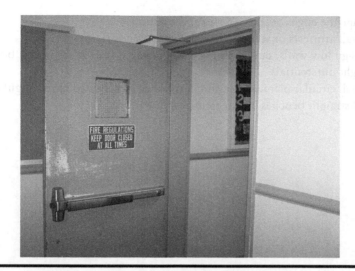

Photo 95.1 **Emergency fire door propped open, in spite of the sign on the door indicating that it is to be kept closed. (Photo taken by Marianna Perry, CPP.)**

- Direct people to safe paths, emergency exits, emergency communications, and so on
- Define a code of conduct for private spaces open to the public

Harden against Vandalism

- Design features and materials that cannot easily be vandalized, stolen, or used to damage the property (e.g., do not use loose rocks)
- Graffiti-resistant paint or anti-graffiti coatings on walls, benches, light poles, signs, and so on
- Screens, wired glass, or other protection for light fixtures and bulbs
- Shiny aluminum or shatter-resistant glass for mirrors
- Protective films on the outside of windows to prevent window damage from graffiti, knife gouging or scratching, and acid etching

To Prevent Skateboarding

- Roughen pavement surfaces or plant grass in front of benches, planter boxes, low walls, steps, and railings
- Plant trees at ground level and not in raised planter boxes

- Shape the edges of seat benches and low walls
- Install armrests or seat dividers on flat seating surfaces
- Design low walls, curbs, railings, and planter boxes with breaks, bumps, or height differentials
- Install circular picnic tables and curved benches instead of rectangular tables and straight benches on concrete paving

Chapter 96

Environment-Friendly Exterior Lighting

The opinion of most security practitioners is that there is a relationship between appropriate lighting and crime, and that appropriate exterior lighting helps to make an area "feel" safe, and may reduce crime as well as the fear of crime. The basic premise is that better lighting will deter offenders who would commit a crime if the area was in darkness. When there is appropriate lighting, offenders are more likely to be seen by someone who may intervene, call the police, or recognize them. "Numerous case studies and related research ... show that simply increasing light levels or maintaining high lighting levels does not necessarily promote or maintain enhanced safety or security."[1] It is important to remember that lighting is just one component of an effective physical security plan along with good environmental design. These components together create a holistic approach to safety and security and will help to deter crime. All research has indicated that improved lighting can have a variety of effects on crime, but there is not a simple answer to the relationship between lighting and crime because there are so many variables to consider.[2]

The Center for Problem-Oriented Policing (www.popcenter.org) is an excellent resource for more information on the relationship of lighting and crime, and numerous research studies are cited.

When designing outdoor lighting, ensure that you consider placement, intensity, timing, duration, and color. Good lighting will help with the following:[3]

---

[1] Exterior Lighting for Energy Savings, Security, and Safety. Retrieved on January 23, 2017, from: http://www.pnl.gov/main/publications/external/technical_reports/PNNL-18173.pdf

[2] How Might Improved Lighting Affect Crime. Retrieved on January 19, 2017, from: http://www.popcenter.org/responses/street_lighting/2

[3] Guidelines for Good Exterior Lighting Plans. Retrieved on January 19, 2017, from: http://www.darkskysociety.org/

Promote Safety

"More light" is not necessarily "better." If lighting is designed incorrectly, there will be unsafe glare that may interfere with facial recognition, cause accidents, and reduce visibility. When lighting is too bright, it affects the ability of the eye to adapt to darker areas.

Save Money

Lighting levels should comply with professionally recommended levels. The Guideline for Security Lighting for People, Property, and Public Spaces (Illuminating Engineering Society of North America [IESNA]), the Army Field Manual, and the Occupational Safety and Health Administration (OSHA) are commonly cited sources for appropriate lighting levels. Consider using shielded fixtures that direct the light downward and cost-efficient light sources (such as LED) because they use less energy.

Conserve Natural Resources

Lighting that is inappropriate or excessive, wastes natural resources, and can pollute the air and water if the source of the electricity supplying the energy is derived from fossil fuels.

Help Be a Better Neighbor

Excessive[4] lighting or lighting that is misdirected can intrude on the property of neighbors when light or glare trespasses over property lines.

Retain a Community's Character and Reduce "Skyglow"

Excessive or misdirected lighting contributes to "light pollution" and can produce an unnatural "sky glow" or brightness of the night sky. This will interfere with a clear view of a dark, starry night sky.[5]

---

[4] International Darksky Association. My Neighbors Lighting. Retrieved from http://www.darksky.org/lighting/my-neighbors-lighting/

[5] International Dark-Sky Association. Light Pollution Wastes Energy and Money. http://www.darksky.org/light-pollution/energy-waste/

Protect Ecology of Flora and Fauna

Research[6] indicates that artificial night lighting disrupts the migrating, feeding, and breeding habits of many wildlife species and may affect the growth patterns of trees.

Reduce Health Risks

Light[7] at night disrupts sleep and also interferes with circadian rhythms. There is some research that indicates that excessive light may reduce the production of melatonin.

For more information on appropriate lighting and reducing "light pollution" and "skyglow," visit the web page of the International Dark-Sky Association (http://darksky.org).

What Is an Acceptable Lighting Plan?

The following should be considered when developing an acceptable lighting plan[8]:

1. Identify any safety or security issues for the area.
2. Determine where lighting is needed by using a light meter along with Illuminating Engineering Society of North America (IESNA) recommendations.
3. Are there specific areas or activities in the area that need to utilize lighting for specific activities?
4. Select the appropriate type and number of luminaires.
5. Select the correct light source. Include the initial lumens for each fixture as well as the depreciated lumens. When there is a shorter lamp life, there will be increased maintenance costs for lamp replacement. LED and high-pressure sodium (HPS) are usually recommended because of high lamp efficacy, even though there is a reduced color rendering index (CRI). Metal halide lighting is more expensive to operate, uses more energy, has a greater impact on the environment, and contributes to "sky glow."[9]

---

[6] Ooutdoor Lighting Ordinance Guide. Prepared by John Batinsey, Member, Eatontown Environmental Commission Revised June, 2006. Retrieved from http://www.nj.gov/dep/opsc/docs/Sample_Lighting_Ordinance.PDF

[7] USAI Lighting. Circadian Rhythm Lighting. http://www.usailighting.com/circadian-rhythm-lighting

[8] Maine State Planning Office. Technical Assistance Bulletin: Lighting Manual: Promoting Quality Outdoor Lighting in Your Community. http://www.maine.gov/dacf/municipalplanning/docs/lightingmanual.pdf

[9] International Darksky Association. Guidelines for Good Exterior Lighting Plans. 2009. Retrieved from http://www.darkskysociety.org/handouts/LightingPlanGuidelines.pdf

6. Use the appropriate amount of light taking into consideration light levels and uniformity ratios.

7. Direct light downward by choosing the correct type of luminaire. Light that shines where it is not needed is wasted energy. The housings, reflectors, ballasts, lenses, and shields of the luminaire determine the proportion of actual lumens emitted. You also have to consider the mounting height of the fixture as well as the reflectance properties of the nearby surfaces (e.g., dark asphalt versus light concrete). The nearby surfaces will determine the distribution of the light.[10]

8. Specify Illuminating Engineering Society of North America (IESNA) "Full Cut Off" or "fully shielded" lighting fixtures so that no light is emitted above the lowest light emitting portion of the fixture.

9. Use sensors or timers to turn off the lights when they are not needed.

10. Determine the height of the luminaires and/or poles for the appropriate foot-candle distribution.

11. Limit the amount of light that crosses property lines to prevent "light trespass."

12. Lighting should not exceed the recommendations of IESNA RP-33 or -20 unless for specific reasons (i.e., high crime area).

Lighting[11] manufacturers are an excellent resource to help you design a lighting plan that will comply with local ordinances and adhere to environmental concerns.

According to the Lincoln Institute of Land Policy, nature should be integrated into urban design, and there should be plans to makes cities and urban infrastructures green, sustainable, and resilient.[12] Appropriate lighting and crime prevention through environmental design (CPTED) concepts are a part of this urban design, and we as security practitioners must do our part for the "green" movement and work with landscape architects, architects, city planners, and urban designers.

---

[10] *Lighting Upgrade Manual,* US EPA Office of Air and Radiation 6202J EPA 430-B-95-003, Lighting Fundamentals, January 1995, U.S. EPA Green Lights Program. Retrieved from http://www.boles.de/teaching/mm/pages/light-fundamentals.html

[11] International Dark-Sky Association. Lighting, Crime, and Safety. http://www.darksky.org/light-pollution/lighting-crime-and-safety/

[12] Lincoln Institute of Land Policy. Fiscally Standardized Cities. Retrieved on January 23, 2017, from: https://www.lincolninst.edu/

Chapter 97

The Seven Qualities for Well-Designed, Safe Places

The following are seven qualities for well-designed, safe places[1]:

1. Access
   a. Design for safe movement and connections.
   b. Clear routes should provide for different modes of traffic.
   c. Movement safety should be maximized, especially after dark.
   d. Safe access is provided between key destinations and entrapment spots eliminated.
   e. All routes necessary should lead to destinations that people want to reach.
   f. Multiple exit points should be provided from public spaces and along pedestrian routes.
   g. Consequences of the number and type of connections should be carefully considered.
   h. Routes should not provide potential offenders with ready and unnoticed access to potential targets.
2. Surveillance and Sight Lines
   a. See and be seen requires good visibility; sight lines and casual surveillance should be provided.

---

[1] Ministry of Justice. National Guidelines for Crime Prevention through Environmental Design in New Zealand. Part 1: Seven Qualities of Safer Places. https://www.justice.govt.nz/assets/Documents/Publications/cpted-part-1.pdf

    b. Opportunities for surveillance from adjacent buildings should be maximized.

    c. Building design should create opportunities for informal surveillance to incorporate crime reduction measures.

    d. Concealment and isolation opportunities should be removed so that areas are kept active.

    e. Concealment spots should be eliminated or secured.

    f. Fencing, landscaping, and street-scape features should be designed to help visibility.

    g. Efforts should be made to eliminate "inactive" frontages and corners.

    h. Lighting should be a primary consideration and integral to the overall design.

3. Layout

    a. Clear and logical orientation.

    b. Design and layout should support safe movement and help with orientation and wayfinding.

    c. Design and layout should be appropriate for the identified crime risk, to maintain or improve environmental conditions and enhance personal safety.

    d. Ground-level building facades should be of a high design quality and provide active frontages to the street (e.g., windows, doors, displays, and visible indoor activity).

    e. Public spaces should be of a high quality, serve a purpose, and support an appropriate level of legitimate activity.

    f. Entrances and exits should be clearly signposted and easily accessible.

    g. Signage should be legible and informative of the surrounding developments, public facilities, and access routes.

    h. Landscaping should support legibility.[2]

4. Activities Sometimes Are Mixed

    a. If You See Something - Say Something™

    b. Informal surveillance should be supported and the legitimate use of public space maximized.

    c. Mixed use/activity generators should be incorporated with various uses and successfully integrated.

    d. Use of the area should be compatible with any potential conflicts and be thoroughly addressed.

    e. Strategies for encouraging residential population in town and city centers are promoted.

    f. Encouraging appropriate night-time uses is considered.

---

[2] Guiducci D. and Burke A. Reading the landscape: Legible environments and hominin dispersals. *Evol Anthropol.* 2016. 25(3):133-41. doi: 10.1002/evan.21484. Retrieved from https://www.ncbi.nlm.nih.gov/pubmed/27312185

5. Developing a Sense of Ownership
   a. Showing a place is well-cared for reflex a positive image.
   b. Spaces should be clearly indicated as to whether they are public, communal, semi-private or private.
   c. Boundaries between these spaces should be appropriately indicated to support their intended use.
   d. Elements that delineate ownership boundaries should be well-designed and do not restrict visibility.
   e. Property numbering and identification should be incorporated within the design.
   f. Community engagement in the planning and design process should be encouraged.
   g. People who feel ownership of a place should be involved in defining its identity.

6. Quality Environments
   a. Environments should be well-designed, well-managed and a well-maintained environment.
   b. Care should be taken to create good quality public areas.
   c. Appropriate management and maintenance systems should be in place.
   d. Design and layout should support management and maintenance.
   e. Materials and fixtures should be vandal resistant.
   f. Users, businesses and residents should be involved in management.
   g. An integrated approach to design, involving a range of disciplines, should be taken.
   h. Alliances or partnerships between stakeholders should be promoted.

7. Physical Protection
   a. Use active security measures.
   b. Potential for target hardening measures with a visually negative impact should be carefully addressed.
   c. Barriers should be designed carefully, be of high quality and appropriate to their local context.

Chapter 98

Parks, Reserves, and Waterways

Parks, reserves, and routes alongside waterways are often perceived as being unsafe areas, especially after dark.[1] The application of crime prevention through environmental design (CPTED) principles can help to increase the usage of these areas and decrease the fear of crime.

The safety of parks, reserves, and waterways will be affected by the following:

- Their location and layout
- Their relationship with surrounding activities
- The activities contained within them
- The design and location of landscaping and structures within them

Generally, good planning and design contribute to increased usage, a good relationship between public and private spaces, and maximized informal surveillance. This can be achieved by

- Locating parks so that they can be easily seen from surrounding houses and streets
- Locating high-use elements, such as toilets, playgrounds, and main paths, so that they are visible from adjoining streets, houses, and from within the park
- Providing a range of recreational opportunities and spaces in order to ensure activity throughout the day and a range of users (e.g., passive open grassed areas as well as active areas such as sports facilities)
- Avoiding the use of high solid fences along park and waterway edges

---

[1] Project for Public Spaces, Understanding Personal Safety. December 31, 2008, Retrieved from https://www.pps.org/article/torontosafety1

- Using fencing that is of a low or open (transparent style) construction, where fencing is required
- Providing facilities for activities that attract people into parks and reserves, and that encourage them to stay longer (e.g., shelters and BBQ facilities)

Encourage a sense of ownership of the park by

- Involving surrounding residents and property owners in the design (or redesign) and ongoing management of the park
- Setting up an "Adopt a Park" scheme and encouraging the reporting of vandalism
- Providing pedestrian gates in residential fences bordering reserves
- Directing people through safe areas with good signage and lighting

Pathways

- Ensure the provision of adequate sight lines along the route.
- Avoid dense planting of tall shrubs within 6 feet of either side of pathways.

Help to make people feel safer in a park by

- Providing pedestrian access ways to enhance the function of public open spaces, but ensuring they are carefully designed and located

Safe route, escape routes, and lines of sight:

- Providing at least one safe route through parks, with frequent "escape routes" back to surrounding streets and car park areas

Lighting

Use of parks at night should be discouraged and only paths that are essential designated routes should be lit. However, lighting alone will not make parks or a route safer. Lighting should be carefully considered and combined with other safety design measures.

Lighting can be used to make parks feel safer by

- Providing lighting that is consistent along the path and at a high level shining down, rather than at eye level, which creates glare and prevents pedestrians from seeing beyond the lighting.
- Providing lighting only where the use of a path is essential at all times.
- Encouraging the use of alternative safe routes by locking park gates, or by not lighting parks at night.

▪ Locating lighting at a height that prevents access and tampering, or using vandal-proof fittings where lighting is provided at a lower level.
▪ Ensuring lighting levels permit users to recognize and identify a face at least 75–80 feet away.
▪ Consider security lighting for all accessible areas including the car park area and also consider solar fixtures.
▪ Security lighting should be movement and sound activated and carefully positioned to ensure that it will be effective.
▪ Care should be taken to prevent lighting causing unwelcome glare in neighboring properties.

Planting and Maintenance/Image

Planting and fencing provide an amenity and safety function, but care should be taken to ensure they do not block views, or create "hiding places" and entrapment spots. A neglected space is likely to invite antisocial behavior and will feel unsafe. Particular care should be taken when considering the area around toilet facilities.

Parks, reserves, and waterways can be made to feel safer by

▪ Ensuring good visibility, with toilet doors opening directly onto public space and planting kept low
▪ Ensuring that planting does not obscure lighting or views by avoiding plants or shrubs that block the field of vision beyond 3 feet above ground level
▪ Pruning trees regularly to ensure clear trunks and avoid obscuring visibility (see section on Landscape Security)

Seating Recommendations for Parks

Careful choice and location of seating can help to make public open spaces more popular and increase safety. This can be achieved by planning seating layouts to encourage social interaction and casual surveillance.[2]

▪ Avoiding potential hiding places through appropriate planting design and incorporating thorny plants into planting mixes.
▪ Using water as a natural barrier between paths and vegetation.
▪ Placing seating in locations which are visible from the park or surrounding streets.
▪ Locating seats so that they face the pathway, as a path going along the back of a seat may make a person who sits there feel uncomfortable or unsafe

---

[2] Safer Canterbury. 3. Parks, Reserves and Waterways. https://cccgovtnz.cwp.govt.nz/assets/Documents/The-Rebuild/Strategic-Plans/CPTEDParksReservesWaterways-docs.pdf

Chapter 99

CPTED Strategies

Crime prevention through environmental design (CPTED) strategies have evolved over time. While many of the actual techniques have been in use for hundreds of years, it has only been in the last few decades that the relationship between the built, urban environment and criminal behavior is understood.

Each of the following CPTED strategies offer guidelines that, as a property owner, builder, or remodeler, you can apply to reduce the fear and incidence of crime and improve the quality of life.

Natural Surveillance

The placement of physical features, activities, and people in a way that maximizes visibility is one concept directed toward keeping intruders easily observable, and therefore less likely to commit criminal acts. Features that maximize the visibility of people, parking areas, and building entrances are as follows: unobstructed doors and windows, pedestrian-friendly sidewalks and streets, front porches, and appropriate nighttime lighting.

Territorial Reinforcement

Physical design can also create or extend a sphere of influence. Users are encouraged to develop a sense of territorial control, while potential offenders, perceiving this control, are discouraged. This concept includes features that define property lines and distinguish private spaces from public spaces using landscape plantings, pavement designs, gateway treatments, signage, and open (CPTED) fences.

Natural Access Control

Natural access control is another design concept directed primarily at decreasing crime opportunity by denying access to crime targets and creating a perception of risk for offenders. People are physically guided through a space by the strategic design of streets, sidewalks, building entrances, landscaping, and neighborhood gateways. Design elements are very useful tools to clearly indicate public routes and discourage access to private areas and structural elements.

Maintenance/Image

Last, care and maintenance allow for the continued use of a space for its intended purpose. Deterioration and blight indicate less concern and control by the intended users of a site and indicate a greater tolerance of disorder. Proper maintenance prevents reduced visibility due to plant overgrowth and obstructed or inoperative lighting, while serving as an additional expression of territoriality and ownership. Inappropriate maintenance, such as overpruning shrubs, can prevent landscape elements from achieving desired CPTED effects.

Communication of design intent to maintenance and landscape staff is especially important for CPTED-related ideas to be effective.[1]

---

[1] City of Virginia Beach, Landscaping Guide, Parking Lot and Foundation Landscaping, March 2009. https://www.vbgov.com/government/departments/planning/zoning/Documents/landscaping_guide_web.pdf

Chapter 100

Broken Windows Theory and CPTED

Before James Q. Wilson and George L. Kelling introduced the "Broken Windows Theory" in 1982, Philip Zimbardo, a Stanford psychologist, conducted experiments on this topic in 1969.[1] He had a car without a license plate parked with its hood up on a street in the Bronx (New York) and a comparable car parked on a street in Palo Alto, California. The car in the Bronx was attacked by "vandals" within 10 minutes of its "abandonment." The first to arrive were a family, and they removed the radiator and battery. Within 24 hours, virtually everything of value had been removed from the car. At that point, there was random destruction—windows were smashed, parts torn off, and the upholstery ripped. Children began to use the car as a playground. The majority of the adult "vandals" were well-dressed, apparently "clean-cut whites." The car in Palo Alto sat untouched for more than a week. Then Zimbardo smashed part of the car with a sledgehammer. Soon, passersby were joining in. Within a few hours, the car had been turned upside down and completely destroyed. Again, the adult "vandals" appeared to be primarily "respectable whites." Untended property becomes fair game for destruction. The vandalism in the Bronx began more quickly because cars and other property are frequently untended and things are stolen or broken, and there is an attitude that no one cares.[2]

[1] J.Q. Wilson and G.L. Kelling. Broken Windows. Retrieved on June 6, 2017, from: https://www.manhattan-institute.org/pdf/_atlantic_monthly-broken_windows.pdf; Broken Windows Theory. https://en.wikipedia.org/wiki/Broken_Windows_theory

[2] National Institute of Justice. Why Crimes Occur in Hotspots. Retrieved on June 6, 2017, from: https://www.nij.gov/topics/law-enforcement/strategies/hot-spot-policing/Pages/why-hot-spots-occur.aspx#brokenwindows

The broken windows theory is based on the premise that if a window in a building is broken and is left unrepaired, all the rest of the windows in the building will soon be broken, also. This is as true in nice neighborhoods as in run-down ones.[3] Disorder and crime are impossible to separate.

CPTED and the broken windows theory suggest that if one nuisance (or broken window) is allowed to exist, it will lead to crime and community issues that will eventually lead to the decline of the entire neighborhood. Properties that are not cared for and poorly maintained are simply breeding grounds for criminal activity.

This is an example of the concepts of image and territoriality, two of Newman's defensible space elements, along with natural surveillance and milieu.[4] Image is basically what an area or property looks like—its appearance. When a property does not look like it is cared for, it communicates to potential offenders that there is no one watching over the property, so there is no one to protect it. If the owners or residents take ownership of the property and demonstrate territoriality, it clearly shows that they will take action to defend it.

Nuisance crimes, untended areas, blight, graffiti, and signs of disorder decrease neighborhood residents' willingness to enforce social order, which in turn leads to more serious crime.[5]

Wilson and Kelling[6] also suggest that "untended" behavior also leads to the breakdown of community controls. If a property is abandoned, weeds will grow and windows will be broken, which will lead to further deterioration of the property and more incivility in the neighborhood.

---

[3] J.Q. Wilson and G.L. Kelling. Broken Windows. https://www.manhattan-institute.org/pdf/_atlantic_monthly-broken_windows.pdf
[4] J. Kushmuk and S.L. Whittermore. 1981. *Defensible Space: People and Design in the Violent City.* New York, NY: Macmillan.
[5] National Institute of Jusice, Why Crimes Occur In Hot Spots, October 2014. Retrieved from https://nij.gov/topics/law-enforcement/strategies/hot-spot-policing/Pages/why-hot-spots-occur.aspx
[6] George L. Kelling and James Q. Wilson. Broken windows: The police and neighborhood safety. *The Atlantic.* March 1982. Retrieved from https://www.theatlantic.com/magazine/archive/1982/03/broken-windows/304465/

Chapter 101

Top 10 CPTED Research and Best Practice Resources on the Web[1]

Periodically I am asked for sources to provide a core body of knowledge on crime prevention through environmental design (CPTED). There are many worthy article contribution candidates to consider, and here are 10 classics to make sure are in your library:

1. *Crime Prevention through Environmental Design* (the updated 3rd ed., Crowe book, edited by Lawrence Fennelly). http://www.amazon.com/Crime-Prevention-Through-EnvironmentalDesign/dp/0124116353
2. Annotated Bibliography on CPTED, by Greg Saville, Sean Michael, and Joel Warren, Utah State University; Today this work remains one of the most expansive CPTED bibliographies in the world. http://www.veilig-ontwerp-beheer.nl/publicaties/a-cptedbibliography-1975-2011
3. DOJ: Center for Problem-Oriented Policing, Community Oriented Policing Services (COPS): Using CPTED in Problem-Solving (Diane Zahm). http://www.popcenter.org/tools/pdfs/cpted.pdf
4. *21st Century Security and CPTED: Designing for Critical Infrastructure Protection and Crime Prevention* (2nd ed.). Randy Atlas, editor; CRC Press. http://www.amazon.com/21stCentury-Security-CPTED-Infrastructure/dp/1439880212

---

[1] Chapter is reproduced with permission from Severin Sorensen, CPP.

5. National Crime Prevention Council - CPTED Best Practices from Weed and Seed Sites https://www.ncpc.org/wp-content/uploads/2017/11/NCPC_BestPracticesCPTED.pdf

6. National Criminal Justice Reference Service—Florida's Approach to CPTED (by Sherry and Stan Carter). https://www.ncjrs.gov/pdffiles1/Photocopy/143817NCJRS.pdf

7. Wikipedia. CPTED. https://en.wikipedia.org/wiki/Crime_prevention_through_environmental_design

8. 1989 Brisbane, Australian Conference on Designing Out Crime, by Susan Geason and Paul R. Wilson. http://www.aic.gov.au/media_library/conferences/cpted/cpted.pdf

9. International CPTED Association. http://www.cpted.net

10. "The" CPTED LinkedIn Group, representing the largest CPTED group with over 3,780 members. https://www.linkedin.com/groups/931077

Special thanks to our group members, Greg Saville, Sue Ramsey, and Paul Van Soomeren, who have added clarity, correction, detail, and color analysis to this growing list.

Chapter 102

The International Dark-Sky Association and CPTED

Outdoor lighting is required for many things, including safety. The International Dark-Sky Association (IDA) recommends that outdoor lighting should be used wisely to lessen the effects of light pollution. Lighting should[1]

1. Only be on when needed
2. Only light the area that needs it
3. Be no brighter than necessary
4. Minimize blue light emissions
5. Be fully shielded (pointing downward)

Increasing urbanization and inefficient use of outdoor lighting has created "light pollution" that obscures the stars from view and can lead to sleep disorders, depression, obesity, and breast cancer in humans.[2] In nature, light pollution is blamed for the decline of lightning bugs, the death of birds during migration, and the fatal disorientation of newly hatched sea turtles.

---

[1] IDA. Outdoor Lighting Basics. Retrieved on June 10, 2017, from: http://www.darksky.org/lighting/lighting-basics/
[2] IDA. Human Health. http://www.darksky.org/light-polution/human-health/

There are three main components of light pollution[3]:

Sky Glow—brightening of the night sky over inhabited areas.
Light Trespass—light that shines where it is not needed or wanted.
Glare—excessive brightness that causes visual discomfort.

Billions of dollars are spent each year to light streets, shopping areas, office complexes, and other properties. Many of the lighting fixtures used are either poorly designed or emit light aimed in the wrong direction, so much of the money spent on lighting is wasted. Outdoor lighting needs to be designed and implemented more responsibly. Responsible lighting means better nighttime visibility, less intrusive light, and less overdone, energy-wasteful installations.[4]

An outdoor lighting ordinance or code can be used to ensure that municipalities implement good, efficient, safe outdoor lighting. A well-written ordinance or code, with enforced proper lighting, can save cities money and increase safety. Thousands of cities have ordinances or codes in place to control light pollution, including glare, light trespass, and skyglow.

In 2011, IDA and the Illuminating Engineering Society of North America (IESNA) approved the Model Lighting Ordinance, an outdoor lighting template designed to help municipalities develop outdoor lighting standards that reduce glare, light trespass, and skyglow.[5]

For more information on the Model Lighting Ordinance and to print the template, visit: http://www.darksky.org/our-work/public-policy/mlo/.

---

[3] IDA. Human Health. http://www.darksky.org/light-polution/human-health/
[4] How I Beat Light Pollution in My Hometown. Sky and Telescope. Retrieved on June 10, 2017, from: http://www.skyandtelescope.com/astronomy-resources/how-i-beat-light-pollution-in-my-hometown/
[5] Lighting Ordinances. Retrieved on June 10, 2017, from: http://www.darksky.org/lighting/lighting-ordinances/

Chapter 103

Workplace Violence Mitigation: Emphasizing Hospitals and CPTED[1]

Workplace violence (WPV) triad, is intended to be a metaphor for the dominant dynamics of a plurality of WPV incidents. Obviously, WPV may include an abundance of other criminal acts outside of the tirade discussed herein. For example, even workplace property crimes have the potential to escalate into crimes of violence, including even homicide. Some episodes of WPV are spontaneous, and unplanned, while other episodes may result from detailed planning and preparation. Many acts are best described as irrational.

Within the health-care arena, the threat of WPV has caught the attention of several state and federal regulatory agencies, who are increasingly becoming involved in the effort to reasonably mitigate WPV. However, because security is a *situational discipline*, specific universal standards may offer only partial solutions at best. This does not imply that goal setting is not praiseworthy. Additionally, due to the risk of relying on universal solutions, given the situational nature of security methodologies, significant vulnerabilities may be overlooked.

Generally speaking, the health-care industry has been on the cutting edge of the development of WPV mitigation strategies, applicable to both staff and the patients under their care. The *Occupational Safety and Health Administration* (OSHA) has published *Guidelines for Preventing Workplace Violence* for health care and social

---

[1] Chapter is reproduced with permission from William (Bill) Nesbitt, CPP.

CPTED FOR HOSPITALS

Figure 103.1 CPTED for hospitals.

service workers.[2] This publication reflects the reality that the health-care industry, when it comes to security, is always held to the highest standard of care for those whom they serve.

Episodes of WPV do not occur in a vacuum. Additionally, WPV is often less predictable than other forms of criminality as evidenced by active shooter episodes in places like Sandy Hook, Danbury, and Columbine. Generally, opportunistic acts of violence are more likely to occur in areas associated with high crime rates. However, this pattern does not necessarily hold true for the purposeful and targeted acts of violence, especially pertaining to hospitals and schools. Parenthetically, these entities are also more likely to receive wall-to-wall media coverage when violence does occur.

---

[2] OSHA. https://www.osha.gov/Publications/osha3148.pdf

WPV, like most criminal behavior, requires the usual preexisting conditions of motive, means, and opportunity. This implies that motive, means, and opportunity must therefore be anticipated, and reasonably mitigated (Figure 103.1).

The challenge, from a crime prevention perspective, is how to specifically anticipate motive, means, and opportunity in a manner to prevent and/or minimize WPV. Many solutions are inculcated in effective security design, including crime prevention through environmental design (CPTED), as well as the enactment of effective security awareness programs, each of which must involve employee participation. Because security programs are site specific, security awareness programs must be situationally determined and reinforced through hands-on employee training.

Frequently, postevent analysis often recognizes that many WPV episodes, given 20/20 hindsight, were predictable, in the absence of perceptual tunnel-vision.

The Workplace Violence Triad

The *WPV triad* broadly describes the morality and casualty of many (not all) WPV incidents, all of which may not be mutually exclusive. Additionally, this triad is generally more applicable to industries that afford public access, and in this case, with emphasis on hospitals, malls, and schools. Awareness of this triad provides a practical initial framework for reasonable prevention. From a criminology perspective, it therefore stands to reason that any mitigation strategy requires the consideration of motive, means, and opportunity *before the fact*.

As with most industries, the threat environment is often unique, in many ways, from one vertical spike to another. This chapter is primarily directed at the health-care audience, with the understanding that the WPV threat affects many verticals. Relevant to the health-care environment, there is generally ease of access (because of soft perimeter control), employee, visitor, and patient density, and weak interior access management, with some exceptions (such as pharmacies). In the health-care arena, WPV carries significantly high levels of potential liability.

Workplace Violence Mitigation

This requires situational awareness, including familiarity of the aggression escalation hierarchy. Situational awareness must consider local crimes rates, cultural factors, and the level of ambient law enforcement. A discussion of some examples follows.

Domestic Violence in the Workplace

For some, the inclusion of domestic violence may seem misplaced. Yet, it is not infrequent that we have seen examples of the domestic violence paradigm invading the workplace, especially within the health-care industry, which incidentally are, *a high percentage of female employees, coupled with a high percentage of female patients.* This means there must be awareness of potential threats associated with orders of protection or restraining orders for both employees and patients. Characteristically, the irrationality of domestic violence has no boundaries. Many of these incidents have resulted in homicide.

Domestic violence, in most cases, is driven by passion and irrationality (ask any police officer).

Active Shooters

Going Postal: The expression derives from a series of incidents from 1986 onward in which a U.S. Postal Service (USPS) worker shot and killed managers. The Colorado school shootings and movie theater shootings victimized individuals simply because they were at the wrong place at the wrong time. Clearly, there is some level of irrationality. Given recent history, there are very few industries that are completely immune from this threat. Disgruntled employees, especially when being discharged, are another source of real and present danger.

Mitigation

There are no simple answers as to how to mitigate WPV. Context counts. Clearly the best first step is a comprehensive threat analysis and security review. The analysis of the ambient threat environment should be followed by security awareness training. Feasible mitigation works best when applied at the incipient stage, assuming that telltale clues are recognizable. Nevertheless, early recognition of the WPV threat is often unavailable, especially in the case of active shooter incidents.

The implementation of a robust *Security Awareness Program* (SAP) will provide cost-effective dividends. The mitigation of WPV is less costly than after-the-fact reaction, including the cost of litigation. With proper training, employees can be provided with the requisite skill-sets to recognize aggressive behavior at or even before the onset of the incipient stage, as well as how to reasonably mitigate the threat, or summon security personnel before harm is done.

In those cases, when WPV is committed by employees, after-the-fact, we usually discover missed opportunities for mitigation. This may include screening failures during the hiring process, or in the case of hospital patents, the failure to identify, upon admission, those patients who may be under pervasive threat as evidenced by *protective orders.*

Additionally, on the mitigation side of the ledger, there organizations, such as AVADE (http://avadetraining.com/), that offer an excellent array of training programs for the early recognition and mitigation of WPV. All the effective WPV mitigation programs include multilevel training for most employees, from recognition of the threat at the incipient stage to managing a WPV event in real time.

Because context counts, security design must be situationally determined. Security awareness training must include the ability to recognize potential threats at the incipient stage. This training should also include basis stage one (on the use of force continuum) recognition skills and basic de-escalation skills, including the notification of the security team.

CPTED

Obviously, need-driven security design is important. Clearly the application of CPTED design is an important component. In part, the role of CPTED is to render the facility as a less likely target for all forms of criminality, including WPV. An understanding of behavioral psychology (B.F. Skinner) can be helpful.

Security personnel, as well as employees, must be taught to recognize industry-specific, early warning signs, such as the local threat environment. Even purposeful acts of violence, including acts of terrorism, are often preceded by reconnoitering activity, including photographic intelligence. Countersurveillance is enhanced by the technical capability of current video surveillance systems. The admonition, "If you see something, say something," is worthy of consideration. Most acts of violence are preceded by some form of incipient behavior. The ability to recognize specific clues is essential to any mitigation strategy.

WPV mitigation strategies must also include effective security design, including the proper application of physical security technologies such as access control, video surveillance, and CPTED design.

Finally, once the security program is in place, the gathering of security information, and analysis of same, is vitally important. This includes the daily recording of routine security mitigation strategies, such as security patrols and the recording and analysis of security breaches. Products, such as REPORT EXEC,[3] provide an excellent platform for the recording of daily preventive security activities, as well as exception reports such as incident reports. These systems provide the means by which to analyze emergency trends, provide the information required to take corrective actions, and subsequently, analyze the impact of corrective actions.

---

[3] REPORT EXEC. http://reportexec.com/solutions/

Systems, such as REPORT EXEC, will provide the C-Suite with the data needed for security budget justification.

When justifying mitigation strategies, hard data is a must. Budgetary justification requires hard data, including longitudinal trend analysis. Merely offering anecdotal opinion data is insufficient. Software such as EXEC REPORT has built-in analytics. These analytics will not only identify trends, it will provide specific information to guide the allocation of scarce resources. These analytics will also quantify return on investment.

Chapter 104

Security Solution Hierarchy[1]

Every security program should be need driven because security is very much a situational discipline. The individual components of each security program should be need driven as defined by the current ambient threat environment and the mission of the enterprise being protected. As we have stated in previous chapters, the backbone of every security program is defined by the *security solution hierarchy* (SSH) (Figure 104.1).

The security solution hierarchy helps to establish a construct of prioritization. The mission of every security program should be to create an environment where various components of the security program (security officers, video surveillance systems, access control systems) and security strategies (such as CPTED) are all synergistically addressing the mission at hand. If the components of the security program are disparate and incongruent, any return of investment will likely be marginalized. For example, the potential benefits to be derived from access control systems may be diminished, to some degree, if they are applied in a vacuum. Every employee should have a role in helping to maintain the integrity of access control programs, as well as all electro-/mechanical security strategies. This creates an effective multiplier effect for every security budget.

Video surveillance systems, if not properly monitored, may well become a liability, in a premises liability lawsuit. Inadequately trained security personnel may potentially increase liability than would the absence of security officers. Inadequately trained security personnel are often manifested in matters such as excessive use of force, if they are not properly trained, and improperly posted.

---

[1] Chapter is reproduced with permission from William (Bill) Nesbitt, CPP.

Figure 104.1 Security solutions hierarchy.

You will note that the bottom of the SSH model begins with CPTED, with security personnel at the top. The purpose of the SSH strategy, is to encourage less costly remedies first, followed by reassessment, prior to moving up through the remaining three levels. As one moves up through the pyramid, there should be a consideration whether the next level is justified, given the ambient threat environment, both internal and external. Two or three levels may be sufficient in some cases. Ironically, the practices of many organizations is to start at the top with security officers, and work downward, thereby assuring *cost-inefficiency*.

Security programs must always be situationally adaptive. This suggests that the starting point should be an objective comprehensive security risk assessment. It is also important to keep in mind that the precursors of criminal activity are *motive, means, and opportunity.* Any security program that fails to identify and quantify these three preconditions will more likely than not, come up short. Of the three preconditions, the primary focus of most security programs is the reduction of opportunity. This challenge requires a combination of both physical deterrence and psychological (behavioral) deterrence.

The preconditions of motive, means, and opportunity must also be considered within the context of a quantified threat environment. Among the plethora of choices of potential security measures available, cost effectiveness will surely become a major factor when considering all available options.

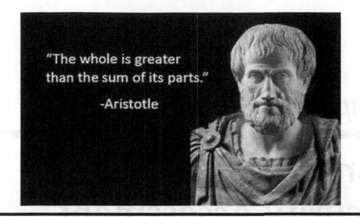

Figure 104.2 "The Whole is Greater than the Sum of it's Parts," Aristotle.

The desired end, with help to justify the means—the value being promoted here—is to ensure that every security program meets the goals of ensuring that the whole is greater than the sum of the parts. This is an achievable and measurable objective goal that will also result in measurable cost efficiency. The Security Solution Hierarchy not only provides a guideline for the sequencing of security remedies, it also implicitly reinforces the notion of a layered approach for effective security.

Security programs that are driven by the notion that the whole should always be greater than the sum of the parts will likely be viewed favorably by the C-Suite. If this concept may seem simplistic, it is. However, the devil is often in the details. This goal is achievable and much more likely to be attained if it is before the fact (Figure 104.2).

In our work, as security consultants, it is not infrequent that we find a number of desperate security strategies that are isolated and completely lacking the linkage of synergy. Security programs, lacking synergy, when the goal does not consider that the whole is greater than the sum of the parts, will almost always come up short.

As one considers the application of security officers, video surveillance systems, access control systems, and barrier systems, the interrelationship of each of these components should also be taken into consideration. It is the interrelationship between various methodologies that ensures that the whole will be greater than the sum of the parts.

Like many security concepts, the fundamentals are simple. The execution may be more complex. Security programs lacking employee or tenant involvement are doomed to mediocrity. When was the last time you conducted a thorough objective security assessment?

Chapter 105

Conducting a Physical Security Assessment

A physical security survey or vulnerability assessment of the facility should be conducted to determine security deficiencies and the potential or probability that a crime will occur at the particular location.[1]

The security process has to address the security vulnerabilities that must be protected. Recommendations should be made to effectively control the risks.

A physical security assessment is a critical on-site examination that is used to[2]

- Determine the security currently in place.
- Identify security deficiencies or excesses.
- Determine what level of security is needed.
- Make recommendations for improvement.

Before you begin the security survey,

- Obtain crime statistics for the property being surveyed and the surrounding area.
- Conduct an interview with the individual who requested the survey.

---

[1] British Home Office, Crime Prevention Program. 2008. https://www.gov.uk/government/publications/2010-to-2015-government-policy-crime-prevention/2010-to-2015-government-policy-crime-prevention

[2] R. Momboisse. 1968. *Industrial Security for Strikes, Riots and Disasters*. Springfield, IL: Charles C. Thomas.

Conducting the security survey:

- Analyze each part of the property as an individual component.
- Determine the potential for criminal activity.
- Be knowledgeable about different types of security devices.
- Make recommendations.

ASIS General Security Risk Assessment Guidelines[3]:

- Assets are people, property, intangible property, and information. What are the risks associated with each of these?
- Conduct a cost-benefit analysis. Are the recommendations affordable, feasible, available, practical, and state-of-the-art?
- Consider the probability and vulnerability that an incident will occur.
- Gather statistical data from local and state police agencies, uniform crime reports, and the current homeland security color code.[4]
- Examine the frequency of events and what can be done to remove or reduce the overall threat.
- Identify the assets.
- Reassess each building or property annually.

Classification of survey recommendations:

- Maximum security
- Medium security
- Minimum security

In 1990, the Crime Prevention Coalition defined crime prevention as, "a pattern of an attitudes and behaviors directed both at reducing the threat of crime and enhancing the sense of safety and security, to positively influence the quality of life in our society, and to develop environments where crime cannot flourish."

In 1972, The National Crime Prevention Institute defined crime prevention as "the anticipation, recognition, and appraisal of a crime risk and the initiation of some action to remove or reduce it."

---

[3] ASIS International Guidelines Commission. 2003. *General Security Risk Assessment Guideline.* Alexandria, VA: ASIS International. https://www.iiiweb.net/files/ASIS_Security_Risk_Assessment_Guidelines.pdf

[4] Homeland Security Advisory System. https://en.wikipedia.org/wiki/Homeland_Security_Advisory_System

Chapter 106

Depression, Dementia, ADHD, Schizophrenia, Alzheimer's, and CPTED

Research as shown that green spaces reduce depression

Design Council, UK 2017

Introduction

We all know someone who is affected by some form of mental health condition. Should it be a close friend or relative, then the concern becomes much greater for their safety and security issues. When it comes to homelessness and mental health, most security practitioners don't have a clue. As a means of full disclosure, Mr Fennelly has a sister with dementia, who is also an alcoholic. Another sister of his has depression, self-medicates with drugs and has alcohol issues. He also has a brother who has had a stroke and is not dealing with long-term memory issues.

Can Crime Prevention through Environmental Design and Urban Design Create a Safer and Healthier Community?

Yes, it can ...

Mental health and homelessness must and needs to be a priority for our politicians to address urban living because those living in our cities are at an increase in risk of depression and a double risk of developing schizophrenia compared with those living in the country. Some causes are: density, crowding, noise, smell, sight, disarray, pollution, feeling overloaded and a lack of brain stimulation.

According to Mayo Clinic,[1] dementia develops in adults with damaged nerve cells in their brains. Many people with Alzheimer's disease display buildup of plaque in certain brain areas, which affects memory. Blood vessel damage, impacting the brain's blood supply, affect patients with vascular dementia.

Symptoms

Dementia symptoms vary depending on the cause, but common signs and symptoms include the following:[2]

Cognitive Changes

- Memory loss, which is usually noticed by a spouse or someone else
- Difficulty communicating or finding words
- Difficulty reasoning or problem solving
- Difficulty handling complex tasks
- Difficulty with planning and organizing
- Difficulty with coordination and motor functions
- Confusion and disorientation

Psychological Changes

- Personality changes
- Depression
- Anxiety
- Inappropriate behavior
- Paranoia
- Agitation
- Hallucinations

---

[1] Dementia. Retrieved on 20 February 2018 from: https://www.mayoclinic.org/diseases-conditions/dementia/symptoms-causes/syc-20352013.

[2] Designing Good Mental Health into Cities: The Next Frontier for Urban Design, Design Council, 201. Retrieved on 20 February 2018 from: www.designcouncil.org.uk/news-opinion/designing-good-mental-health.

Solutions Aside from Medical Intervention
Urban Design

Crime prevention through environmental design (CPTED) practitioners, architects, and planners need to also be doing more in this area. For example:

1. The development of green space is needed for the reduction of depression.
2. Areas for regular exercise, walking, or swimming. Research has indicated that exercise can be just as effective as anti-depressant medication for mild and moderate depression. It can also reduce stress and anxiety, and help alleviate some of the symptoms associated with ADHD (attention deficit hyperactivity disorder), dementia, and even schizophrenia.[3]
3. Reduce dark corners or hidden spots and create natural surveillance or sight lines.
4. Reduce feeling unsafe or the fear of crime.
5. Maintain the area and create a positive image.
6. Community activity is an important part for mental health. (Read below the section on *The Villages* and all the working activities they have.)
7. Good street lighting increases the perception of safety.
8. In landscape architecture, the built environment is understood to mean a human-made landscape, as distinguished from the natural environment; for example, a city park is a built environment.[4]
9. Implement landscape security principles.[5]
10. One study in Denmark found health benefits for bicycle commuting far beyond calories burned in the saddle. Bike commuters also ate healthier diets and felt less stress at work, among other positive effects. If biking transportation could be made fully safe and accessible in our cities, the health impacts would be immense.[6]
11. Eat healthy foods, such as fruit and whole grains, take vitamin D and limit caffeine.
12. Listen to soft music, get a pet, have massages and get exercise.
13. Set your hot water heater to below 120 degrees Fahrenheit.

It is our intention with the items above to pass on information needed to aid in the improvement of the quality of life of those affected by these mental health issues.

---

[3] Green Infrastructure. Retrieved on 15 February 2018 from: http://www.deeproot.com/blog/blog-entries/urban-design-is-affecting-our-brains.
[4] Urban Design. Retrieved on 15 February 2018 from: https://en.wikipedia.org/wiki/Urban_design.
[5] Fennelly, Lawrence and Perry, Marianna, *150 Things You Need To Know About Security*, Second Edition, Boston: Elsevier, 2018.
[6] Cycling Industry of Denmark. Retrieved on 21 February 2018 from: http://www.cycling-embassy.dk/2015/04/30/cycling-is-healthier-than-you-think/.

Current Trends

Urban design seeks to create sustainable urban environments with long-lasting structures, buildings, and overall livability. Walkable urbanism is another ideal that is defined as the *Charter of New Urbanism*. The goal is to reduce environmental impact by altering the built environment to create smart cities that support sustainable transport.[7] Compact urban neighborhoods encourage residents to drive less. These neighborhoods have significantly lower environmental impacts when compared to sprawling suburbs.[8] To prevent urban sprawl, circular flow land-use management was introduced in Europe to promote sustainable land-use patterns.

As a result of the recent New Classical Architecture movement, sustainable construction aims to develop smart growth, walkability, architectural tradition, and classical design.[9] Traditionalists, however, believe that in time things change, but there are basic human values which do not change. Our values with respect to the built environment are an example of this. This is clear for when we look at the great architectures of 100, 500, 2000 years ago and see that it's power is not diminished. This contrasts from modernist and globally uniform architecture.[10] In the 1980s, urban design began to oppose the increasing solitary housing estates and suburban sprawl that we had become accustomed to.

For more information on this topic, the following terms can be used for research:

- Activity centers
- Automobile dependency
- Behavioral sciences
- Circles of sustainability
- Complete streets
- Context theory
- Crime prevention through environmental design
- Environmental psychology
- Landscape architecture
- Landscape urbanism
- Neighborhood character
- New pedestrianism
- New urbanism
- Placemaking

---

[7] Boeing et al. (2014). "LEED-ND and Livability Revisited". *Berkeley Planning Journal.* **27**: 31–55. Retrieved on 15 February 2018.

[8] Ewing, R "Growing Cooler—The Evidence on Urban Development and Climate Change." Retrieved on 23 February 2018.

[9] Charter of the New Urbanism. Retrieved on 24 February 2018 from: https://www.cnu.org/who-we-are/charter-new-urbanism.

[10] "Beauty, Humanism, Continuity between Past and Future". Retrieved on 24 February 2018 from: http://www.traditionalarchitecture.co.uk/aims.html

- Principles of intelligent urbanism
- Smart growth
- Sustainable urbanism
- Transition design
- Unified settlement planning
- Urban acupuncture
- Urban consolidation
- Urban density
- Urban economics
- Urban planning
- Urban village
- Urbanism
- Walkability
- Zoning

Urban Designers[11]

Urban designers are similar to urban planners when preparing design guidelines, regulatory frameworks, legislation, advertising, etc. Urban planners also overlap with building design architects, landscape architects, transportation engineers, and industrial designers. They must also deal with 'place management' to guide and assist the use and maintenance of urban areas and public spaces.

There are professionals who identify themselves specifically as urban designers. However, architecture, landscape and planning programs incorporate urban design theory and design subjects into their curricula. There are an increasing number of university programs offering degrees in urban design at post-graduate level.

Urban design considers:

- Pedestrian zones
- Incorporation of nature within a city
- Aesthetics
- *Urban structure*—arrangement and relation of business and people
- *Urban typology, density* and sustainability—spatial types and morphologies related to intensity of use, consumption of resources and production and maintenance of viable communities
- *Accessibility*—safe and easy transportation
- *Legibility and wayfinding*—accessible information about travel and destinations
- *Animation*—Designing places to stimulate public activity
- *Function and fit*—places support their varied intended uses

---

[11] Urban Design. Retrieved on 24 February 2018 from: https://en.wikipedia.org/wiki/Urban_design.

- *Complementary mixed uses*—Locating activities to allow constructive interaction between them
- *Character and meaning*—Recognizing differences between places
- *Order and incident*—Balancing consistency and variety in the urban environment
- *Continuity and change*—Locating people in time and place, respecting heritage and contemporary culture
- *Civil society*—people are free to interact as civic equals, important for building social capital

The Villages in Florida Calls Itself the Healthiest Hometown in America

Alice Grimes is a good friend of ours and she also is a proofreader of books. In talking with her over the past year while working on this CPTED book she told us about her community and all the activities they have. We asked her to take a minute and tell us in detail about all the activities. Below is her reply:

"Apart from what's shown on the web-links from the Villages, which I believe is now over 300 activities, we all have heated swimming pools and recreation centers within one or two miles, there are 38 executive golf courses with nine holes, and 12 championship golf courses, most with 27 holes. The executive courses are included in our dues of $148 a month along with all the activities, pools, and common maintenance. Classes are taught by volunteers, most by retired people experienced in that field. What's great is that there should be something for everyone. If they don't like to exercise, there are social activities, like card games, group's making things for charities, clubs for train enthusiasts, etc. Most streets have frequent get-togethers with their neighbors, whether it's monthly Flamingo parties in the street (a Flamingo is placed in the front yard when that person is hosting), groups meals out, or parties for events such as Super Bowl, etc. If anyone has surgery, loses a partner, etc., the neighbors rally round and take food and give support. This is a great place for widows and widowers because there's so much going on and it's easy to make friends and keep busy. The other thing is that if there isn't an activity or club someone is interested in, they can start one! We even have support groups for those with diseases like Parkinson's, so they can learn from each other. Oh, and I forgot the three town squares with restaurants and shops, and free, live entertainment every night except Thanksgiving and Christmas Day, where people go to watch or dance."

For more information on The Villages, visit:
https://www.thevillages.com/lifestyle/marketSquare.asp
https://www.thevillages.com/Calendar/index.html
www.thevillagesdailysun.com/app/recnews/index.html#2
www.virginiatrace.com/clubs/ClubsListing_march2017.pdf

First-Generation CPTED

The implementation of first generation CPTED concepts may have more than one effect on the environment—some of which may not be positive. For example, when potential crime targets are made into fortresses or target hardening is taken to extremes, crime and the fear of crime may be reduced, but this will also have a negative affect legitimate users of the space and their quality of life. One of the concepts of the first-generation CPTED that is sometimes omitted is as follows.

Activity Program Support

a. Space to reduce crime
b. Increasing the level of human activity in particular space
c. Additional eyes on the street

Second-Generation CPTED

Second-generation CPTED *"seeks to cultivate while building or rebuilding our Urban Areas"* (Saville and Cleveland 2008).

There are few opportunities for positive and social interactions between people and groups within the community (Green et al., 1998; Saville and Clear 2000).

What are the concepts of second-generation CPTED?

1. Social cohesion
2. Connectivity
3. Community culture
4. Threshold capacity

Second-generation CPTED reduces crime motives by dealing with the cultural, social, and emotional needs of people at the specific locales where crime is or maybe most acute.

Social Cohesion

A few of the characteristics that define social cohesion include:

■ Participation in local events and organizations
■ Presence of self-directed community problem solving
■ Extent to which conflicts are positively resolved within the community, for example, restorative justice programs.
■ Prevalence of friendship networks within the community
■ Extensive positive relations between friendship networks

Connectivity

Connectivity means the neighborhood has positive relations and influence with external agencies such as government funding sources.

Some characteristics of connectivity include:

- Existence of networks with outside agencies, for example, shared websites
- Grant writer or access to a grant writing service
- Formal activities with outside groups organizations and neighborhood
- Adequate transport facilities (ride-sharing, bicycle paths, public transit) linking to outside areas.

Community Culture

CPTED practitioners sometimes forget what is significant about Jane Jacob's "eyes on the street,"[12] not the sight-lines of the streets, but the eyes. We don't need neighborhoods of watchers; we need a sense of community where people care about who they are watching. Community culture brings people together in a common purpose. This is how local residents begin to share a sense of place and why they bother to exert territorial control in the first place (Adams and Goldbard, 2001).

A few characteristics that define culture within a community include:

- Presence and effectiveness of gender and minority equality strategies
- Gender-based programs, for example, violence against women
- Extent of social and cultural diversity within a neighborhood
- Prevalence of special places, festivals, and events
- Extent of community traditions and cultural activities, for example, art fairs, sports role models
- A unique sense of pride or distinctiveness based on the attributes or characteristic of the residents, occupants, or users of the space involved.

Conclusion

We realize this is a complicated topic that sometimes appears difficult to implement at the onset, but there are solutions and remedies to most issues in society. We can no longer ignore social issues that may be controlled and/or eliminated with changes in the environment. CPTED practitioners, building design architects, landscape architects, urban designers and planners, transportation engineers and industrial designers must work together to develop and implement strategies that have a positive effect on social issues in our society to help create safe and healthier communities.

---

[12]Eyes on the Street. Retrieved on 18 February 2018 from: https://www.npr.org/2016/09/28/ 495615064/eyes-on-the-street-details-jane-jacobs-efforts-to-put-cities-first.

Chapter 107

Tips on Crime Prevention Design Techniques for Businesses

- Locate checkout counters near the front of the store, clearly visible from outside.[1]
- Window signs should cover no more than 15% of the windows to provide clear visibility into and out of the store.
- Use shelving displays no higher than 4 feet to help see who is in the store.
- Avoid creating outdoor spaces that encourage loitering.
- Ensure lighting is consistent throughout the parking lot and the store.
- Remove any graffiti immediately to deter future occurrences and reduce fear of crime for customers.
- Communicate with other businesses on your block; look out for each other.

---

[1] Designing Out Crime. Retrieved on June 12, 2017, from: http://cms.cityoftacoma.org/CRO/PW%20405600%20003%20DesignSafeCPTED72.pdf

Chapter 108

Problem-Oriented Policing

Problem-oriented policing is a strategy used by the entire police department aimed at solving persistent community problems.[1] Police identify, analyze, and respond to the underlying circumstances that create incidents. The theory behind community policing is that underlying conditions create problems (Goldstein, 1979).[2] Police officers use the information gathered in their responses to incidents, together with information obtained from other sources, to get a clearer picture of the problem (Eck and Spelman, 1987).[3] The basic idea is to ensure that the root cause of a problem is being addressed, not just the symptoms of a problem.[4]

As a part of this process, the SARA problem-solving model is used.

Scan

Identify problems and prioritize them incorporating community input.

---

[1] Community Oriented Policing Services. www.cops.usdoj.gov; National Criminal Justice Reference Service. www.ncjrs.gov

[2] National Institute of Justice. Practice Profile Problem-Oriented Policing. Retrieved from https://www.crimesolutions.gov/PracticeDetails.aspx?ID=32

[3] Office of Juvenile Justice and Delinquency. Literature Review. A Product of the Models Program Guide. 2010. Retrieved from https://www.ojjdp.gov/mpg/litreviews/Community_and_Problem_Oriented_Policing.pdf

[4] Office of Juvenile Justice and Delinquency Prevention. Community- and Problem-Oriented Policing. https://www.ojjdp.gov/mpg/litreviews/Community_and_Problem_Oriented_Policing.pdf

Analyze

Study information about offenders, victims, and crime locations.

Respond

Implement strategies that address the chronic character of priority problems by thinking "outside the box" of traditional police enforcement tactics and using new resources that were developed by the city to support problem-solving efforts.

Assess

Evaluate the effectiveness of the strategy through self-assessments to determine how well the plan has been carried out and what good has been accomplished.

The goal of the process is to find alternative responses to persistent community problems. Some of the alternative responses that police agencies implement "fit" well with crime prevention through environmental design (CPTED) strategies. For example,

- Target hardening (i.e., reducing opportunities)
- Changes in government services
- Provision of reliable information to residents
- Specialized training for police officers
- Use of community resources
- Increased regulation
- Changes in city ordinances or zoning

Chapter 109

Community Policing

Community policing is "a philosophy that promotes organizational strategies, which supports the systematic use of partnerships and problem-solving techniques, to proactively address the immediate conditions that give rise to public safety issues such as crime, social disorder and fear or crime."[1,2]

The goal of community policing is to redefine the relationship between the police and the community, so that the two collaborate to identify and solve community problems.

The following are usually associated with community policing[3]:

- The empowerment of the community
- A belief in a broad police function
- The reliance of police on citizens for authority, information, and collaboration
- The application of general knowledge and skill
- Specific tactics targeted at particular problems rather than general tactics such as preventive patrol and rapid response
- Decentralized authority to better respond to neighborhood needs

---

[1] United States Department of Justice. *Principles of Good Policing: Avoiding Violence between Police and Citizens* (Revised September 2003). Retrieved from https://www.justice.gov/archive/crs/pubs/principlesofgoodpolicingfinal092003.htm

[2] D. Diamond and D.M. Weiss. *Community Policing: Looking to Tomorrow.* U.S. Department of Justice, Department of Community Oriented Policing Services. https://ric-zai-inc.com/Publications/cops-w0520-pub.pdf

[3] Office of Juvenile Justice and Delinquency Prevention. Community- and Problem-Oriented Policing. https://www.ojjdp.gov/mpg/litreviews/Community_and_Problem_Oriented_Policing.pdf

Instead of responding to crime after it occurs, community policing encourages law enforcement agencies to proactively develop solutions to the underlying conditions contributing to public safety problems. Problem-solving must become a part of all police operations and guide department-wide decision-making efforts.[4]

Community policing strategies include foot patrols, school resource officers, storefronts and mini-substations, the geographic assignment of officers, and neighborhood-based crime prevention activities (Zhao, He, and Lovrich 2003).[5]

The goals of community policing include the overall safety of the community, a reduction in crime, and a reduction in the fear of crime. These goals work well with crime prevention through environmental design (CPTED) strategies.

For further information, the U.S. Department of Justice has compiled several publications on key community policing topics for quick and comprehensive reference[6]:

- Alternatives to Incarceration
- Child and Youth Safety
- Community Partnerships
- Diversity
- Drugs
- Ethics and Integrity
- Healing Communities
- Homeland Security
- Officer Safety and Wellness
- Organizational Transformation
- Policing in the 21st Century
- Problem Solving
- Procedural Justice

---

[4] Community Oriented Policing Services. U.S. Department of Justice. https://cops.usdoj.gov/ Default.asp?Item=2558

[5] Office of Juvenile Justice and Delinquency. Literature Review. A Product of the Models Program Guide. 2010. Community Oriented Policing. Retrieved from https://www.ojjdp.gov/ mpg/litreviews/Community_and_Problem_Oriented_Policing.pdf

[6] Community Oriented Policing Services. U.S. Department of Justice. https://cops.usdoj.gov/ resources

Chapter 110

Reactive Policing versus Proactive Policing

The following are principles of reactive versus proactive policing[1]:

Reactive Policing

- Police respond to citizen calls for assistance.
- Patrol is routine and unstructured.
- 9-1-1 calls drive police activity.
- The dispatch section dictates police activity.
- The emphasis is on solving crimes.

Proactive Policing

- Police seek crime solutions before the crimes occur.
- Patrol is targeted.
- Crime patterns drive police activity.
- Records management/research dictates police activity.
- The emphasis is on preventing crimes.

---

[1] Center for Problem-Oriented Policing. Model POP Curriculum—Detailed Syllabus. http://www.popcenter.org/learning/model_curriculum/?p=syllabus

Chapter 111

A Working Knowledge of Advanced CPTED Principles

> The secret of SUCCESS in business is in detecting where the world will go and getting there FIRST.
>
> **Bill Gates**

There has been an increased interest in crime prevention through environmental design (CPTED) in recent years, both nationally and internationally. More and more people are conducting CPTED assessments and applying CPTED concepts in an effort to reduce crime and the fear of crime. In September 2016, we were lecturing at the Annual ASIS International Seminar about security and CPTED assessments and were describing the issues of a specific location where we had just finished an assessment. After the presentation, a seminar attendee told us that he knew the exact location that we were talking about and that it was in Atlanta. We both laughed and told him that the location was in New Jersey. This added credence to our research that many communities throughout the United States have similar issues that can be addressed through application of CPTED strategies.

We both strongly feel if you want to advance yourself in CPTED you must

1. Be aware of the contributions of Jane Jacobs.
2. Understand defensible space and Oscar Newman's research.
3. Grasp the meaning and use of the broken windows theory.
4. Know how to control physical deterioration and disorder.

5. Read the publications of Tim Crowe, Randy Atlas, Paul Cozen, Lawrence J. Fennelly, Marianna Perry, and others.
6. Have an understanding of the following breakdown of *first-generation CPTED*:
   a. Natural Surveillance
      i. Clear windows
      ii. Law enforcement
      iii. Delineate boundaries
   b. Natural Access Control
      i. Security awareness
      ii. Reporting and reactions
      iii. Reducing the number of entrances and access
   c. Territoriality Reinforcement
      i. Sphere of influence
      ii. Physical design
      iii. Maintenance
   d. Image Management
      i. Positive and negative indicators
      ii. Perception of space
      iii. Behavioral effects
   e. Activity Program Support
      i. Space to reduce crime
      ii. Increasing the level of human activity in particular space
      iii. Additional eyes on the street
   f. Target Hardening
      i. Securing of property
      ii. Installation of physical security components
      iii. Use of security officers or law enforcement
   g. Geographical Juxtaposition (Wider Environment)
      i. Land use
      ii. Vacant or derelict sites
      iii. Lack of pedestrian movement
7. The first generation of CPTED focuses on strategies and concepts that will reduce and discourage criminal opportunity:
   a. Defines boundaries
   b. Clear line of sight
   c. Users of space and types of space
   d. Urban zones prone to criminal activity
   e. Street lighting
   f. Security surveillance systems (closed-circuit television [CCTV])
   g. Digital technology to make the offender visible to others (digital signage)
   h. Proper maintenance of space to signify a sense of ownership that is influential in reducing fear of crime
   i. Spatial design

     j. Reinforcing positive behavior within the physical space through the use of physical attributes

     k. Public and private space

     l. Acceptable patterns of usage

8. Understand the *second and third generations of CPTED.*
9. Participate in Neighborhood Watch and Business Watch.
10. Understand community policing concepts and theory.
11. Know how to formulate public and private sector partnerships.
12. Understand the displacement of crime theory.
13. Understand the fear of crime and how to reduce it.
14. Know how to implement crime prevention concepts and applications.
15. Study the 25 techniques of situational crime prevention by Ronald V. Clarke.
16. Understand risk, risk factors, and the different types of risk.
17. Know about the three D's of CPTED: definition, designation, and design.
18. Have knowledge of city building codes.
19. Know how to read blueprints and architectural design.
20. Be capable of conducting assessments.

Chapter 112

The Premise of Third-Generation CPTED

The premise of third-generation crime prevention through environmental design (CPTED) is that a sustainable green urban environment is perceived by its members, as well as outsiders, as "safe." Focus on sustainable, green environmental design strategies and insist on practical measures that foster the perception of urban space as safe.

Elements of third-generation CPTED[1]:

- Addresses energy crisis, urban pollution, recycling, and minimizing waste
- Reprograming the physical space and material, based on consumption, online services, and cyberfunctionality
- Going "green"
- Natural energy as a power source, solar lighting and solar closed-circuit television cameras
- Reprograming the urban space
- Urban-scale green and green space
- Design strategies
- Portal of digital information—smart signs
- Smart signs
- Perception of safety and security
- Recycle of waste

---

[1] Unicri. Improving Urban Security through Green Environmental Design: New Energy for Urban Security. http://www.unicri.it/news/files/2011-04-01_110414_CRA_Urban_Security_sm.pdf

Chapter 113

Description of Second-Generation CPTED

Second-generation crime prevention through environmental design (CPTED) focuses on strategies to eliminate the reasons for criminal behavior via sustainable livable environments:

- Supporting social interaction and promoting "eyes on the street" activity
- Relying on a triad of community culture, cohesion, and connectivity
- Enhancing a sense of belonging, the web of personal relationships, groups, networks, traditions, and patterns of behavior
- Neighborhood management committees taking full advantage of what is defined as resources:
  - Social (people)
  - Economic
  - Technological
  - Environmental
  - Natural esources
  - Ecological
- Making the best of habitat spaces and ecosystems
- Bringing private ownership to single tenure social housing
- Building affordable housing
- Low energy designing in new developments
- Providing educational opportunities for young people

- Developing walk-able streets
- Laying out a master plan
- Creating neighborhoods that are close to stores and public transportation
- Fostering community and social welfare
- Following Americans with Disabilities Act (ADA) guidelines

Chapter 114

Community Culture

Crime prevention through environmental design (CPTED) practitioners sometimes forget what is significant about Jane Jacob's "eyes in the street." We are not talking about the sight lines or particulars about the streets, but the "eyes."

According to Adams and Goldbard, we do not need neighborhoods of watchers; we need a sense of community where people care about whom they are watching. Community culture brings people together in a common purpose. This is how local residents begin to share a sense of place and why they exert territorial control in the first place.[1]

What if we were to say ... in our opinion, Adams and Goldbard are wrong ... we believe that Adams and Goldbard have misinterpreted some of the key concepts outlined by Jane Jacobs in her book, *The Death and Life of Great American Cities* (1961), when she first introduced "eyes on the street." Jacobs supported the concept of Neighborhood Watch within the community, and she wanted the community to come together and to report suspicious activity to the police as a means to create a safer environment. This is the same concept currently being used by the Department of Homeland Security (DHS) campaign, "If You See Something, Say Something."

---

[1] D. Adams and A. Goldbard. 2001. *Creative Community. The Art of Culture Development.* New York, NY: Rockefeller Foundation.

Chapter 115

Emerging Trends in Security in 2018 and Beyond

There is no doubt that technology will and has advanced the security profession. Almost monthly, we read about new developments in the industry. China, for example, is trying to be proactive and address "pre-crime," with the help of the China Electronic Technology Group, who seek to develop software to collate data on jobs, hobbies, consumption habits, and other behavior for the purpose of predicting terrorist acts before they strike.

In California, a group of individuals are attempting to prevent crime by utilizing software that is based on crime analysis that records crime data in real time. The program tracks the location of law enforcement in specific locations to help reduce crime.

Research into new software programs will continue to develop, and it is predicted that radio-frequency identification (RFID) technology and smart home devices will play a more significant role in the future. Applications for new technology will expand over time, and we will find new ways to use it.

Magnetometers (metal detectors) will continue to play a large role in safety and security (especially the Garrett model PD-6500i unit) and will be accepted as commonplace in all public environments, including schools and houses of worship.

We are currently experiencing an increase in cyber investigations, cyber forensics, and cyber certifications. The field of security will continue to evolve as new threats and different types of vulnerabilities emerge. Physical security and cybersecurity will mesh even closer.

Photo 115.1 Marianna Perry with an Allied Universal Security Services robot that was patrolling the convention center at the 2016 ASIS Annual Seminar and Exhibits in Orlando, Florida. (Photo taken by Lawrence J. Fennelly.)

The security workforce will continue to become more diverse and include more women, ethnic groups, and cultures working in the industry. We will see more security "professionals" with certifications and advanced academic degrees entering the security industry. Security officers working in the field will be better trained, and body cameras will become a standard part of the security uniform. Technology, such as drones and robots, will support human personnel (Photo 115.1).

The security industry as a whole will see phenomenal growth as law enforcement officers struggle to combat rising crime rates. There are currently two and a half times as many private security officers as law enforcement officers in the United States,[1] and the numbers will continue to increase as private security officers take on

---

[1] Private Security and Public Police Officer Similarities. Retrieved on March 15, 2017, from: www.cengage.com/resource_uploads/downloads/0314067329_57038.ppt

more responsibility for crime and disorder. As the industry grows, the relationship between contract security companies and the organizations they protect will be more of a partnership, instead of the typical organization-contractor relationship we see today.

Optical turnstiles combined with biometrics will be the "go-to" access control solution, especially those with high-security or very controlled environments. Stand-alone access control systems will continue to be used to solve "everyday" ingress and egress at most facilities. Technology is not *the* answer to security; it is part of a holistic security program. Humans will still be needed and security professionals will still oversee the operation of technology.

CPTED design approaches focus on both the proper design and the effective use of the physical environment. The concept of proper design and effective use emphasizes the designed relationship among strategies to ensure that the desired results are achieved. For example, improved street lighting alone (a design strategy) is ineffective against crime without the conscious and active support of citizens (in reporting what they see) and of police (in responding and conducting surveillance). CPTED involves the effort to integrate design, citizen and community action, and law enforcement strategies to accomplish surveillance consistent with the design and use of the environment.

CPTED Strategies

There are now seven overlapping strategies in CPTED because needs emerged that were beyond the original concepts, so CPTED had to evolve to meet those needs. These seven concepts are as follows:

1. Natural access control
2. Natural surveillance
3. Territorial reinforcement[2]
4. Image and/or maintenance[3]
5. Activity program support[4]

[2] T. Crowe and L.J. Fennelly. 2013. *Crime Prevention through Environmental Design* (3rd ed.). Cambridge, MA: Elsevier.

[3] S. Kajalo and A. Lindblom. Formal and informal surveillance and competitiveness of shopping centers in Nordic countries. *Journal of Management and Marketing Research.* "Theoretical Background" p. 3. Referenced from http://www.aabri.com/manuscripts/10564.pdf

[4] S. Kajalo and A. Lindblom. Formal and informal surveillance and competitiveness of shopping centers in Nordic countries. *Journal of Management and Marketing Research.* "Theoretical Background" p. 3. Referenced from http://www.aabri.com/manuscripts/10564.pdf

6. Target hardening[5]
7. Geographical juxtaposition (wider environment)[6]

Trends Going Forward

■ *Crime Prevention through Environmental Design* (3rd ed.), by T. Crowe and L.J. Fennelly has been translated into Mandarin Chinese and Korean. This demonstrates the increased worldwide interest in CPTED.
■ Color scheme designs have been identified for CPTED.
■ Music and light strategies have been identified for CPTED.

Traditional Security Countermeasures

■ Solar panel lighting and solar panel cameras
  – "The Cloud"
  – IT infrastructure
  – IP video and digital video
  – IP-based access control
  – Standards, ISO 31010-2009-11
  – Emergency management and preparedness
  – Soft targets and traditional target hardening
  – Robots and drones on patrol
  – Social media, Facebook, LinkedIn, and Twitter
  – Closed-circuit television (CCTV) is now referred to as security surveillance systems
  – Visitor management systems and access control
  – Background checks and drug testing in schools—for all personnel, including bus drivers, maintenance, custodial employees, and so on
  – Mass notification system
  – Digital video analytics

---

[5] P. Cozens, G. Saville, and D. Hiller. 2005. A review and modern bibliography. *Journal of Property Management* 23(5): 328–356.

[6] P. Cozens and T. van der Linde. 2015. Perceptions of Crime Prevention through Environmental Design (CPTED) at Australian railway stations. *Journal of Public Transportation*, 18(4): 73–92. Referenced from https://www.researchgate.net/publication/287805123_Perceptions_of_Crime_Prevention_Through_Environmental_Design_CPTED_at_Australian_Railway_Stations

Creating a Master Plan

In a recent assessment, the company wanted a security master plan for their property. Since we had a set of best practices, they were re-worked to fit the needs of the company. A security master plan should state: "A Master Plan for Security should dovetail with the corporation's Master Plan and Mission Statement." Master planning is a catalyst for defining a vision for security that touches all aspects of service delivery, including technology, emergency management, IT integration, command and control, and communication with stakeholders and employees. The plan should identify specific areas where security can be re-positioned as a part of a core business function.

Formulation of Partnerships

Partnerships are often formed in response to a rash of crimes that target a particular type of business or a particular neighborhood. Existing groups of individuals and organizations are beginning to see the value in the formulation of partnerships. Bill Gellar and Lisa Belsky were instrumental in developing positive results between the community, residents, businesses, and law enforcement to address community concerns. A case study was conducted in New Haven, Connecticut, in an area that had high rates of violent crime, urban blight, abandoned homes and businesses, illegal drug activity, and vehicles being set on fire. The neighborhoods were magnets for crime. It was only through the formulation of partnerships that the community was able to regain control over their neighborhoods. Individuals and businesses, local houses of worship, local government offices, law enforcement, community leaders, and community members joined together, with each member or group bringing a different area of expertise and value to the partnership.

Future discussions on security should include the following:

- Urban safety
- Public safety and security
- Role of local government in community safety
- Digital intelligence
- Safety–reality versus perceptions
- Promoting safety and reducing crime within our communities
- Crime and violence prevention
- Re-design of Neighborhood Watch

Chapter 116

Youth Violence: Using Environmental Design to Prevent School Violence

For more than a century, public health practitioners have modified the environment to prevent disease and injury. For example, in the mid-1850s Dr. John Snow removed the pump handle from a contaminated well in London to stop a deadly cholera outbreak. Modern environmental modifications, such as seat belts and airbags in vehicles, have saved countless lives. Other environmental modifications, such as sidewalks and community parks, have increased physical activity while helping to reduce obesity.

In the early 1960s, criminologists became particularly interested in identifying the environmental characteristics associated with crime. These characteristics include, but are not limited to, the physical design of a particular space, weapon availability, number of people in the space, and the purposes for being there.[1,2] These characteristics are associated with the immediate environment rather than broader social factors, such as poverty, racism, gender inequality, exposure to violence through the media, and criminal laws.

In 1971, C. Ray Jeffrey coined the phrase "Crime Prevention through Environmental Design (CPTED)." According to this approach, the "proper design

---

[1] CDC. Youth Violence: Using Environmental Design to Prevent School Violence. Retrieved on June 12, 2017, from: https://www.cdc.gov/violenceprevention/youthviolence/cpted.html

[2] J.S. Mair and M. Mair. 2003. Violence prevention and control through environmental design. *Annual Review of Public Health* 24: 209–225. Referenced from http://www.annualreviews.org/doi/10.1146/annurev.publhealth.24.100901.140826

and effective use of the built environment can lead to a reduction in the fear and incidence of crime and an improvement in the quality of life."[3] CPTED focuses on reducing crime opportunities and on promoting positive social behavior. It does not change the motivation of individual perpetrators.

School Violence

The Centers for Disease Control and Prevention (CDC) are studying how CPTED can be applied to school violence prevention. While schools in the United States remain relatively safe, any amount of violence is unacceptable. Approximately 40% of public schools reported to police at least one incident of violence during the 2009–2010 school year. Of these public schools, approximately 10% reported at least one serious violent incident during the same time period.[4] A nationwide survey of high school students in the United States found that 4.1% of students carried a weapon (such as a gun, knife, or club) on school property in the 30 days preceding the survey. The same survey found that 6% of students missed school in the 30 days preceding the survey because they felt unsafe at school or on their way to or from school. CPTED principles that schools can consider include the following[5]:

1. *Natural surveillance* refers to the placement of physical features that maximize visibility. Example: The strategic use of windows that look out on the school entrance so that students can see into the school and know that others can see them.
2. *Access management* involves guiding people by using signs, well-marked entrances and exits, and landscaping. It may also include limiting access to certain areas by using real or symbolic barriers. Example: Landscaping that reduces access to unsupervised locations on the school grounds.
3. *Territoriality* is defined by a clear delineation of space, expressions of pride or ownership, and the creation of a welcoming environment. Example: Motivational signs, displays of student art, and the use of school colors to create warmth and express pride.
4. *Physical maintenance* includes repair and general upkeep of space. Example: Removing graffiti in restrooms in a timely manner and making the necessary

---

[3] T.D. Crowe. 2000. *Crime Prevention through Environmental Design: Applications of Architectural Design and Space Management Concepts.* Boston, MA: Butterworth-Heinemann.

[4] A. Zhang, L. Musu-Gillette, and B.A. Oudekerk. 2016. *Indicators of School Crime and Safety: 2015* (NCES 2016-079/NCJ 249758). Washington, DC: National Center for Education Statistics, U.S. Department of Education, and Bureau of Justice Statistics, Office of Justice Programs, U.S. Department of Justice. https://nces.ed.gov/pubs2016/2016079.pdf

[5] L. Kann et al. 2016. Youth risk behavior surveillance—United States, 2015. *Morbidity and Mortality Weekly Report: Surveillance Summaries* 65(SS-06): 1–174. https://www.cdc.gov/mmwr/volumes/65/ss/ss6506a1.htm

repairs to restrooms, light fixtures, and stairways to maintain safety and comfort.

5. *Order maintenance* involves attending to minor unacceptable acts and providing measures that clearly state acceptable behavior. Example: Maintaining an obvious adult presence during all times that students transition from one location to another.

The principles of CPTED can potentially benefit schools by[6]

- Creating a warm and welcoming environment
- Fostering a sense of physical and social order
- Creating a sense of ownership by students
- Sending positive messages to students
- Maximizing the presence of authority figures
- Minimizing opportunities for out-of-sight activities
- Managing access to all school areas

CDC Activities

The CDC contracted with Carter and Carter Associates, a partnership of urban planning and law enforcement professionals specializing in CPTED, to develop a tool to assess the consistency of physical characteristics of schools with CPTED principles. This tool, the CPTED School Assessment (CSA), assesses the application of CPTED principles in three geographic areas of schools: grounds, buildings, and interiors.

The CDC is implementing a study that assesses the association between ratings of adherence to CPTED principles and measures of student fear and violent behaviors on school property. Ultimately, the data may be used to develop and evaluate school interventions that reduce violence through the design or redesign of the physical environment and the creation of relevant policies and procedures.

Environmental design alone will not prevent all violent acts within schools. However, CPTED is a promising prevention strategy that, if shown to be effective, may lead to reducing fear among students and teachers, to more positive social interactions, and to safer schools.

---

[6] Centers for Disease Control and Prevention. Youth Violence: Using Environmental Design to Prevent School Violence. Referenced from https://www.cdc.gov/violenceprevention/youthviolence/cpted.html

Chapter 117

CPTED and Private Country Clubs[1]

The conceptual thrust of a crime prevention through environmental design (CPTED) program is that the physical environment can be manipulated to produce behavioral effects that will reduce the incidence and fear of crime, and improve quality of life.[2] This concept fits nicely into the private club setting. There are natural built-in measures that most country clubs have without realizing they have aligned with the principles of CPTED. CPTED is not a new concept, but it has gained popularity in recent decades because of the proven effectiveness of the environmentally pleasing crime prevention techniques. The goal of a CPTED program is to design a physical environment that positively influences human behavior. There are some basic theories of first-generation CPTED theory, including natural access control, natural surveillance, territoriality, and maintenance, all of which are a part of the overall image a country club wants to project to not only the members of the club, but to members of the community as well.

Traditionally, access control and surveillance, as design concepts, have emphasized mechanical crime prevention techniques while overlooking or minimizing the use of the physical environment. More recent approaches to physical design of environments have shifted the emphasis to natural crime prevention techniques, attempting to use natural opportunities presented by the environment for crime prevention.[3] Channelization and territoriality are two of the fundamental principles that are present in the private club setting. Begin with the aesthetically

---

[1] Chapter is reproduced with permission from John O'Rourke, CPP.
[2] L.J. Fennelly and M.A. Perry. 2017. *Effective Physical Security* (5th ed.). Boston, MA: Elsevier, p. 1.
[3] L.J. Fennelly and M.A. Perry. 2017. *Physical Security: 150 Things You Should Know* (2nd ed.). Boston, MA: Elsevier, p. 19.

appealing "No Trespassing" carved into wooden signs attached to the fancy wrought iron fencing. This will portray a sense of ownership that figures into the principles of territoriality. Moreover, the mandatory dress codes of private clubs support territoriality and ownership. These exclusive establishments require a "look" that members must adhere to, and those not adhering to this standard are easily spotted and approached. This helps at a very basic level of situational awareness and can prevent, and often does prevent, unwanted access by unauthorized users. Not only does this figure nicely into territoriality, but it also will bring attention to security awareness, which is supported by landscaped natural surveillance schemes.

Building along the natural surveillance lines are neatly manicured bushes and trees that allow a visual sight line from the fairways to the clubhouse. The architecture and building designs of many clubhouses are enhanced by an overattentive grounds superintendent (and crew) to ensure that the shrubbery and trees are trimmed and aesthetically appealing. This brings natural surveillance or sight-lines to those visiting the property, so they can enjoy the architectural splendor of the clubhouse and grounds, and at the same time, they are conducting "informal surveillance" of the property without realizing the part they are playing in crime prevention.

These environmental concepts have strong security results that are fundamental to the goals of CPTED, most of which are unbeknownst to legitimate users of the club, but embraced by security professionals, who can build upon these "built-in" CPTED principles to enhance and reinforce existing measures. The ultimate goal of any CPTED program is to not only reduce crime and the fear of crime, but to also improve the quality of life for everyone who utilizes the property for work or play.

CPTED can reduce crime and the fear of crime through[4]

- Territoriality—fostering residents' interaction, vigilance, and control over their neighborhood
- Surveillance—maximizing the ability to spot suspicious people and activities
- Activity support—encouraging the intended use of public space by residents
- Hierarchy of space—identifying ownership by delineating private space from public space through real or symbolic boundaries
- Access control/target hardening—using physical barriers, security devices, and tamper-resistant materials to restrict entrance
- Environment—a design or location decision that takes into account the surrounding environment and minimizes the use of space by conflicting groups
- Image/maintenance—ensuring that a building or area is clean, well maintained, and graffiti free

---

[4] Royal Canadian Mounted Police. Crime Prevention through Environmental Design (CPTED). http://bc.rcmp-grc.gc.ca/ViewPage.action?siteNodeId=50&languageId=1&contentId=4814

Chapter 118

CPTED Principles for Shopping Mall Design

Shopping malls often provide much of the public space in suburban communities and as such can be a mixed blessing.[1] On one hand, they perform the important function of a town center, serving as a gathering place for the community. On the other hand, a mall can serve as an attraction for criminal activity.

While shopping malls continually grow in size and popularity, they also become a haven for abnormal users and sites of a growing number of parking lot crimes. It is now more important than ever for the shopping mall designers and re-modelers to implement crime prevention through environmental design (CPTED) principles.

---

[1] Crime Prevention through Environmental Design. Albemarle County Police Guide to Creating a Safer Community. Retrieved on June 12, 2017, from: http://www.albemarle.org/upload/images/forms_center/departments/Police/forms/CPTED%20Manual%20III.pdf

Chapter 119

Translating CPTED Principles into Action

Following are ways that crime prevention through environmental design (CPTED) principles are put into action.[1]

Fencing

Fence design should maximize natural surveillance from the street to the building and from the building to the street and minimize opportunities for intruders to hide.

Entrances to Buildings

Provide entrances that are in prominent positions and allow users to see into them before entering.

Blind Corners

Avoid creating blind corners in pathways, stairwells, hallways, and car garages. Pathways should be direct. All barriers along pathways should be permeable

---

[1] CPTED, fact sheet (TRIM: Z11/156852). 2015. Wollongong City Council. http://www. wollongong.nsw.gov.au

(see through), including landscaping, fencing, and so on. Consider the installation of mirrors to allow users to see ahead of them and around corners.

Communal and Public Areas

Provide natural surveillance for communal and public areas by

- Positioning active observation or windows of habitable rooms adjacent to communal public areas (e.g., playgrounds, swimming pools, gardens, and car garages)
- Making communal laundries and garage areas easily seen
- Locating seating in areas actively used
- Locating foyers/waiting areas where they are both visible from the building entry and close to actively used areas
- Providing open-style or transparent materials on doors and walls or both of elevators and stairwells

Landscaping

Avoid landscaping that obstructs causal surveillance and allows intruders to hide.

Generally, visual surveillance corridors can be maintained by limiting growth of shrubbery to a maximum height of 3 feet and trees to a minimum height of 7–8 feet at the lowest branches, thus ensuring that visibility between 3 and 7–8 feet from the ground will always be relatively unimpaired. Another function of landscaping in crime prevention is aesthetics; because aesthetics are important, an attractive environment brings about a feeling of pride and ownership (Gardner, 1995).[2]

Lighting

Ensure lighting does not produce glare or dark shadow. Areas well used after dark should be lit.

A bright, cheerful environment is much more pleasing than one that appears dark and lifeless. As used in CPTED, lighting plays a part in creating the ability to feel good about one's environment, which is important in developing a sense of pride and ownership and a feeling of territoriality. Lighting can influence an individual's feelings about his or her environment from an aesthetic as well as a safety standpoint.

---

[2] Robert A. Gardner, CPP. 1995. Crime Prevention Through Environmental Design. Referenced from http://www.crimewise.com/library/cpted.html

Mixed Land Uses

Where permitted, provide appropriate mixed uses within buildings to increase opportunities for natural surveillance. For example, businesses can be observed by residents after hours, and residences can be observed by businesspeople during business hours.

Building Identification

Ensure buildings are clearly identified by street numbers to prevent unintended access and to assist persons trying to find the building.

Security Devices

Use quality locks, and ensure they comply with the building code in respect of egress. Security grilles, shutters, and doors should allow natural observation of the street.

Spaces

Spaces should be clearly defined to express a sense of ownership and reduce unauthorized access.

Maintenance/Image

Finally, care and maintenance allow for the continued use of a space for its intended purpose, as well as contributing to territorial reinforcement. Deterioration and blight indicate less concern and control by the intended users of a site and a greater tolerance of disorder. Proper maintenance protects the public health, safety, and welfare in all existing structures, residential and nonresidential, and on all existing premises by establishing minimum standards, best practices, as well as a master plan. Maintenance is the responsibility of the facilities manager, owners, and occupants.[3]

---

[3] Crime Prevention through Environmental Design (CPTED) Fact Sheet. Wollongong City Council. http://www.wollongong.nsw.gov.au/customerserviceonline/factsheet/Factsheets/Crime%20Prevention%20through%20Environmental%20Design%20(CPTED).pdf

Studies

"Many crime prevention programs work, others do not. Most programs have not yet been evaluated with enough scientific evidence to draw conclusions."[4,5]Experimental designs are more difficult to conduct with CPTED strategies. A multitude of CPTED studies have been conducted, trying to determine the impact of the strategies on specific geographic areas. When the units of measurement are areas instead of individuals, experimental designs are more challenging because random assignment is more difficult to accomplish. Plus, it is often difficult to identify comparable areas to serve as controls, and it can be challenging to ensure that the intervention does not inadvertently affect the control area. Use of statistical techniques control for other variables influencing outcomes will help increase scientifically a more stringent control of the evaluations. Environmental factors require longer data collection periods. Although research indicates that fear of crime and perceptions of safety are affected by time of year, many CPTED studies have not had long enough follow-up periods that report seasonal variations.

We feel the CPTED programs have several advantages over the other programs, by planning strategies that avert or eliminate crime opportunities. CPTED treats whole areas at a time, instead of the emphasis being on treating problems on an individual basis, or person-to-person basis, thereby bringing swifter results, and affecting whole communities. CPTED is flexible; its variables can be integrated into most crime programs as part of the solution to avert crime through readdressing public area problems, commercial areas, residential communities or public housing, parks, government facilities, and schools. It can embrace the best components and strategies of other programs, such as surveillance technologies, policing, and psychological tools, as well as parts of other successful programs with proven successful strategies in the reduction of crime.

The criterion principle is to make the quality of life safer for people residing in communities by making the environment safer through various scientific and design methods that discourage criminal acts. CPTED has proven to work successfully as a method of modern crime control alone, and combines with other crime prevention programs. In new schools being built, CPTED planning is a prerequisite to getting government contracts and funding in certain towns and states. We think its future is very promising and will be implemented and integrated into many future projects.[6]

---

[4] L. W. Sherman, D. C. Gottfredson, D. L. MacKenzie, J. Eck, P. Reuter, and S. D. Bushway. July 1998. Preventing Crime: What Works, What Doesn't, What's Promising. National Institute of Justice. Research in Brief. Jeremy Travis, Director. Referenced from https://www.ncjrs.gov/pdffiles/171676.pdf

[5] UKEssays. Reviewing Crime Prevention through Environmental Design Criminology Essay. March 2015. Referenced from https://www.ukessays.com/essays/criminology/reviewing-crime-prevention-through-environmental-design-criminology-essay.php

[6] Ibid.

Chapter 120

Improved Street Lighting

Practice Goals/Practice Components

Interventions that focus on improving street lighting aim to prevent crime by modifying an environment and reducing opportunities for offenders to commit crimes.[1] These interventions may occur in public or private settings, such as residential neighborhoods, parking lots, shopping malls, campuses, hospitals, or various other facilities. Installation and street light components vary by setting. For example, in a neighborhood or residential setting, improved street lighting may include trimming bushes so that lights are more visible, or replacing old or broken lamps with new light fixtures to achieve the street light's intended purpose. Through modifying and improving environmental measures in various settings, the overall goal of these interventions is crime prevention (Clark, 2008; Welsh and Farrington, 2008).[2]

Program Theory

Improving street lighting to prevent crime is grounded in two main perspectives: (1) situational crime prevention and (2) strengthening informal social control and community cohesion. Taken together, situational crime prevention and informal social controls hold that crime is influenced by environmental conditions in interaction with resident and offender characteristics. Therefore, by improving street

---

[1] National Institute of Justice. Practice Profile: Improved Street Lighting. https://www.crimesolutions.gov/PracticeDetails.aspx?ID=38

[2] National Institute of Justice. Practice Profile: Improved Street Lighting. https://www.crimesolutions.gov/PracticeDetails.aspx?ID=38

lighting, the offender is believed to perceive greater risks of apprehension, while residents are believed to invest more in their community and thus work to prevent crime in their community.

Situational crime prevention focuses on reducing the opportunities for crime, while also increasing an offender's perceived risk of apprehension. It is believed that modifying the nighttime visibility within urban areas should reduce opportunities for crime by increasing the perceived risk of detection (Jacobs, 1961; Welsh and Farrington, 2008).[3]

Informal social controls and community cohesion also play a key role in these interventions. According to Sampson (1997),[4] a low degree of "collective efficacy," also referred to as social control, in a neighborhood typically results in high crime rates. Therefore, installing or improving street lighting in an area, a sign of positive investment, might signal to residents that efforts are being made to improve their community. This improvement might lead to community pride and cohesion for residents. As a result, residents may have a personal investment in the area, causing an increased interest in watching over their community (Welsh and Farrington, 2008).[5]

---

[3] National Institute of Justice. Practice Profile: Improved Street Lighting. https://www.crimesolutions.gov/PracticeDetails.aspx?ID=38

[4] R.L. Sampson, S.W. Raudenbush, and F. Earls. 1997. Neighborhoods and violent crime: A multilevel study of collective efficacy. *Science* 277: 218–224.

[5] National Institute of Justice. Practice Profile: Improved Street Lighting. https://www.crimesolutions.gov/PracticeDetails.aspx?ID=38

Chapter 121

Measuring and Evaluation of CPTED

> Crime prevention is a pattern of attitudes and behaviors directed at reducing the threat of crime and enhancing the sense of safety and security, to positively influence the quality of life in our society and to develop environments in which crime cannot flourish.
>
> **National Crime Prevention Council (1990)**

Introduction

Very little has been written on how to measure the effectiveness of your crime prevention through environmental design (CPTED) program. Some work was done in 2005, but overall very little has been written on this topic. So here are some guidelines in order to evaluate properly: Let's call the site in question "the complex" since CPTED covers the full spectrum.

You get 3 years of data from the local police department and from the complex. After a full assessment and review of the natural surveillance (landscape security) and natural access and territoriality, the complex hardens the target.

The job of security now must change to be more proactive. Crimes of the past 3 years are to be addressed, and programs such as awareness or neighborhood are implemented followed by security making monthly reports on the status of aspects of physical security.

Include Awareness

Become aware of your community and who the strangers are—the guy walking down the street with the black dog, who is he?

Look for signs of behavior that do not fit the normal pattern. "Can I help you?" you ask. Now evaluate the response.

Ever go for a walk and see four newspapers on the lawn? What does that tell you? Thieves also do assessments and evaluate your complex.

Fear of Crime

We have seen fear many times on television when a school is in lock-down and parents have been outside for an hour waiting to see their child. It is not a pretty sight, and the look of a mother's fear is in their eyes.

CPTED Strategies with the Goal of CPTED to Reduce Opportunities for Crime to Occur

The previous discussion suggests a series of general design strategies that can be applied in any situation to improve natural access control, natural surveillance, and territorial behavior.

- Provide a clear border definition of controlled space.
- Provide a clearly marked transition from public to semipublic to private space.
- Locate gathering areas in places with natural surveillance and access control and away from the view of potential offenders.
- Place safe activities in unsafe locations and unsafe activities in safe locations.
- Provide natural barriers to conflicting activities.
- Improve the scheduling of space to provide the effective and critical intensity of uses.
- Design spaces to increase the perception of natural surveillance.
- Overcome distance and isolation through improved communications and design efficiency (e.g., emergency telephones, pedestrian paths).
- Turn soft targets into hard targets.

Obtaining Results

After all of the above have been completed and security is maintained at the highest level, you should have a reduction in crime risks and crime as well as a reduction in fear of crime. Then after 3 years, you compare the data with the previous 3 years to see your results (Fennelly, 2017).[1]

Common Goals

- Reduction to removal of drug dealers
- Reduction to removal of crime and police calls
- Creation of safe housing
- Encouragement to address problem-solving issues
- Encouragement to upgrade neighborhoods with planting of trees and flowers
- Development of neighborhood pride
- Development of crime prevention workshops
- Building away of crime
- Development of a checklist for direction[2]

[1] L. J. Fennelly. 2017. *Effective Physical Security*, Fifth Edition. Butterworth-Heinemann Ltd.

[2] Reference material used for this chapter: S.R.M. Sakip and A. Abdullah. 2012. Measuring crime prevention through environmental design in a gated residential area: A pilot survey. *Procedia—Social and Behavioral Sciences* 42: 340–349.

Chapter 122

CPTED Success: A Blend of Factors

The intent of crime prevention through environmental design (CPTED) is to discourage crime, while at the same time encourage legitimate use of an environment.[1] "The security program [for the building or area] is integrated into the environment, not just added on." Although the concept originated as a result of research to reduce crime in public housing projects, it has applicability to single-family homes, neighborhoods, apartment complexes, public buildings, schools, parks, and recreation areas.[2]

The use of CPTED principles in the planning and design of buildings, office and shopping complexes, and neighborhoods can reduce the creation of problem areas in which the criminal element feels less risk of discovery and possible apprehension. With an atmosphere of safety, persons are more likely to frequent businesses and shops. With repeated presence in an area, an individual's sense of territorial ownership increases, and that individual is more likely to want to protect that area. With increased ownership, the individual's awareness of what is happening and the desire to alert the authorities to the problem increases, and this behavior is vital to the prevention of crime in that area.

But an environment with CPTED design principles does not guarantee an absence of crime and vandalism. To be effective and truly implement the CPTED principles, the design (industrial) factors must be blended with the social (human) factors of the environment. This blend requires the involvement of trained and

[1] M. Krehnke. Crime Prevention through Environmental Design. Retrieved May 2017 from: http://www.infosectoday.com/Article/CPTED.html

[2] R.A. Gardner. Crime Prevention through Environmental Design. http://www.crimewise.com/library/cpted.html

dedicated individuals—a mix of government, neighborhood, and business representatives—from its design through its use. Individuals from very diverse disciplines must come together to design an environment for people to experience life without fear, and improve the quality of life for all individuals—where they live, where they work, and where they play or relax—not just for now but into the future.

Chapter 123

Premises Liability and CPTED

Premises liability cases may offer insights into the application of crime prevention through environmental design (CPTED). It is apparent that judges and juries can appreciate the logic of CPTED and decide in specific cases that the way properties are designed can influence criminal behavior.

Design is usually not a singular cause of a criminal act. Invariably, several factors contributed to the crime: not having a security plan, not being aware of what is happening on the property, not having enough security officers, or not having security officers who are properly recruited and trained. In other words, the crime was driven by a variety of factors, design being just one of them.

When testifying as an expert witness, more and more security professionals are basing their testimony not only on best practices in the industry and traditional security countermeasures, but on CPTED concepts and strategies as well.

Chapter 124

Security Design for Schools

In designing security for schools, architects and facilities committees should include objectives in the educational specifications with descriptions and expectations for providing a safe learning environment. Document the institution's security philosophy, systems approach, and special considerations for operations and management. When designing an education facility, have a security specialist on the design team to help integrate security into architectural, electrical, technology, mechanical, and site elements.

Architects designing secure learning environments incorporate "intuitive" and "active" design:

Intuitive design consists of facility layouts and design standards that promote safety. Visitors approaching a site are guided via architectural and landscape features and other wayfinding means. These security measures include

- A welcoming site entrance with appropriate signage detailing areas for learning and community engagement
- Easily identifiable vehicular and pedestrian pathways to route visitors immediately toward designated areas
- Appropriately designated and ample visitor parking near the main entrance
- A well-marked main entrance to the building
- Labeled entrances to communicate after-hour access

For the perimeter of the building, consider the following:

- Landscaping, which minimizes shadowed areas against the building (low-height shrubs and higher trees)

- Entrances open to view for patrol visibility and camera recording (avoiding wide columns and screen walls)
- Walls of appropriate height with secure gates to prevent access to unsupervised areas (e.g., courtyards, screen wall enclosures at loading docks)
- Entrance doors clustered together instead of numerous, dispersed single doors, which are difficult to supervise
- Glare-controlled, well-lighted areas at window locations
- Fish-eye viewers in windowless exterior doors
- Numbered windows to aid emergency responders

For the building interior, consider the following:

- At main circulation areas, transparent glazing that is visible from the exterior for ease of supervision
- A direct view from administrative areas to the main entrance, and a direct view to the reception area for the visitor
- Controlled access at the main entrance that directs visitors to a reception area for check-in
- Building zoning that enables after-hours community use while securing unused areas
- Staff planning areas with glazing into student areas for supervision during school hours
- Low-height student lockers in commons areas for easy supervision by staff
- Well-maintained door and window hardware, and exterior door latch plates to prevent break-ins
- Numbered doors to aid emergency responders

Active design uses technology and electrical systems for the final measure of providing a secure learning environment. For active site design, provide nonglare, well-lighted approaches, parking lots, and entrances. Consider providing the following "active" features for secure exteriors:

- Cameras at site and building entrances and fenestration
- High-resolution cameras with appropriate recording times
- Interior lighting at glazed main entrance areas with evenly distributed lighting to the exterior
- Card readers at main entrances and other heavy-use areas (staff entrances, receiving areas, playground areas, etc.)
- Card readers in lieu of keyed entries to control key-distribution issues

Consider providing the following for building interiors:

- Cameras situated by building zone to protect users

- Two-way communications from central administration to all rooms
- Cameras for authorities to find an intruder during lockdown
- Panic or duress alarm at the reception desk
- Cameras used as a deterrent to protect property from vandalism
- Walk-through security lighting
- Cameras for evidence documentation
- Radio-frequency communication
- Cameras with adequate recording time and high resolution at appropriate distances
- Generator backup power supply for phones and emergency communications

Secure, Yet Welcoming

Appropriate planning and design can result in life-saving experiences. Make sure administrators and the community define and understand the desired level of security. A place for learning must be both secure and welcoming to its users (metal detectors usually are a distraction). Have a consistent plan for maintaining security equipment operational (a nonoperating camera is a false sense of security, and does more harm than good).

Involve security designers early in the design process to avoid costly reconstruction, which also can affect aesthetics negatively. Uncontrolled entrances and hallways permit security breaches. (Main reception areas and entrance vestibules should be connected.) Zone building areas so that code-required exits can be maintained (zones with double doors swinging in both directions provide no security). An improperly designed area may need to be covered by security cameras that otherwise would not be needed.

Through proper planning, design, and management, a facility and its surrounding site can be a welcoming place, yet be highly secure through intuitive and active strategies that are simple and cost effective. Proper facility management and training for handling daily procedures, visitor sign-in practices, lockdown protocol, and equipment maintenance are keys to comprehensive security solutions. The goal is to provide a safe haven for learning, limit the probability of crime, and promote social control through a variety of measures and design strategies.

Chapter 125

Examples of CPTED Success

Crime prevention through environmental design (CPTED) is a multidisciplinary approach to the reduction of crime and the associated enhancement of the perception of personal safety by inhabitants of an environment.[1] Because of their direct concern for these objectives, law enforcement agencies around the world have embraced these concepts and worked diligently within their communities and the local community resources to implement these principles in ways that are appropriate for their environments. Some cities, such as Federal Way, Washington, have incorporated the CPTED design principles into their city code requirements for project design. Others utilize the concepts to guide businesses and homeowners to assess their environment and its characteristics to reduce opportunities for crime.[2]

In Bridgeport, Connecticut, the Phoenix Project resulted in a 75% decline in crime, the lowest since 1972, by controlling street drug trafficking with the used of CPTED plans that included traffic control devices with one-way street design, increased tactical law enforcement, and mobilization of area businesses and residents.

In Knoxville, Tennessee, police, traffic engineers, public works officials, and residents participated in CPTED training and its implementation to address drug trafficking and excessive vehicle traffic in residential areas. This effort required street redesign, revised park schedules, and volunteer-led security survey teams. Vehicle

---

[1] Mollie Krehnke. Crime Prevention through Environmental Design. From http://www.infosectoday.com/Articles/CPTED.htm

[2] Crime Prevention through Environmental Design (CPTED) Checklist Instructions, Bulletin 21, August 18, 2004, and Crime Prevention through Environmental Design (CPTED) Checklist, Bulletin 22, August 18, 2004, Department of Community Development Services, Federal Way, WA. http://caldoca.webstarts.com/uploads/CPTED_checklist.pdf

cut-through traffic was reduced by 90%, and there is no more drive-through drug trafficking.

In Sarasota, Florida, a successful plan to reduce crime in one neighborhood has resulted in the integration of CPTED principles into the local planning process for all development and redevelopment in that city.

In Cincinnati, Ohio, a CPTED partnership plan with the housing authority management, residents, and police officials has resulted in a 12%–13% decline in crime in the first three successive years after the plan was implemented.[3]

Participants in CPTED Implementation

There are four general groups that use the CPTED concepts: environmental designers (e.g., architects, landscape architects), land managers (e.g., park managers), community action groups (e.g., neighborhood watch groups), and law enforcement groups (e.g., park rangers, metropolitan police). No group alone can successfully implement these principles because each has a unique perspective and knowledge base. The combination of that knowledge into a unified approach is necessary for the creation of an environment that deters crime and creates an environment where persons want to live, work, and shop and feel "ownership" so that they will do their part to ensure its protection.[4] These groups must work with the city planners, commissioners, traffic engineers, and construction managers who must review the designs and implement the planned construction—hopefully in a manner that effectively implements the desired CPTED principles.

Community Benefits

There are definite benefits to the utilization of CPTED principles in a community for municipal leadership (ML), local law enforcement (LLE), and community residents (CR). Following are some of those listed in the *Design Safer Communities Handbook*:

- Improved perception of safety and livability in public areas and neighborhoods (ML)
- More revenue from safer and busier business districts (ML)
- Increased use of public parks and recreation facilities by residents (ML)
- Increased opportunities to develop crime prevention partnerships with residents (LLE)

---

[3] *Designing Safer Communities: A Crime Prevention through Environmental Design Handbook.* Washington, DC: National Crime Prevention Council, pp. 2–3.

[4] Mollie Krehnke. Crime Prevention through Environmental Design. From http://www.infosectoday.com/Articles/CPTED.htm

- Identification of potential crime problems in the community before they become serious (LLE)
- Recognition that crime prevention is everyone's responsibility (LLE)
- Improved sense of security and quality of life through reduced fear of crime (CR)
- Increased interaction among residents and stronger neighborhood bonds (CR)
- New crime prevention and problem-solving skills (CR)
- Enhanced knowledge of city government agencies and other resources (CR)[5]

The implementation of CPTED principles can help support community crime prevention goals. The implementation of the principles, when considered early in the design process for a community, does not increase the costs to residents or business owners. The decision process for the review and acceptance of a project will generally not be lengthened. If CPTED principles conflict with local building and fire codes, then a trained CPTED professional should be consulted to identify suitable alternatives. In some circumstances, the community design groups have worked to modify the local codes for future projects, to incorporate the CPTED principles, and to further enhance the safety and use of environments in that community.

---

[5] *Designing Safer Communities: A Crime Prevention through Environmental Design Handbook.* Washington, DC: National Crime Prevention Council, p. 4.

Chapter 126

CPTED Design and Planning Process

Depending on the scale of the development, there are multiple stages of review and construction that take place. The following is a generic process that reflects key considerations in site design and instruction, and examples of crime prevention through environmental design (CPTED) concerns that should be addressed during each phase.[1]

Predesign

Preapplication Meeting: Some communities require a preapplication meeting to discuss and review the expected land use before the design process begins. Discussions on the location, siting, and design of new or remodeled facilities can reduce the costs of retrofitting a design to address the desired CPTED principles.

CPTED concerns are as follows: Once the design has been established, changes may be limited to those required by law or policy—no matter how useful (from a CPTED viewpoint) they may be. Therefore, CPTED input before the plan is reviewed can save the owner a significant amount of money and time. Such a review is not a standard practice in municipal and corporate developments.

---

[1] M. Krehnke. *Crime Prevention through Environmental Design*. Boca Raton, FL: CRC Press, online May 2017.

Design

Schematic Design: This level of the design presents a list of the requirements regarding the intended uses of the property. This document includes the general site organization, including the building location, parking location, site entrances and exits, and building entrances and exits.

CPTED concerns are as follows: How will the development affect the existing neighborhood and how will the neighborhood affect the security of the development? These relationships will affect later decisions regarding access control measures, surveillance opportunities from various locations on and adjacent to the site, design details, and policies regarding use.

Design Development: This level of design lists the sizes and shapes of buildings, parking, and other site features. Building structural features defined at this time include plumbing, lighting, and communications systems, and door and window types and locations.

CPTED concerns are as follows: What are the design influences with regard to opportunities for crime, particularly the location of "public" and "private" activities, automobile and pedestrian routes, and the use of landscaping to provide places of concealment or reduce surveillance opportunities. Other features that have to be considered are the placement of fences, walls, dumpsters, signs and graphics, and lighting.

Chapter 127

CPTED Construction Documentation

Construction documents for crime prevention through environmental design (CPTED) include the construction drawings and a manual of materials and product specifications.[1] These documents are used to solicit bids for construction services and building materials and products, and to guide the site and building construction and installation of related materials.

CPTED concerns are as follows: This documentation is often overlooked as a source of information that is beneficial in assessing the ability of a site and its buildings to reduce crime. The specifications manual can be useful in identifying problems that could result from the use of certain materials with regard to life expectancy and required maintenance. Breaking and entering, vandalism, and graffiti increase the life costs of such materials by the cost to replace the materials or to repair the damage done to the site in a timely manner, in order to implement the CPTED maintenance principle.

Bidding and Negotiation

During bidding and negotiation, the contractors may request material or product substitutions to reduce cost. Contractors may not understand that the substitutions are not "equivalent" and may negatively impact the CPTED principles that should be addressed.

---

[1] M. Krehnke. *Crime Prevention through Environmental Design.* Boca Raton, FL: CRC Press, online May 2017. http://www.infosectoday.com/Articles/CPTED.htm

CPTED concerns are as follows: The substitutions can "appear" to be beneficial to the client but significantly reduce the ability of the resulting environment to reduce crime. Examples of CPTED desirable materials are graffiti-resistant materials on walls and other surfaces, the use of constant (rather than average) lighting standards for pedestrians in designated areas, and the use of landscaping materials that only grow to a certain height or can easily be maintained for ease of surveillance by persons in the area.

Construction

Observation of the construction activities throughout the construction process is vital to the success of the design to ensure that the design is true to the plan and the specified materials are used in the construction process.

CPTED concerns are as follows: Unauthorized substitutions in materials may be contrary to the CPTED principle to be implemented in the design.

Site Use—After Construction

The way that the property will be used when it is completed is as vital to the prevention of crime as its design, including the hours of activity and scheduling, assignment of space, property maintenance, and disciplinary code for violators.

CPTED concerns are as follows: The implementation of CPTED principles by property owners, managers, and residents is necessary to the deterrence of crime and the sense of safety for the residents.

CPTED Guidelines for Various Environments

The Department of Community Development Services in Federal Way, Washington, has created a CPTED Checklist to assist the designer of a proposed project in implementing the CPTED principles that are identified in the Federal Way City Code (FWCC) Section 22–1630.[2] The checklist states the functional area performance standards by topic area, indicating whether the standard is applicable during the Site Plan Review or during the Building Permit Review; possible strategies for implementation of that principle include a write-in section and provide a column for the results of the agency analysis, including whether the design conforms, requires revision, or is not applicable. The topic areas for natural surveillance include blind corners, site and building layout for non-single-

---

[2] City of Federal Way. Crime Prevention through Environmental Design (CPTED) Checklist Instructions. http://caldoca.webstarts.com/uploads/CPTED_checklist.pdf

family development, commercial/retail/industrial and community facilities, surface parking and parking structures, common/open space areas, entrances, fencing, landscaping, exterior lighting, mix of uses, and security bars/shutters/doors. The topic areas for access control include building identification, entrances, landscaping, landscaping location, security, and signage. The topic areas for ownership are maintenance and materials.[3]

---

[3] City of Mesa. *Crime Prevention*. 2018. Crime Prevention through Environmental Design PDF. http://www.mesaaz.gov/home/showdocument?id=4536. Referenced from http://www.mesaaz. gov/residents/police/divisions/crime-prevention

Chapter 128

Two Important CPTED Concepts

The following text presents two important crime prevention through environmental design (CPTED) concepts.[1]

Activity Support

Activity support involves both passive and active efforts to promote the presence of responsible pedestrian users in a given area, thus increasing the community value of the area, while discouraging actions by would-be offenders who desire anonymity for their actions. Passive examples are design elements that make an area appealing to appropriate pedestrian use, such as attractive landscaping, safety from car traffic, and public art. Active examples involve scheduling events for an area to attract appropriate users, such as picnics, concerts, children's play groups, or sports events.

Management and Maintenance

Proper maintenance of landscaping, lighting, and other features is vital to ensuring that CPTED elements serve their intended purpose. Unfortunately, failure to maintain property—and its management parallel, the failure to stop harmful use of property—will rapidly undermine the impact of even the best CPTED

---

[1] City of Portland. Crime Prevention through Environmental Design. https://www. portlandoregon.gov/oni/article/320548

design elements. While CPTED principles supplement effective maintenance and management practices, they cannot make up for the negative impacts of ineffective management. Damaged fencing, overgrown hedges, graffiti left to weather and age, litter and debris, broken windows, as well as such factors as inattentive or overly permissive management practices will attract would-be offenders and, equally, drive away responsible users of the space. While effective design is an important part of good crime prevention, following through with consistent maintenance and management practices ensures that the designed-in elements keep their effectiveness. For CPTED principles to accomplish the goals of enhanced livability and better natural safety, each principle must work together with the others. For example, activity support can be undermined if a property is stripped bare of landscaping in the interests of natural surveillance alone. Installing a tall opaque wall or fence will take the concept of territoriality too far by undermining natural surveillance benefits. Access control solutions that are aggressive in appearance (such as window bars, harsh lighting treatments, or hostile-looking fencing) can undermine activity support. The intent, therefore, is to use the combined balance of these principles to promote a safer, more livable environment for all.[2]

---

[2] City of Portland. Crime Prevention through Environmental Design. https://www.portlandoregon.gov/oni/article/320548

Chapter 129

Effectiveness and Criticism of CPTED

Crime prevention through environmental design (CPTED) strategies are most successful when they inconvenience the end user the least and when the CPTED design process relies on the combined efforts of environmental designers, land managers, community activists, and law enforcement professionals.[1]

In terms of effectiveness, a more accurate title for the strategy would be crime deterrence through environmental design. Research demonstrates that offenders cannot be literally prevented from committing crimes by using CPTED.

CPTED relies on changes to the physical environment that will cause an offender to make certain behavioral decisions. Those changes are crafted so as to encourage behavior, and thus they deter rather than conclusively "prevent" behavior.

Beyond the attraction of being cost effective in lowering the incidence of crime, CPTED typically reduces the overall costs of preventing crime. Retrofitting an existing environment to meet CPTED can sometimes be costly, but when incorporated in the original design phase of facility planning, cost of designing to CPTED principles are often lower than with traditional approaches. Operational costs are often lower also, as CPTED lighting designs can significantly lower energy use. Adding to the attraction of CPTED is that it lowers liability.

The area of liability has led to the questioning of how much crime prevention is really necessary for a given place. It has been mooted that a risk management approach might be superior to a fear-driven one. The question is, "does a community

---

[1] Crime Prevention through Environmental Design. https://en.wikipedia.org/wiki/Crime_Prevention_through_environmental_design

give up too much freedom, usually in terms of movement and assembly, to be free from fear of crime?"[2]

This was a question that was not widely asked in the 1990s; note the rise around the world of gated communities and the use of closed-circuit television (CCTV) in public spaces.

---

[2] Talk: Crime Prevention through Environmental Design. https://en.wikipedia.org/wiki/Talk:Crime_Prevention_through_environmental_design

Chapter 130

Four Obstacles to Adopting CPTED

There are four primary obstacles to the adoption of crime prevention through environmental design (CPTED).[1]

First is a lack of knowledge of CPTED by environmental designers, land managers, and individual community members. For this reason, allocating substantial resources to community educational programs is often required.

The second major obstacle is resistance to change. Many specifically resist the type of cooperative planning that is required to use CPTED. Beyond that, skeptics reject the research and historic precedents that support the validity of CPTED concepts.

The third obstacle is the perception that CPTED claims to be a panacea for crime that will be used to displace other more traditional approaches rather than a small, but important, complementary tool in deterring offender behavior.

The fourth obstacle is that many existing built areas were not designed with CPTED in mind, and modification would be expensive, politically difficult, or require significant changes in some areas of the existing built environment.

[1] P. Cozens and T. Love. Crime Prevention through Environmental Design (CPTED), Subject: Prevention/Public Policy. March 2017. Referenced from http://criminology.oxfordre.com/view/10.1093/acrefore/9780190264079.001.0001/acrefore-9780190264079-e-2

Chapter 131

Perceptions and Feelings of Safety

Sometimes the perception of a lack of security can make people avoid using public transportation.[1] In bigger cities, especially, older people avoid using public transport after dark. They might feel vulnerable about passing groups on the street or at isolated stations or bus and tram stops. They might consider themselves easy targets for pickpockets and other petty criminals. Some older people have no qualms with using public transport at all, while some younger people might have the same fears as some older people often have. And of course, there are parents who are not too keen for their children to use public transport, especially at night.

Perception of safety is not based only on gender or age, but also one's own behavior. One design that fits all is utopic. Society is changing and developing all the time, and areas that are new today are subject to reconstruction tomorrow. Areas with mainly young families change over the years into areas full of older people. This means that we need to stay focused on the changes and adjust. Together with the community, we can establish the most safe and secure environment possible.

Elements That Influence a Person's Perception of Security in a Public Space

- Clear purpose of the area with adequate references
- Sight lines with no obstacles

---

[1] UITP. Design Out Crime to Increase Feelings of Safety. http://www.uitp.org/design-out-crime-increase-feelings-safety

- Transparency with no obstacles
- Art and decoration
- Use of transparent materials
- Use and color of material
- Social interaction, not only at platforms or in stations but also outside
- Natural boundaries (guiding lines on the street, flowerbeds, illuminated routes, etc.)
- Natural illumination, low intensity and color to avoid dramatic contrast with light and dark
- Use of music or fragrance (though fragrance can be controversial)
- Natural associations to engender desired behavior (e.g., people in a library usually silent)
- Mirrors to activate self-image (you do not want to see yourself throwing your litter or cigarette away)

Elements of Design That Make Users Feel Unsafe

- Dark, hidden places
- Large obstacles that obstruct sight lines and transparency
- Dark, solid materials like concrete
- Bad or absent illumination
- Easily accessible walls for graffiti
- Absence of litter bins without communicating you are not allowed to eat, drink, and so on
- Possibilities for youth to hang around
- Nonrepaired acts of vandalism

Chapter 132

Suspicious Behavior

There are many ways in which you play a role in security at your workplace. Watch people's behavior and what they tell you or even ask you. While at work, being aware of your surroundings is important. If you notice anything suspicious, like someone taking pictures, anyone sneaking around with unusual behavior, or even something that just does not look right, tell security. It is always your right and responsibility to move away from, or leave your immediate area if you feel uncomfortable or something seems wrong, and report it. If you feel that a co-worker is having personal problems that may become a security issue if the problem is not addressed, we strongly encourage you to help by telling a manager. You need to report any information that raises doubt as to whether another employees' continued eligibility for access to classified information might be compromised by their behavior.

Some behaviors that could be viewed as suspicious are as follows:

- Someone taking unusual interest in the office building, parking lot, or a surrounding area
- Unusual requests for information
- Suspicious activity by unauthorized persons
- Suspicious activities regarding documents
- Someone running from a car or building

What Is Suspicious Activity?

A total stranger entering your neighborhood or your neighbor's home while your neighbor is away or someone crossing your or your neighbor's yard for no apparent lawful reason is suspicious activity. If you observe this same person trying to open your neighbor's door, this is suspicious behavior. If you see a moving truck pull into your neighbor's driveway while the neighbor is away, this is suspicious behavior. Keep in mind that burglaries occur 24/7/365, and not just at night. It may look less suspicious during broad daylight, in full view of observers, but that is when most residential burglaries occur.

Let's take the case of a suspicious person who enters your workplace and is stopped at the front desk. The person then asks to use the bathroom. If this person gets by the front desk, he or she is inside the complex.

If there is a door-to-door solicitor without proper identification, that is a suspicious person.

You have to use your senses in many of these cases. Breaking glass, for example, could be a signal of a possible burglary, vandalism, or larceny in progress. Screams, yelling, loud noises, a fight, an armed robbery, a life-threatening event—again your senses telling you, *we have a problem.*

An improperly parked car, an abandoned vehicle, a stolen car with the dashboard broken, combined with screaming, may be a sign someone is being forced into a vehicle.

Call the Police, 9-1-1

Successful efforts to combat crime require a community working closely with law enforcement. Today just about everyone has a cell phone. The police cannot be everywhere, so success against crime is dependent on the community being involved with a safe and secure environment. Crime can be reduced when the community is alert to suspicious activity and law enforcement is notified.

New Jersey Bomber, 2016

Lee Parker was homeless and digging through trash, but thanks to a startling discovery, he now has a home and job prospects lined up. Parker and Ivan White are being hailed as heroes after they found a bag full of pipe bombs at the Elizabeth Train Station, moved the bag away from people, and alerted authorities.

The two men may have saved lives. Their discovery was made on the same weekend bombs went off in Manhattan's Chelsea neighborhood and Seaside Heights, New Jersey.[1]

This should remind you of the Department of Homeland Security's *If You See Something, Say Something* initiative.

Neighborhood Watch programs are specifically designed to prevent, detect, and report criminal activity and leave the enforcement action always to the police.

---

[1] Homeless 'Hero' who found bombs at New Jersey train station gets a home, money. NEWS, September 26, 2016 - Maya Chung. Referenced from http://www.insideedition.com/headlines/18892-homeless-hero-who-found-bombs-at-new-jersey-train-station-gets-a-home-money

Chapter 133

Crime and Effective Community Crime Prevention Strategies

Community crime prevention programs or strategies target changes in community infrastructure, culture, or the physical environment in order to reduce crime.[1] The diversity of approaches includes Neighborhood Watch, community policing, urban or physical design, and comprehensive or multidisciplinary efforts. These strategies may seek to engage residents, community and faith-based organizations, and local government agencies in addressing the factors that contribute to the community's crime, delinquency, and disorder.

1. *Alley-gating* involves placing durable, lockable gates to restrict access of an alley to local residents with the aim of reducing opportunities for potential offenders. *The program is rated Effective.* The analysis found that the greater the "intensity" of the intervention (i.e., the number of gates fitted, blocks protected, or houses protected), the larger was the reduction in burglary, and spatial diffusion was observed in four out of seven buffer zones along with some tactical displacement.

2. A program designed to *reduce repeat victimization* in domestic burglary and thefts from cars. *The program is rated Effective.* There was a greater decrease in recorded and repeat crime than the surrounding areas. There was an increase in satisfaction with police services and no evidence of displaced crime.

---

[1] National Institute of Justice. CrimeSolutions.gov. Crime and Crime Prevention. https://www.crimesolutions.gov/TopicDetails.aspx?ID=10

3. *Engine immobilizers are devices that prevent a vehicle from starting* unless they receive the correct signal from the driver. The goal of these systems is to reduce car theft. *The program is rated Effective.* Cars fitted with immobilizers reduced rates of theft compared with cars not fitted with the device.

4. A problem-oriented policing program that aims to eliminate *overt drug markets* and the problems associated with them through a deterrence-based, pulling-levers framework. *The program is rated Effective.* The intervention had a statistically significant impact on reducing violent incidents in the target areas.

5. *Public surveillance systems* include a network of cameras and components for monitoring, recording, and transmitting video images. The ultimate goal of installing public surveillance cameras is to reduce both property and personal crime. The practice was rated *Promising* for reducing overall crime and property offenses (i.e., vehicle crimes) but rated *No Effects* on impacting violent crime.

6. *Problem-oriented policing strategies* that follow the core principles of deterrence theory. *The practice is rated Promising.* The evaluation found that focused deterrence strategies (also referred to as "pulling levers" policing) can reduce crime.

7. A crime prevention strategy that aims to improve the *lighting on streets* to reduce crime through modifying and improving environmental measures. *The practice is rated Promising* for reducing crime and property offenses, but rated *No Effects* for violent offenses.

8. Also known as *Block Watch, Apartment Watch, Home Watch, and Community Watch*, these programs involve citizens trying to prevent crime in their neighborhood or community. Citizens remain alert for suspicious activities and report those activities to the police. *The practice is rated Promising* in reducing crime in the control area compared to the experimental area, and rated *No Effects* in reducing victimization.

9. These *analytic methods* are used by police to develop crime prevention and reduction strategies. *The practice is rated Promising* and led to a significant decline in crime and disorder.

10. *Reducing gun violence* is a persistent public policy concern for communities, policymakers, and leaders. To reduce gun violence, several strategies have been deployed including public health approaches (e.g., training and safe gun storage); gun buy-back programs; gun laws; and law enforcement strategies. *The practice is rated Promising* for reducing violent gun offenses.

11. *Sobriety checkpoints* are police operations that aim to reduce the number of alcohol-related car crashes by preventing people from driving under the influence of alcohol and other substances. Driving under the influence (DUI) is prevented by increasing the perceived and actual risk of detection and apprehension by the police. *The practice is rated Promising* for reducing the number of car crashes.

12. This practice includes *targeted-policing approaches* for reducing drug and drug-related offenses. *This practice is rated Promising* in reducing reported, drug-related calls for services and offenses against persons. *This practice is rated No Effects* in reducing reported property offenses, public order calls for service, and total offenses.

13. *Juvenile curfew laws* are designed to restrict juveniles (below ages 17 or 18) from public places during specific hours such as nighttime (e.g., between 11 p.m. and 6 a.m.) or during the school day (e.g., 8:30 a.m. to 1:30 p.m.). The primary purpose is to reduce juvenile crime and victimization by keeping them at home with their families or in school. *This practice is rated No Effects* for reducing juvenile crime during curfew hours.

Chapter 134

Displacement of Crime and Diffusion of Crime

Crime displacement is the relocation of crime from one place, time, target, offense, or tactic to another as a result of some crime prevention initiative.

The possible forms of displacement are as follows:[1]

Temporal—offenders change the time at which they commit crime;

Spatial—offenders switch from targets in one location to targets in another location;

Target—offenders change from one type of target to another;

Tactical—offenders alter the methods used to carry out crime;

Offense—offenders switch from one form of crime to another.

Crime diffusion entails the reduction of crime in areas or ways that are related to the targeted crime prevention efforts, but not targeted by the response itself. Diffusion effects are referred to as the "bonus effect," the "halo effect," the "free-rider effect," and the "multiplier effect."[2]

As with displacement, diffusion of benefits can occur in many forms. Spatial and target diffusion occurs when areas or other crime targets near the intervention zone also experience a reduction in crime. Temporal diffusion occurs when other time periods experience a reduction in crime even though the intervention was not applied during those times.

---

[1] Analyzing Crime Displacement and Diffusion. Center for Problem-Oriented Policing. Retrieved on June 12, 2017, from: http://www.popcenter.org/tools/displacement

[2] Analyzing Crime Displacement and Diffusion. Center for Problem-Oriented Policing. Retrieved on June 12, 2017, from: http://www.popcenter.org/tools/displacement

If crime will simply move around the corner in response to targeted police interventions at "hot spots," there is little reason for carrying out hot-spots policing programs. This idea that the police cannot reduce crime but can only push it to other areas has traditionally been an objection to focusing intervention programs on high crime places.[3] The research evidence regarding displacement as a result of focused policing interventions in contrast suggests overall that threats of displacement are overstated.[4] Indeed, studies to date have been more likely to identify a "diffusion of crime control benefits"[5] around targeted areas than evidence of displacement. In a number of studies, an unanticipated crime decline has been found in untargeted areas surrounding intervention sites.[6]

Over the years, we have read quite a bit of material from many criminologists, but we find we disagree with many of them when it comes to displacement of crime. Ask a security practitioner or someone in law enforcement if crime displacement works, and they will tell you, "Yes, it does." Many times, it does not just move around the corner; in many cases it totally disappears and goes away. Consider the victims, and the increase in the fear of crime. If an apprehension cannot be made, then by all means displacement and diffusion of the "hot spots" is in order. This is a proactive approach.

[3] T.A. Reppetto. 1976. Crime prevention and the displacement phenomenon. *Crime and Delinquency* 22(2): 166–177. https://www.ncjrs.gov/App/Publications/abstract.aspx?ID=32897

[4] A.A. Braga. 2008. *Problem-Oriented Policing and Crime Prevention* (2nd ed.). Lynne Rienner Publishers. http://www.rienner.com/title/Problem_Oriented_Policing_and_Crime_Prevention_2nd_edition

[5] R.V. Clarke and D. Weisburd. 1994. Diffusion of crime control benefits: Observations on the reverse of displacement. In R.V. Clarke (Ed.), *Crime Prevention Studies* (Vol. 2). Monsey, NY: Criminal Justice Press, pp. 165–182.

[6] D. Weisburd et al. 2010. *The Police Foundation Displacement and Diffusion Study.* https://www.scribd.com/document/111422217/Weisburd-Et-Al-2010-The-Police-Foundation-Displacement-and-Diffusion-Study

Chapter 135

Crime Prevention: Watching Out, Helping Out

Crime and fear of crime remain major problems, and statistics do not tell the whole story.[1] According to the 2016 FBI Uniform Crime Reports and Census Bureau's victimization surveys, Part I crimes have decreased slightly, but the level is still unacceptable. Each individual crime hurts us all—our neighborhoods, schools, children, and businesses. All who are harmed by crime become possible resources for combating it.

Business can become an active partner, helping you take positive action to reduce crime and develop a safer community in which to live and work. Stable communities allow business to prosper, and businesses know it. Let business executives know that crime prevention is not a "them and us" but a "we" situation. When they recognize that their involvement can be visibly productive, they will join you. It is important to demonstrate your willingness to assist them in their efforts and just ask for money, printing, or other services for your program. When people assume responsibility for getting the job done in partnership, they tend to come through.

Businesses are concerned with at least three kinds of crime victimization:

- Thefts of the company assets—fraud, embezzlement, and shoplifting
- Crimes against them and employees at the work-site—armed robbery, arson, vandalism of equipment, and so on

---

[1] L. Bickman, M.D. Maltz, and P.J. Lavrakas. 1977. *Evaluation of Crime Prevention through Environmental Design Programs.* https://www.ncjrs.gov/App/Publications/abstract. aspx?ID=50378

■ Street crimes—assault, burglary, and robbery—that have produced overlooked effects on the victim, his or her family, or his or her work

Any business or individual who thinks there is no percentage in community crime prevention or who thinks such programs are good only for public relations and have no real effect on people and profits, should be acquainted with the following facts by police managers:

■ A prime factor in making business decisions such as expansion, relocation, reduction, or discontinuing operations is the perceived quality of life in site localities. Crime is one of the major determinants of quality of life (Joint Economic Committee of the U.S, Congress, 2016).[2]
■ Most employees feel safe at their workplace, but getting to and from work can be dangerous. One study showed that the prime crime hours are those during which most employees are away from the work-site and therefore more vulnerable (Bell of Pennsylvania, 2015).[3]
■ About one-third of all households in this country have been victimized by crime annually in the past several years. One study shows that more than half the victims are employed (Criminal Victimization in the U.S. Government Printing Office, 2016).[4]
■ Workers, as a group, have a high probability of victimization because victimization rates for major crimes are highest in the center city and suburban areas from which businesses draw most of their employees (Crime Victimization in the U.S., 2016).[5]
■ Laborers have the highest rate of victimization by violent crime of any occupational group. Professional/technical workers have the highest rate of theft. Service workers follow close behind for both violent crime and theft. The higher the level of education, the more likely a person is to be the victim of property crime (Criminal Victimization in the U.S., 2016).[6]
■ When people become crime victims, the fear of crime can be debilitating—especially if the work-site is located in a high crime environment. Turnover

---

[2] The 2016 Joint Economic Report. Report of the Joint Economic Committee Congress of the United States on the 2016 Economic Report of the President. Referenced from https://www.jec.senate.gov/public/_cache/files/0db793da-5e90-4f9d-ad9e-487f28652c7a/3-2-2016-joint-economic-report-w-minority-views-final.pdf

[3] Roy Maurer. Survey: Most employees feel secure at work - But 1 in 4 are unsure how they would protect themselves in an emergency. June 19, 2015. Referenced from https://www.shrm.org/resourcesandtools/hr-topics/risk-management/pages/survey-employees-feel-secure-work.aspx

[4] R. E. Morgan and G. Kena. December 2017. Criminal Victimization, 2016. U.S. Department of Justice, Office of Justice Programs, Bureau of Justice Statistics. NCJ 251150. Referenced from https://www.bjs.gov/content/pub/pdf/cv16.pdf

[5] Ibid.

[6] Ibid.

increases, workers become reluctant to work overtime at certain locations, and productivity declines (Dr. Georgette Bennett, Bennett Center for Policy Research, New York, 1982).[7]

■ Recruitment of quality executives is more difficult if the company is located in places where the crime rate is perceived to be high (Dr. Georgette Bennett, Center for Policy Research, New York, 1982).[8]

A variety of program possibilities exist both for working with the community and for employee education. The contact person at the business should be the chief executive officer, but it is important to note that the initial contact should be coordinated through the security director of the business if there is one. Businesses located in core city areas with a majority of female employees who use mass transit face much different crime concerns than those with a workforce located in a suburban area. They must analyze the nature breadth and impact of crime in the community on their business, but their responses will certainly differ. At this point, law enforcement can provide suggestions for action, utilizing crime analysis and crime prevention techniques.

---

[7] National Institute of Justice. Practice Profile: Neighborhood Watch. Referenced from https://www.crimesolutions.gov/PracticeDetails.aspx?ID=13

[8] Ibid.

Chapter 136

CPTED Strategies: Prince William County, Virginia

The Neighborhood Watch Program is designed to reduce crime and enhance the quality of life.[1] The concept is simple: it involves cooperation between the police department and the community where the residents become the "eyes and ears" of the police department. The program has many benefits:

- Creates a greater awareness of crime
- Increased support from the police department
- Greater community pride
- Brings neighbors closer together
- Potential increased property value
- Crime prevention training
- Increases reporting of crime and suspicious activities
- Sign serves as a warning to criminals
- Provides residents with access to crime patterns and trends that may affect them
- Home security inspections
- Gives residents a contact within the police department
- Results in a better and safer community

---

[1] CPTED Strategies. Prince William County Police Department. Retrieved on June 12, 2017, from: http://www.pwcgov.org/government/dept/police/documents/002035.pdf

Business Watch

Business Watch is one of the most effective and inexpensive ways to prevent crime and reduce fear. Business Watch fights the isolation that crime creates and feeds on. It creates bonds among area businesses and helps reduce burglaries, robberies, and vandalism. It also increases the knowledge of frauds and scams, which improves the relationship between the police and the business community.

Benefits of Business Watch include the following:

- Creates a greater awareness of crime
- Greater community pride
- Brings businesses together
- Crime prevention training
- Sign serves as a warning to criminals
- Provides business owners with access to crime patterns and trends that may threaten them
- Business security inspections
- Results in a better and safer community

Worship Watch

The purpose of the Worship Watch program is to involve members of a church, synagogue, mosque, or temple, with the police department and the surrounding community in working together to create and maintain a safe environment by utilizing accepted crime prevention practices.

Fleet Watch

This is a program that uses businesses with mobile communication capabilities. Employees of the businesses are trained by the police department to report suspicious or dangerous activity. This program enhances the safety of the community by putting hundreds of extra "eyes" on the streets.

Chapter 137

Street Safety

Landscaping, lighting, natural surveillance, and territoriality can all play a part in safety while on urban or rural streets.[1]

Street Safety Tips:

- Be aware of your surroundings at all times and trust your instincts. If you think you are in an area you should not be, you probably are.
- Know where you're going and the safest way to get there, particularly when moving about the city during hours of darkness. Walk/run in well-traveled, well-lit areas avoiding short cuts through alleys and parking lots.
- Have a plan of action in mind. Decide where you would go and what you would do should some dangerous situation occur. Know where the nearest police/fire station is located, how to contact the police in the event of an emergency, what establishments are open late where you could seek refuge if needed, etc.
- Walk with confidence on the street and at a good, steady pace. Keep your head up, observe your surroundings, and don't look down at the ground.
- Carry a whistle or similar type of noisemaker. In the event of an emergency, the sound may scare off a would-be attacker.
- Take special care when jogging or biking. Vary your route, go with a friend, and avoid isolated areas.
- Do NOT wear headphones or listen to music. These can distract you from being aware of your surroundings and who may be approaching you.

---

[1] City of Cambridge, MA. Street Safety. Permission obtained to reproduce. Retrieved on June 12, 2017, from: https://www.cambridgema.gov/cpd/communityresources/CrimePrevention/streetsafety

- Keep purses and packages tucked securely between your arms and body. Don't overload yourself with packages and bags—it is distracting and it can make you look defenseless.
- Carry only what you need. Don't carry a large amount of cash or numerous credit cards and avoid wearing flashy and excessive amounts of jewelry.
- Exercise caution when using ATM machines. Only use ATMs located in well lit, well trafficked areas those physically located in stores are the safest.

If You Are Being Followed:

- Show you are suspicious and turn to look at the person. It sends a clear message that you will not be taken by surprise.
- Change directions. If someone is following you on foot, cross the street and vary your pace. If the person following you is in a car, turn and walk in the opposite direction.
- Go into the nearest store or public place. If the person follows you, ask to use (or find) a phone and call for help. If there isn't a store or public area nearby, keep moving. If you have to scream (or blow your whistle) to draw attention to your situation, do it.

If You Are Robbed:

- DO NOT RESIST, especially if you know or believe the robber to be armed. The best course of action is to hand over money and whatever other belongings are demanded as quickly as possible and try to disengage from this confrontational, and potentially dangerous. Remember, belongings can always be replaced, but you cannot.
- Try to remain calm. Note the robber's appearance and report the crime immediately to the police.

Chapter 138

Safety While Using an Automatic Teller Machine

Because of the variety of automatic teller machines (ATMs), the unique characteristics of each installation, and crime considerations at each location, no single formula can guarantee the security of ATM customers.[1] Therefore, it is necessary for ATM customers to consider the environment around each ATM and various procedures for remaining safe when using an ATM.

Criminals select their victims and targets, focusing on the unaware or unprepared. Criminals are also drawn to environmental conditions that enhance the opportunity to successfully complete their crime. The attitude and demeanor you convey can have a tremendous effect on potential assailants. There are a number of things you can do to increase your personal security and reduce your risk of becoming an ATM crime victim.

The following crime prevention tips can help make the use of ATMs safer for everyone:

- Walk purposefully and with confidence. Give the appearance that you are totally aware of your surroundings.
- Be aware of your environment and what is going on around you. Criminals tend to avoid people who have this type of demeanor.
- Perform mental exercises and plan out what you would do in different crime or personal security situations.
- Follow your instincts. If you feel you are in danger, respond immediately. Remember that your personal safety is the top priority.

---

[1] City of Cambridge, MA. ATM Safety. Retrieved on June 6, 2017, from: https://www.cambridgema.gov/cpd/communityresources/CrimePrevention/atmsafety

ATM selection considerations:

The law sets minimum standards for ATM lighting, procedures for evaluating the safety of ATMs and requires notices to ATM users outlining basic safety precautions for using ATMs. Although ATM environmental design issues are covered in the law, there are other considerations that an ATM customer needs to consider prior to selecting and using an ATM, for example:

■ Select an ATM that is in a well-lit, well-traveled location.
■ Whenever possible, select an ATM that is monitored or patrolled by a security officer.

Considerations prior to/during transactions:

■ Always watch for suspicious persons or activity around an ATM. Be aware of anyone sitting in a parked car in close proximity to or at a distance from the ATM location.
■ If you notice anything strange, leave and return some other time. Even if you have already started a transaction, cancel it and leave.
■ Maintain a small supply of deposit envelopes at home, in your car or office. Prepare all transaction paperwork prior to your arrival at the ATM site. This will minimize the amount of time spent at the ATM.
■ Maintain an awareness of your surroundings throughout the entire transaction. Do not become so involved with your transaction that you are not aware of changing conditions in the area
■ Do not wear expensive jewelry or take other valuables to the ATM. This is an added incentive to an assailant.
■ If you get cash—put it away right immediately. Do not stand at the ATM and count it.
■ Never accept offers of assistance with the ATM from strangers; ask the bank for help.
■ Never lend your ATM card to anyone; treat it as if were cash or a credit card.
■ If you use a drive-up ATM, ascertain your vehicle doors and windows are locked.
■ During evening hours consider taking a companion along, park close to the ATM in a well-lighted area, and lock your car. If the lights around the ATM are not working properly, do not use it.
■ When leaving an ATM location, make sure you are not being followed. If you are being followed, drive immediately to a police, sheriff, or fire station, crowded area, well-lighted location, or open business. Flash your lights and sound your horn to bring attention to your situation.
■ If you are involved in a confrontation and the attacker is armed with a weapon and demands your money or valuables, GIVE IT TO THE SUSPECT. Do not resist, property may be recovered later or replaced.

Chapter 139

Space Management and Design

Space Management

Space management is linked to the principle of territorial reinforcement. It ensures that space is well used and maintained, and involves the formal supervision, control, and care of urban space. Space management strategies are an important means of generating and maintaining activity, surveillance, and natural community control. Strategies include activity coordination, site cleanliness, rapid repair of vandalism and graffiti, and the refurbishment of decayed physical elements.[1]

Design

Facilitate any existing community and stakeholder participation in the design process. This may involve but is not limited to the following:

- Developer
- Design architects or design team
- Local planning authority
- Community members

---

[1] Lake Macquarie City Council. Crime Prevention through Environmental Design (CPTED) Guideline. Referenced from https://www.lakemac.com.au/downloads/AA1A6F5091D28E8C8A207576313D37A2876FAAD2.pdf

Ensure that the crime prevention through environmental design (CPTED) strategy is carried through from the planning phase to the design phase and the microlevel of pathway design, lighting, signage, and so on.[2]

Healthy Space

We were fascinated by a recent article in *Building* magazine (May 2017) titled "Boost productivity with healthy space." Here are some brief quotes from this article[3]:

1. Showers are an important component of exercise space.
2. Know your company's culture.
3. Instead of vending machines, healthy snacks are available.
4. Green walls, moss walls, and other interior plantscaping encourage occupant health and are in the design budget.
5. Consider a living wall or a selection of trees, plants, or flowers in place of artwork. Also referred to as a living wall.
6. Game rooms, indoor soccer, and fun space.
7. Scooters and scooter racks, because many employees bike to work—another reason for a shower facility.

The proper use of both natural light from open space window design and ceiling light, plus the use of color schemes, combined with modern furniture and polished floors all give you that ambiance for healthy space.

---

[2] Lake Macquarie City Council. Crime Prevention through Environmental Design (CPTED) Guideline. Referenced from https://www.lakemac.com.au/downloads/AA1A6F5091D28E8C8A207576313D37A2876FAAD2.pdf

[3] J. Feit and J. Penny, Renovate offices to revitalize occupants. *Buildings, Smarter Facility Management.* April 28, 2017. Referenced from https://www.buildings.com/article-details/articleid/21099/title/energetic-interiors-that-don-t-break-the-bank/viewall/true

Chapter 140

Crime Prevention through Environmental Design

Crime prevention through environmental design (CPTED) is a crime prevention strategy that outlines how physical environments can be designed in order to lessen the opportunity for crime.[1]

This is achieved by creating environmental and social conditions that

- Maximize risk to offenders (increasing the likelihood of detection, challenge, and apprehension)
- Maximize the effort required to commit crime (increasing the time, energy, and resources required to commit crime)
- Minimize the actual and perceived benefits of crime (removing, minimizing, or concealing crime attractions and rewards)
- Minimize excuse-making opportunities (removing conditions that encourage/facilitate rationalization of inappropriate behavior)

The CPTED guidelines consider design and use, identify which aspects of the physical environment affect the behavior of people, and then uses these factors to allow for the most productive use of space while reducing the opportunity of crime. This might include changes to poor environmental design such as street lighting and landscaping.

CPTED concepts and principles are ideally incorporated at the design stage of a development but can also be applied to existing developments and areas where crime and safety are a concern.

---

[1] Queensland Police. Crime Prevention through Environmental Design. https://www.police.qld.gov.au/programs/cscp/safetyPublic/

Chapter 141

The 10 Principles of Crime Prevention

The following principles can assist you in reducing the opportunity for crime to occur at your home, your place of work, or your business.[1] They can be considered for development and implementation by individuals, communities, partners, or businesses and act as a checklist to see what steps you may be able to take for your own particular circumstances. It is not a case of having to use all of the 10 principles at once; you may find using just one of them could help you or it may be a combination of several of them to be added to your overall master plan.

The 10 Principles of Crime Prevention

1. Target Hardening
   This basically refers to making something harder for an offender to access and making it more resistant to approaches made by offenders. You do not want your complex to be a soft target. This could be
   a. Upgrading the locks on your doors or windows
   b. Replacing ineffective doors or windows if they are particularly weak or the frames are in a poor state of repair
   c. Fitting sash jammers to doors or windows, adding peepholes in doors
   d. Ensuring that outbuildings are all secure
   e. Installing LED lighting for return on investment

---

[1] West Yorkshire Police. The 10 Principles of Crime Prevention. https://www.westyorkshire. police.uk/help-advice/what-crime-prevention/10-principles-crime-prevention

    f. Prevent double-hung windows from opening more than 5 inches

    g. Solar lighting and/or solar cameras

2. Target Removal

This principle can be cost free in most cases and is all about ensuring that a potential target for an offender is out of view, so as not to attract their attention in the first place. This could be

    a. Not leaving items in an unoccupied vehicle

    b. Putting your vehicle in the garage if you have one

    c. Ensuring that you do not leave attractive items on view through your kitchen window (i.e., laptops, cell phones, keys, bags)

    d. Not leaving attractive objects such as game consoles, iPads, collectibles, or antiques on full view in downstairs rooms

3. Removing the Means to Commit Crime and Reduce Opportunity

As with Target Removal, this principle can also be relatively cost free and relates to ensuring that items are not accessible to offenders that may help them commit an offense. This could be

    a. Not leaving garden tools out once you have finished with them

    b. Ensuring that ladders are not left in an accessible position

    c. Keeping wheelie bins out of reach from an offender, as they may be a climbing aid or used to transport items away from a scene

    d. Making sure that bricks or rubble are cleared up

    e. Through maintenance creates a positive image

4. Reducing the Pay-Off

An offender will want to maximize the amount gained from taking the risk of committing an offense and there are ways to reduce their potential pay-off. This could be

    a. Security marking your property

    b. The use of a domestic safe to secure valuable or sentimental items

    c. Using dummy stock in shop windows

    d. Ensuring that you do not leave vehicle keys in an obvious place

5. Access Control

As the principle suggests, this is simply looking at measures that will control access to a location, a person, or an objective. This could be

    a. Locking your doors and windows and removing the keys from the lock once you have done it

    b. Making sure that car doors are locked and that sunroofs and windows are shut

    c. Ensuring that fencing, hedges no higher than 3 feet, walls, and other boundary treatments are in a good state of repair and provide no unintentional access points

    d. Putting a security system in place at a commercial site (i.e., entrance/ exit barriers, security officers, ID Card systems, and mass notification systems)

6. Surveillance

Offenders obviously do not want to be seen and look for concealment opportunities to assist them commit their crimes. Improving surveillance around homes, businesses, or public places is very important. This could be
   a. Not having an 8 foot high hedge in front of your home that simply provides a barrier for an offender to work unseen behind
   b. Adding video surveillance to a commercial site or public place
   c. Establishing a Neighborhood Watch Scheme in your street
   d. Encouraging neighbors or employees to be more alert in their day-to-day business (i.e., while walking the dog or taking their lunch break around places of work

7. Environmental Change

Offenders like familiarity with an area, they like knowing routes in and out of an area and knowing that they can leave with ease if required. Environments should also not look like they have been forgotten about and that no one cares. This could be
   a. Working with the police and local authority to close a footpath
   b. Ensuring that graffiti and domestic/commercial waste is cleared up
   c. Reporting issues as broken street lights to the relevant authority
   d. Organizing or taking part in environmental action days
   e. You want to change the behavior of the criminal and reduce opportunity

8. Rule Setting

Changing our habits may require the setting of rules and informing people of rules may require the positioning of signage in appropriate locations. This could be
   a. Introduce a new rule in your home that the last person leaving or entering the property should lock the door and remove the keys
   b. Informing visitors to commercial sites that they must report to reception on arrival
   c. Making sure employees wear ID badge at all times
   d. Informing users that a particular site is closed between certain times and should not be accessed between them

9. Increasing the Chances of Being Caught

As previously mentioned, offenders do not want to be seen and they look for concealment points around the site where they are looking to commit an offense. There are ways that we can increase the chances of an offender being seen. This could be
   a. Making sure that domestic security lighting is in place and in working order
   b. The use of good quality security digital surveillance systems (CCTV), especially on commercial sites and around public places
   c. Reducing the height of hedges to the front of properties to no higher than 3 feet and making sure overgrown shrubbery does not provide concealment points

d. Improving boundary protection or upgrading security to delay an offender, meaning they would have to spend more time in/at a location
10. Deflecting Offenders
Deterring an offender or deflecting their intentions can be done in a number of ways. Some approaches will be done in partnership with specific agencies/organizations. Others can be done around the complex. This could be
a. The use of timer switches to make your homes look occupied if vacant after the hours of darkness, also turn on a talk show on the radio so voices can be heard
b. Running youth diversionary schemes with partner agencies
c. Referring offenders to drug rehabilitation programs
d. Taking every opportunity to implement crime prevention measures around homes and businesses

When you are looking at using the principles of crime prevention to improve security around your home or business, the best way to approach it is to look at your home or premises as if you were the offender. Identify the weak spots, vulnerable areas, and concealment points and prioritize the areas for improvement.

Chapter 142

Security Lighting

Lighting by itself does not prevent crime.[1] Lighting provides the opportunity for "choice," the choice to walk forward because you can see clearly that the path is clear and free of danger. If the user can see a potential danger (a person hiding, a group of misbehaving young people at the corner), they may choose to walk a different way.

However, lighting can illuminate a target for a criminal as easily as it allows a legitimate user to see a potential threat or criminal. For this reason, lighting must be applied properly. Unless you have natural surveillance of an area, lighting may not always prevent crime. In fact, good lighting without surveillance may actually encourage criminal activity.

Lighting is a powerful tool that management and residents can use to control and reduce the "fear" and opportunity of crime.

Goals of Lighting

Security lighting should be energy efficient (used consistently), and tamper proof (use special screws) with break-resistant lenses (Polycarbonate-Lexan).

Building lighting should illuminate building numbers, building accesses, front and back areas; porch lights under control of the building, not by the apartment user; and the corners as well as walls.

Grounds lighting should provide a cone of light downward to walkways, preferably from the side. Provide a level of lighting between buildings to distinguish forms and movement.

Energy-efficient, outdoor lighting fixtures help reduce your energy costs.

---

[1] Oakland Police Department. Crime Prevention through Environmental Design (CPTED) Security Handbook. http://rockridgencpc.com/documents/fliers/CPTED%20Security%20 Handbook-rev%20simlin.pdf (updated May 2017).

Various Types of Lighting

■ LED are currently the most efficient and come in white light, incandescent are not used as much, and flood lights as well are in LED and white light.

■ High-pressure sodium, hermetically sealed, lamps have 24,000 hours of dependable life. Built for outdoor uses, they absorb wind and vibration, are insulated against high voltage pulses, and have minimal freezing or rusting in the socket.

■ Quartz Light Metal Halide have 500 watt brilliant white light.

■ Incandescent Bulbs: Supreme incandescent bulbs are rated to last 5,000 hours compared to 750 hours for regular bulbs. They have a cooler burn with 85% longer lamp life. They withstand voltage fluctuations, and their brass base offers reduced socket freezing.

■ White light incandescent flood lights have a one-piece weatherproof construction with a brass base to reduce socket freezing. Cooler burn.

■ White light fluorescent tubes cast cool, bright, economical light indoors.

Another key performance characteristic, color rendering, is the ability of a light source to represent colors in objects. This is important for natural surveillance considerations, because different types of lighting cause colors to appear differently at night. For example, a criminal wearing a white sweater and gray sweatpants under a high-pressure sodium light would look like he was wearing a tan sweatsuit. Color rendering and the planned location for security lighting must always be considered before the final installation of a light.

Purposes of Security Lighting

■ Reduce crimes
■ Reduce trespassers
■ Reduce concealment
■ Increase security
■ Increase confidence
■ Increase territoriality
■ Increase surveillance

Types of Lighting

1. Metal Halide: Recreation areas, parking lots
2. High-Pressure Sodium: Parking lots, common areas
3. Fluorescent: Covered parking, porch lights, walk paths

4. LED and Incandescent: Porch lights, inside units working of a solar panel
5. Low-Pressure Sodium: Dumpsters, maintenance shops[2]

Lighting Terminology

1. Foot-candle: Equals light from one candle at 1 foot away
2. Lux: European scale for foot-candle
3. Lumen: Quantity of light from source
4. Watt: Amount of energy consumed
5. Life: Number of hours bulb will last
6. Light and lamp comparison

Lighting Recommendations

When you are conducting assessments, you need to take into consideration the comfort level of the legitimate users of the property. What is the message being transmitted? The comfort level of an area should be that which lets you use your senses of sight, sound, and smell—so that you "feel" safe.

1. Lighting is an important element in any site design. Whether a single house or a shopping mall, appropriate lighting techniques should be used. Good lighting will help people to feel more comfortable with their surroundings.
2. It should provide clear paths for movement and highlight entryways without creating harsh effects or shadowy hiding places.
3. Provide lighting systems that provide nighttime vision for motorists to increase the visibility of pedestrians, other vehicles, and objects that should be seen and avoided.
4. Design lighting systems for pedestrians, homeowners, and business people to permit pedestrians to see one another, and to see risks involved in walking at night.
5. Provide lighting systems that will enhance the ability for surveillance and observation.
6. Provide lighting systems that minimize glare, shadow, light pollution, and light trespass.

---

[2] City of Virginia Beach, Virginia. 2000. Crime Prevention through Environmental Design. https://www.vbgov.com/government/departments/planning/areaplans/Documents/Citywide/Cpted.pdf

Chapter 143

Design Out Crime from the Start

Design has an important role to play in preventing crime and reducing criminal activity without compromising the enjoyment and usability of products, places and services by legitimate users.[1] Designers must remain focused on those they are designing for, as well as those they are designing to thwart.

Designing out crime is not simply a case of designing better locks and bolts. For it to be most effective (and cost effective), crime prevention needs to be designed-in at the start of a project. If designers consider the ways in which the object, systems or environments they are designing might be susceptible to crime early in the design process, they can prevent crime from occurring, or at least reduce the opportunities for offender behavior.

Through design interventions and new ways of thinking, real solutions can cut the cost and burden of the problem while creating new enterprise and revenue opportunities for businesses and designers alike.

The Design Out Crime initiative worked to collect evidence and insight towards a better understanding of business-related crime. The goal was to help designers, manufacturers and policy makers comprehend the scale and effects of the problem and encourage more design commissions to tackle it.

---

[1] Permission to reproduce obtained from: Design Council. 2015. Case Study: Design Out Crime. http://www.designcouncil.org.uk/resources/case-study/design-out-crime

Chapter 144

Creating a Plan to Improve Environmental Conditions

Creating a plan to improve environmental conditions is a critical point in problem-solving, because it is time to make decisions about what to do.[1] Stakeholders should be engaged in developing the plan and are likely to have very concrete ideas about what they want and why. Opportunities for input are important because broad community support for the plan enhances the potential for success during plan implementation.

Plan development is not an isolated activity, but one that comes near the end of a potentially very long process. It is focused on solving a well-defined problem. It uses the data that have been collected and the analyses that have already been completed. It relies on previous input from stakeholders and asks for more advice along the way. (In fact, the plan should include regular opportunities for stakeholders to offer their opinions on how well things are going.)

The process can be organized into five steps:

1. Identify the full range of options available to solve the problem, which may include
    a. Physical improvements
    b. Alterations in the building design, floor plan, room layouts

---

[1] Creating a plan to improve environmental conditions. Using CPTED in Problem Solving. Page 4. 2017 POP Conference, October 2017. Referenced from http://www.popcenter.org/tools/cpted/4

    c. Changes to site layout

    d. New or improved site amenities like lighting and landscaping

      Not all of these alternatives should be included for every problem. The actual list depends on the problem and the setting.

2. Narrow the list to include programs and strategies most likely to have an impact.

3. Decide which of these should be included in the plan for improvement, and in what order of priority, giving due consideration to

    a. Criticality of need

    b. Ease of implementation

    c. Cost

    d. Legality

    e. Technical feasibility

    f. Positive and negative externalities

    g. Client or community support

      One question that frequently arises during this step is whether programs with popular support should be included, even if they hold little potential for addressing the problem or improving environmental conditions. Decisions about trade-offs and the relative weight given to the community's priorities are also situational, and best handled on a case-by-case basis. But it is important to be prepared for such controversy.

4. Develop the plan document, with details on funding and staffing resource requirements, responsibilities, implementation (immediate, short-term, long-term schedules), and indicators of success, tied to the evaluation.

5. Implement the strategies in the plan using the schedule and responsibilities outlined in the plan document. Though community support for the plan should be in place, some attention may need to be given to community education, participation and input, and other strategies to engage stakeholders and garner support for the plan.

Engaging Stakeholders in Problem Solving

It has been noted in previous sections that stakeholder involvement is an important aspect of the environmental analysis. "Stakeholders" are individuals, departments, organizations, and agencies impacted by the problem; with resources to commit to understanding and solving the problem; who make decisions about funding or other priorities; or that have some interest in the outcome. The array of stakeholders actually included in any problem-solving process will depend on the problem, its location, and the circumstances in which the problem is situated.

Crime Prevention through Environmental Design Stakeholders

Neighborhood

- Homeowners, nonresident property owners, tenants
- Community association representatives from the study neighborhood, from adjacent neighborhoods, from adjacent localities
- Business community
- Business owners and managers, employees, business association representatives
- Institutions
- Schools (public and private), places of worship, clubs, cultural facilities (theater, art gallery, museum)

Nonprofit Organizations

- Community development, corporations, social services providers
- Government
- Elected officials, administration and management, police, community/ neighborhood planning, and, depending on the issue, traffic and transportation, transit, parks and recreation, housing and redevelopment, economic development, etc.

Choices about which stakeholders will participate and how they will be engaged in problem-solving will depend upon the complexity of the problem, size of the impacted area, availability of resources, and existence of established community organizations.

Remember that area residents and employees are familiar with the place and the problem. They frequently recognize crime-environment relationships, and can explain events and anticipate trends that will not be revealed through data analysis. They bring critical information to the process. They also represent critical data collection resources and can serve as the line of communication with the rest of the community.

If the neighborhood has no network of communication among tenants and property owners, homeowners, or local institutions and the clients they serve, the plan may need to include community organizing and programs like Neighborhood Watch.

Owners, residents, visitors, and others must be engaged in problem-solving so they understand crime prevention through environmental design (CPTED), and can make or recommend legitimate design, security, and policy choices. Lack of agreement—even outright controversy—can stall progress.

Stakeholder involvement is an important aspect of the environmental analysis. Groups such as area residents and employees can bring critical information to the process. They also represent critical data collection resources and can serve as the line of communication with the rest of the community.

Keeping Tabs on Progress

The last step in the problem-solving process is not a single step, but an ongoing program of monitoring and evaluation. Evaluation is an ongoing activity because change sometimes occurs in small increments so that measurable improvements take a long time to emerge; because immediate change may be an outcome of engagement in the process that disappears over time as interest and attention wane; because the improvement plan is likely to include short-term projects as well as long-term investments, and all of them must be evaluated; and because programs and strategies will need to evolve as environmental conditions change.

The purpose of the evaluation is to decide whether

- The problem has been eliminated, either temporarily or permanently
- The problem is occurring less frequently
- The impact of the problem has been reduced (i.e., fewer victims, less violence, smaller losses)
- Fewer problems are noted in areas adjacent to the problem location
- The problem has moved to another location
- A new or different problem is emerging
- The problem remains, unchanged[2]

Because CPTED engages a variety of organizations and agencies on a problem-solving team—including police officers—the problem may never actually be "removed" from police consideration, even if it becomes the responsibility of another team member.

If the assessment shows the problem has been eliminated or reduced in its frequency or severity, then no additional measures are necessary. The other results, though, suggest it is time for a new problem-solving process linked to new or different outcomes and approaches.

An earlier section of this guide outlined eight categories of data that are used to establish goals and indicators of success linked to those goals. Many police programs rely on indicators such as crime, victimization, and fear, or response times or clearance rates. These measures continue to be important, but other indicators may prove equally useful depending on the problem, the setting, and the circumstances. A return to the eight categories of data offers some perspective on the options

---

[2] National Criminal Justice Reference Service. https://www.ncjrs.gov

available. Each is discussed in greater detail as follows, including an estimated time before noticeable and measurable change might be evident.

Crime Data

In most cases, reductions in calls for service and reported crime are the goal; however, this is not true in all instances. Some communities may instead be working toward an improved relationship with police, or for greater participation in programs like Neighborhood Watch. Increases in calls for service or reported crime are legitimate outcomes under those circumstances.

It is also possible that the number of incidents will not decrease, but the types of incidents that take place are less violent, involve fewer victims, and result in fewer losses, leading to the perception that conditions have improved.

Alternatively, the evaluation may show that the distribution of incidents has changed either temporally or spatially. These changes may mean the crimes are more easily observed, that the police agency can respond more quickly, or that there are fewer complaints about the problem.

It is also possible that when strategies are successfully implemented at the problem site or location, areas surrounding the site also experience reductions in crime. These types of circumstances suggest the need for broad geographic coverage during both data collection and during the evaluation.

Population Characteristics

A neighborhood improvement program may be focused on increasing the diversity of residents with regard to age, gender, race, ethnicity, or income; creating a more stable population base indicated by an increasing number of family households; improving resident quality of life by increasing household income; or establishing an enclave for a specific racial or ethnic community; etc. But in some cases, the goal may be to support the existing population and see that its characteristics do not change.

Institutional and Organizational Relationships

Indicators of success in this category might include active community groups with widespread participation; an increase in the number of associations/organizations/institutions working with the community; an increase in property investment; or an increase in support services targeted to residents. Each of the support services may have its own set of indicators—and the organizations involved should participate in, or be linked to, the CPTED evaluation.

Land Use and Development Patterns

Land use and neighborhood stability are very much related. Indicators of stability include

- Constant, or increasing, property values and rental rates
- A higher proportion of owner-occupied property (rather than rental property)
- Fewer vacant lots, dwelling units, or commercial spaces, and/or increases in construction or rehabilitation activity
- A more compatible mix of uses, or a more diverse mix of uses
- Fewer building, fire, health, and zoning code violations
- Reduced turnover time (time for property to sell or rent)
- Increasing contributions of taxes or fees

Traffic, Transportation, and Transit Systems

Speeding and traffic enforcement are common issues in problem neighborhoods. Evidence of increased enforcement, through the number of citations issued, leading eventually to fewer complaints about speeding problems, is one possible indication of improvement.

When a plan includes changes to traffic patterns through street closings or traffic calming measures, indicators of success are required for the target neighborhood, and also for surrounding communities that may be impacted by new travel patterns. This can include numbers of complaints or numbers of accidents, changes in traffic volumes or turning movements, etc. Alternatively, the evaluation may consider the number of pedestrians, bicyclists, or others using sidewalks, trails, and green-ways.

Transit ridership is an important aspect of that system's successful operation. Real and perceived safety during travel to and from stops or while waiting for or riding the bus or train can be critical. Increased ridership, a more diverse user population, and ridership that is more distributed geographically may be indicators of a successful campaign to improve transit safety. Alternatively, the goal may simply be to increase ridership and the perception of safety for one transit stop or along one route.

Resident or User Surveys and Stakeholder Interviews

Reductions in fear and victimization are critical, but are not the only opportunities for improvement in this category. For example, one goal for the program might be a better relationship with police, so that increased reporting of victimization, or greater cooperation during investigations, are the ideal outcomes. Additionally, look for changes in activities and schedules showing that people are less afraid to use various places and spaces, or an improved opinion about the overall quality of life in the community.

On-Site Behavioral Observations

The evaluation should show a reduction in problem behaviors and more widespread activity by a critical mass of "good" users. As with other categories, greater diversity with regard to age, race, income, etc., can be important.

Safety Audits and Security Surveys

Follow-up safety audits and security surveys should reveal that critical recommendations have been implemented. This allows for testing or evaluation of the results of those implementation activities, which might include changes to policies and procedures such as key control; modifications to building layout or site landscaping; additional security measures like locks or CCTV; etc. For example, one indicator of success might be better record keeping, resulting in better information and a quicker and more targeted response to emerging problems.

What should become clear from this summary is that indicators of success absolutely must be tied to program goals, because different goals equate to different results for some measures. What is also clear is the need for quality data collection and analysis during the early phases of problem solving, so that baseline measures are available and the data afford an opportunity to understand the true impacts of program implementation.

The problem is that evaluation is frequently ignored, overlooked, or under-appreciated. Three possible reasons for this are

1. For many participants, the goal of the problem-solving process is to "do something." Once a program, project or strategy is in place and underway, they are satisfied. They see the process as complete.
2. Evaluation can be time consuming and costly. Other tasks such as those related to implementation, are given higher priority.
3. Problem-solving using CPTED can result in multiple programs or projects. In a setting where many other circumstances and conditions are constantly changing, it is often difficult to determine which changes are the outcomes of specific CPTED initiatives or of CPTED generally, and which changes are produced by other factors in the environment.

Given its role in the problem-solving process, evaluation is an essential and valuable tool for decision-making. It affords an opportunity to understand what is working, where it is working, and why it is working (or is not working). Evaluation aids in recognizing change, and information from one evaluation can be used as part of the problem-solving process somewhere else. This means that data collection and analysis need adequate time and attention early in the process, and evaluation needs adequate time and attention later on.

Additional information on methods for data collection and evaluation are available at the POP Center website: www.popcenter.org

CPTED and the Problem-Solving Process: Reexamining the Three Introductory Cases

The introduction of this guide used three cases to illustrate the potential applications of CPTED as a problem-solving tool. The guide then offered an overview of CPTED principles and a guide for problem solving, including data collection, stakeholder participation, and the evaluation of crime-environment relationships. This section returns to those three original cases as a way to examine the process in greater detail. As a reminder, the three problems are

Case 1: Smoking, drinking, and vandalism in a high school lavatory
Case 2: Graffiti on the back wall of an office center
Case 3: Robbery of nighttime ATM patrons

Scanning includes understanding the problem, identifying stakeholders, and deciding on a process to engage stakeholders in problem-solving. While items like stakeholder interviews are consistent across the three cases, each case has its own unique set of stakeholders. The high school case could also make use of a CPTED task force for problem-solving.

Analysis offers some detail on the kinds of data that could and should be collected. In the first two cases (both of which are about vandalism), maintenance reports rather than crime reports are critical. Population data are not necessary for the school case because this problem involves only the high school students, faculty, staff, and administrators. The two other cases consider user populations rather than the more general community. Community involvement would only be appropriate if these problems were spread over a larger geographic area.

Policies and procedures are an important consideration in all three cases. More types of policies appear relative to the high school lavatory case, as this problem involves lunchtime cafeteria and building use, faculty monitoring assignments, and school rules regarding student behaviors like smoking and drinking.

Response includes three additional segments that distinguish between the three CPTED strategies of natural access control, natural surveillance, and territorial reinforcement.

Assessment is a variety of outcomes that might be experienced as a result of strategy implementation. The goal is to remove or reduce crime and other problem behaviors, but it is also possible for problems to move to a new location or change in character as a result of an intervention. In the worst-case scenario, the problem continues, even after the strategies have been put into place.

The SARA Process is a way to organize thinking about problems and problem-solving using CPTED. It demonstrates why each problem deserves its own detailed examination, one that focuses on the unique circumstances in which that problem is situated. When intervention strategies are specific to the problem, they are more likely to be successful.

Chapter 145

Crime Opportunity Theory and CPTED

Crime opportunity theory suggests that when offenders want to commit a crime, they look for an opportunity or a practical target. By implementing crime prevention through environmental design (CPTED) strategies, opportunities for crime will be reduced.[1]

In the 1998 publication, *Opportunity Makes the Thief* (which is somewhat dated and controversial, but still has relevant applications today), Marcus Felson and Ronald V. Clarke present 10 principles of crime opportunity theory, which describe how opportunities, or vulnerabilities, are the root cause of crime:

1. Opportunities play a role in causing all crime.
2. Crime opportunities are highly specific.
3. Crime opportunities are concentrated in time and space.
4. Crime opportunities depend on everyday movements.
5. One crime produces opportunities for another.
6. Some products offer more tempting crime opportunities.
7. Social and technological changes produce new crime opportunities.
8. Opportunities for crime can be reduced.
9. Reducing opportunities does not usually displace crime.
10. Focused opportunity reduction can produce wider declines in crime.

---

[1] M. Felson and R.V. Clarke. Opportunity Makes the Thief. Police Research Series. Paper 98. Retrieved on June 23, 2017, from: http://www.popcenter.org/library/reading/pdfs/thief.pdf

The first principle implies that since opportunities play a role in all crime, security decision-makers can design facilities that will either encourage or discourage crime.

The second principle states that the specific nature of each type of crime must be analyzed in order to select proper countermeasures. Security measures should be custom tailored to the crimes in question. For example, robberies in a parking lot of a grocery store require different security measures than a robbery of the grocery store's cash handling office.

The third principle emphasizes that dramatic differences in crime levels can be found from one facility to the next, even when both are in high crime areas. The reason for this is that crime shifts temporally (time and day) as opportunities change.

Felson and Clark's fourth principle expands on principle 3, that crime shifts are due to criminals and their victims moving about in time (hour of the day, day of the week) doing their routine activities of work, school, home, and recreation.

Principle 6 describes how repeat attacks by the same or different offenders lead to major increases in risk to the facility. Assets that are high in value and easily accessible are at higher risk than low-value or inaccessible assets. For example, over-the-counter drugs are often targeted by criminals in grocery stores.

Principle 7 discusses how social and technological changes produce new crime opportunities. For example, popular electronic items such as iPads, cell phones, and computers are high-theft items.

Principle 8 is the basic premise behind vulnerability assessments, which is that crime can be prevented by reducing opportunities. This is accomplished by increasing risks to would-be offenders and reducing rewards if the crime is successful.

Principle 9 implies that when opportunities are reduced, it does not usually displace crime. *Crime displacement means that by blocking crime at one facility, security measures will force crime to another, less hardened facility. While displacement does occur, it is not absolute.*

Principle 10 is focused on opportunity reduction, which can produce additional declines in crime. This is the concept of diffusion of benefits. Diffusion is a process where increased security measures at one location may also benefit neighboring facilities.[2]

---

[2] Threat Analysis Group. Ten Principles of Opportunity and Crime. Retrieved on June 23, 2017, from: https://www.threatanalysis.com/2010/10/21/ten-principles-of-opportunity-and-crime/

Chapter 146

Social Disorganization Theory and CPTED

Poverty is the mother of crime.

Marcus Aurelius[1]

Criminologists Clifford Shaw and Henry D. McKay developed the social disorganization theory in 1942, but it is still used today to predict youth violence and crime. The theory behind social disorganization theory is that an individual's physical and social environments are primarily responsible for the choices they make. Shaw and McKay found that neighborhoods with the highest crime rates had at least three problems in common: physical dilapidation, poverty, and a higher level of ethnic and cultural residents. The theory of social disorganization states a person's physical and social environments are primarily responsible for the behavioral. The premise behind their research is that delinquency is not caused at the individual level, but delinquency is caused by a normal individual's response to abnormal conditions.[2]

Using spatial maps to determine the residential locations of juveniles referred to Chicago, Illinois, courts, Shaw and McKay discovered that rates of crime were not evenly distributed across time and space in the city. They found that crime was concentrated in particular areas of the city, regardless of the continual residential

---

[1] B. Kavanagh. 2017. "Poverty is the mother of crime." Prosper Australia. Retrieved on June 23, 2017, from: https://www.prosper.org.au/2017/03/16/poverty-is-the-mother-of-crime/

[2] M. Bond. 2015. Criminology: Social Disorganization Theory Explained. Retrieved on June 24, 2017, from: https://www.linkedin.com/pulse/criminology-social-disorganization-theory-explained-mark-bond

turnover and change of residents who lived in the areas. This finding led Shaw and McKay to the conclusion that crime was a function of neighborhood dynamics, and not necessarily a function of the individuals who lived within the neighborhoods.[3]

A renewed interest in the social disorganization theory began in the 1980s and continues today. The research indicates that social disorganization is an important predictor of youth violence and crime, and that social disorganization has an impact on youth violence and crime. Criminologists and practitioners are conducting research on the relationship between economic deprivation and social disorganization when attempting to explain the origins of youth violence. The basic premise of social disorganization theory is that crime occurs when community relationships and local institutions fail or are absent. For example, a neighborhood with high residential turnover may have more crime than a neighborhood with a stable residential community.[4]

---

[3] Ontario Ministry of Children and Youth Services. Review of the Roots of Youth Violence: Literature Reviews. Retrieved from http://www.children.gov.on.ca/htdocs/English/professionals/oyap/roots/volume5/index.aspx

[4] National Institute of Justice. Why Crimes Occur in Hot Spots. Retrieved on June 24, 2017, from: https://www.nij.gov/topics/law-enforcement/strategies/hot-spot-policing/Pages/why-hot-spots-occur.aspx#socdisorg

Chapter 147

Calming the Traffic

Visual changes can be made to roads to encourage more attentive driving, reduced speed, reduced crashes, and a greater tendency to yield to pedestrians. Visual traffic calming includes *lane narrowing* (9–10 feet), *road diets* (reduction in lanes), use of trees next to streets, on-street parking, and buildings placed in urban fashion close to streets.

Physical devices to calm traffic include speed humps, speed cushions, and speed tables, sized for the desired speed. Such measures normally slow cars to between 10 and 25 miles per hour (16 and 40 km/h). Most devices are made of asphalt or concrete but rubber traffic calming products are emerging as an effective alternative with several advantages.

Traffic calming can include the following engineering measures, grouped by similarity of method[1]:

- Narrowing traffic lanes makes slower speeds seem more natural to drivers and are less intrusive than other treatments that limit speed or restrict route choice. Narrowing measures include narrowing lanes by extending sidewalks, adding bollards or planters, or adding a bike lane or on-street parking.
- *Curb extensions* (also called bulb outs) narrow the width of the roadway at *pedestrian crossings*.
- Chokers are curb extensions that narrow roadways to a single lane at certain points.[2]

---

[1] Fitzgerald and Halliday, Inc. Traffic Calming Resource Guide. South Central Regional Council of Governments. http://scrcog.org/wp-content/uploads/upwp/studies/TrafficCalming_ResourceGuide_Final.pdf

[2] Single lane choker. Institute of Transportation Engineers (ITE). Traffic Calming Measures—Choker. http://www.ite.org/traffic/choker.asp

- Road diets remove a lane from the street. For example, allowing parking on one or both sides of a street to reduce the number of driving lanes.
- *Pedestrian refuges* or small islands in the middle of the street can help reduce lane widths.
- Converting *one-way streets* into two-way streets forces opposing traffic into close proximity, which requires more careful driving.
- Construction of a change of surface, such as asphalt to brick, can be used to indicate a high-traffic crosswalk.
- A vertical deflection is created by raising a portion of a road surface to create a discomfort for drivers traveling at high speeds. Both the height of the deflection and the steepness affect the severity of vehicle displacement.

These include

- *Speed bumps*, sometimes split or offset in the middle to avoid delaying emergency vehicles.
- *Speed humps*, parabolic devices that are less aggressive than speed bumps.
- *Speed cushions*, two or three small speed humps sitting in a line across the road that slow cars down but allow wider emergency vehicles to straddle them so as not to slow emergency response time.
- *Speed tables*, long flat-topped speed humps that slow cars more gradually than humps.
- Raised *pedestrian crossings*, which act as speed tables, often situated at *intersections*.
- Changing the surface material or texture may also include a change in color to indicate to drivers that they are in a pedestrian centric zone.

Horizontal deflection (i.e., make the vehicle swerve slightly). These include

- *Chicanes*, which create a horizontal deflection that causes vehicles to slow as they would for a curve.
- *Pedestrian refuges* again can provide horizontal deflection, as can *curb extensions* and chokers.

Block or restrict access. Such traffic calming means include

- Median diverters to prevent left turns or through movements into a residential area
- Converting an intersection into a *cul-de-sac* or dead end
- *Boom barrier*, restricting through-traffic to authorized vehicles only
- Closing of streets to create *pedestrian zones*

See Photo 147.1.

Photo 147.1 Traffic radar speed sign.

Traffic Calming Benefits

Benefits may include the following[3]:

- Slower speeds = Safer streets
- Slower speeds = Lower emissions
- Slower speeds = Higher perceived value in home pricing

Photo 147.2 Marked crosswalk for pedestrian safety.

---

[3] The Catholic University of America. Education and Awareness Programs. http://publicsafety. cua.edu/programs.cfm

- ■ A traffic calming benefit of neighborhood radar speed sign avoids all the negatives of speed humps, including
  - – Slower response times of emergency vehicles: police, fire and ambulance
  - – Added wear and tear on your vehicle
  - – Increased noise
  - – Pits neighbor against neighbor (for versus against)
  - – Required expense of maintenance
  - – Perceived neighborhood speeding problem could lower house values

See Photo 147.2.

Chapter 148

Risk Reduction for the University Campus Community

The following are factors to reduce crime risk for the university campus community[1]:

- *Proactive Police Patrol*
  Campus Police Officers patrol the campus 24 hours a day 7 days a week. Patrol methods include vehicle patrol, foot patrol, and bicycle patrol. Officers utilize fixed posts at various, designated locations on the campus.
- *Residence Hall Security*
  All residence halls are equipped with access control systems which allow entry for authorized individuals only. Housing security will also check visitors in and out of the residence halls. Safety and security presentations are periodically given for building residents to obtain information about safety.
- *Crime Prevention through Environmental Design (CPTED)*
  The Campus Crime Prevention Unit routinely conducts safety and security surveys on campus and makes recommendations for alterations in landscaping, physical security, and lighting. Students, faculty, and staff are encouraged to report lighting outages or unsafe conditions.

---

[1] The Catholic University of America. Campus Safety and Security. Retrieved on May 12, 2017, from: http://publicsafety.cua.edu/programs.cfm

- *Emergency Telephones*
  There are emergency telephones and panic buttons located throughout the campus. Emergency phones connect the caller directly to the Public Safety Communications Center.
- *Safety and Security Literature*
  A variety of safety and security literature is available through the Department of Public Safety. The Crime Prevention Unit regularly distributes literature at meetings and in community areas. All printed material distributed by the department lists the Campus Police telephone number which can be used to report incidents and obtain police service 24 hours a day.
- *Safety Escorts*
  Safety escorts are offered to students, faculty, and staff, 7 days per week. This is an on-campus service only. Escorts are performed by DPS uniformed officers and Public Safety Assistants (PSAs). Escorts are provided during non-bus service hours, during late and unusual hours, and whenever someone has a concern for their personal safety.
- *Shuttle Services*
- *Education and Awareness Programs*

The following programs are available to the campus community:

Women's Self-Defense Classes: The Department of Public Safety offers self-defense classes for women in order to "develop and enhance the options of self-defense, so they may become viable considerations to the woman who is attacked."

Campus Watch: University community members are encouraged to immediately report suspicious persons, vehicles, and activities to the Department of Public Safety. Public Safety utilizes Watch Captains in each building to disperse emergency information, distribute crime prevention literature, post crime alerts, and act as a safety and security liaison for their area of responsibility.

Safety and Security Presentations: Throughout the year, the crime prevention unit provides safety and security presentations in residence halls and other campus locations. Safety information is distributed at all presentations, meetings, and seminars, and is available at the Department of Public Safety.

New Student Orientation: A variety of presentations are available to share knowledge about DPS services and increase awareness of safety and security on and around campus. DPS staff members are available to answer questions from parents and students.

Operation Street Smart: This program will provide information about personal and property safety that will reduce the risk of becoming a victim of crime on campus and the surrounding areas.

Participation in National Campus Safety Month: DPS participates in National Campus Safety month each September by providing a variety of programs and activities for the campus community.

Chapter 149

CPTED Concepts from a Fire Department Perspective[1]

Crime prevention through environmental design (CPTED) has been effective in reducing crime and creating safer buildings when applied appropriately. CPTED has significant benefits to improving fire safety as well, multiplying benefits received. CPTED philosophies that focus on proper design and effective use of the environment are providing operational value during a fire or other emergency incident.

Natural surveillance sight lines provided for occupants also benefit responding fire units. Windows or doors that are obscured by vegetation block views inside that provide essential indicators to the type and severity of a fire that may be occurring. Responding fire units will provide a size-up report as they arrive. This size-up information is critical to protocols that additional responding units may follow. Not being able to see smoke in a building may provide a false sense that there is no problem when in fact there is. A 360-degree walk-around of a building is an additional essential activity in identifying potential problems. In both cases, natural surveillance features support identification of events on the interior. In one notable instance, a fire that was started in mulch rapidly spread to bushes that covered the front of the house. Burning landscape allowed the fire to extend inside through an open window.

Natural access control is another area of mutual benefit. Providing a clear view from the street to the driveway can provide responding emergency crews critical

---

[1] Chapter is reproduced with permission from Greg Benson.

clues as to the presence of occupants. Fires vary depending on a number of factors; however, the ability to easily mount an attack is important in saving lives and limiting losses. The driveway often makes a good area to stage equipment. Clear access will support a faster fire attack.

Maintenance of property remains an additional constructive area. Property that is poorly maintained with broken windows, lack of lighting, and so on, may also have similar interior safety or fire hazards such as broken smoke detectors, electrical system problems, and so on. Exterior property maintenance may encourage similar efforts inside, increasing occupant safety and decreasing likelihood of an incident.

Having visible street addresses as well as definition of public/private areas establishes territorial reinforcement. Lacking a street address or specific property definition can make identification of the emergency location difficult, creating dangerous response delays.

Too often police and fire priorities are seen as incompatible. CPTED establishes a common platform that provides a proactive benefit to residents as well as response agencies. Each CPTED area has benefits for fire and other emergency responses. Use of CPTED strategies to influence a criminal's decisions before an incident is also effective at reducing risk from other types of emergencies. This integration provides both a greater safety awareness by the occupants as well as actions to reduce risk.

Chapter 150

Space Management and Design

Space management is linked to the principle of territorial reinforcement. It ensures that space is well used and maintained, and involves the formal supervision, control, and care of urban space. Space management strategies are an important means of generating and maintaining activity, serviceability, and natural community control. Strategies include activity coordination, site cleanliness, rapid repair of vandalism and graffiti, and the refurbishment of decayed physical elements.

Design

The seven crime prevention through environmental design (CPTED) strategies of territorial reinforcement, natural access control, natural surveillance, image and/ or maintenance, activity program support, target hardening, and geographical juxtaposition (wider environment)[1] are inherent in the Three-D concept. Does the space clearly belong to someone or some group? Is the intended use clearly defined? Does the physical design match the intended use? Does the design provide the means for normal users to naturally control the activities, to control access, and to provide surveillance? Once a basic self-assessment has been conducted, the Three-Ds may then be turned around as a simple means of guiding decisions about what to do with human space. The proper functions have to be matched with space that can support them—with space that can effectively support territorial identity, natural

---

[1] P.M. Cozens, G. Saville, and D. Hillier. 2005. Crime prevention through environmental design (CPTED): A review and modern bibliography. *Property Management* 23(5): 328–356.

access control, and surveillance—and intended behaviors have to be indisputable and be reinforced in social, cultural, legal, and administrative terms or norms. The design has to ensure that the intended activity can function well, and it has to directly facilitate any existing community and stakeholder participation in the design process. This may involve but is not limited to the following:

1. Developer.
2. Design architects or design team.
3. Local planning authority.
4. Community members.
5. Refine the CPTED strategy.
6. Ensure that the CPTED strategy is carried through from the planning phase to the design phase and the microlevel of pathway design, lighting, signage, and so on.
7. Engage an experienced or certified professional to peer review the proposed plans.

Design Out Crime from the Start

Design has an important role to play in preventing crime and reducing criminal activity without compromising the enjoyment and usability of products, places and services by legitimate users.[2] Designers must remain focused on those they are designing for, as well as those they are designing to thwart.

Designing out crime is not simply a case of designing better locks and bolts. For it to be most effective (and cost effective), crime prevention needs to be designed-in at the start of a project. If designers consider the ways in which the object, systems or environments they are designing might be susceptible to crime early in the design process, they can prevent crime from occurring, or at least reduce the opportunities for offender behavior.

---

[2] Permission obtained to reproduce from: Design Council. 2015. Case Study: Design Out Crime. http://www.designcouncil.org.uk/resources/case-study/design-out-crime

Conclusion

What we did in this text was to discuss not only crime prevention through environmental design (CPTED) in the United States, but CPTED internationally, as well. Our research showed us that many communities are working hard to create safer environments and have explored the advancements of CPTED utilizing various strategies. We believe that Neighborhood Watch and community policing programs need to be updated and improved to include CPTED concepts as well as available technology.

The bottom line is, "It is people who are the ones who can prevent crime by focusing on the many social issues that lead to crime and the reduction of opportunity." We believe that there is still a lot of work to be done educating people in CPTED strategies and concepts. The direction that we see law enforcement and CPTED practitioners heading in is to have a working knowledge of all three generations of CPTED, understanding the concept behind the broken windows theory, and applying the research principles of Oscar Newman.

Jack Morse, a good friend of ours, always asks two questions, "What's new in crime prevention?" "Where is the innovation coming from?" We designed this text with these two questions in mind. We hope it is of help to you, and it is our hope that you stay ahead of the curve with CPTED and security countermeasures, because we have just raised the bar.

Appendix A: Fear of Crime

Even though the majority of people have a low chance of being a victim of crime, the number of people who are afraid or worried about being a victim of crime is relatively high. One of the reasons for the high fear of crime is that crime rates are generally overrepresented in media coverage, compared to actual crime rates in society. Research has discovered that the vast majority of the public depends on the media for information about crime, so they form their opinions about crime according to what the media reports. We can assume then that the general picture of crime provided by the media is inaccurate.[1]

Fear of crime is considered a serious social problem and has been studied for almost 40 years. Research that was conducted found that even when crime rates decline, fear of crime rates stay relatively stable. Research has attempted to determine why the fear of crime does not match up with actual victimization. One of the explanations focused on vulnerability (individuals felt vulnerable to crime even if they were not vulnerable) and a focus on differences in groups (women were more afraid of crime than men, even though they were less likely to be victims). This explanation has led researchers to study individual fear of crime predictors, such as sex, race, age, and social class, and contextual predictors, such as neighborhood disorder, incivilities, and social cohesion. Both psychological and behavioral consequences of the fear of crime were studied.[2]

Fear of crime can deter people from using public spaces, such as parks and public transportation. Some groups of people are affected more than others. Fear of crime among black and minority ethnic people is higher than that of white people. Some

---

[1] A. Emanuelsson and R. Mele. The Mean World Syndrome. http://www.svj.hvu.nl/mediahype/risk4/page2.htm

[2] N. Rader. Fear of Crime. *Criminology and Criminal Justice.* http://criminology.oxfordre.com/view/10.1093/acrefore/9780190264079.001.0001/acrefore-9780190264079-e-10

people, especially women, will not travel after dark. Some parents restrict their children's usage of public transportation because of this fear.[3]

New approaches to reduce and prevent crime and also the fear of crime (feelings of insecurity) throughout the world have been developed in recent decades primarily because of reports about violent crimes reported on media, such as television and in print.

Many times, the risk of being a victim of crime can be mitigated with some simple precautions. For example, a woman afraid of being assaulted in a parking lot can go to and from the lot with a friend or security officer and also lock her car doors. She can also park in well-lit areas to further reduce the likelihood of victimization. Each one of these measures will make the woman a less attractive victim, and therefore reduce the likelihood that a criminal will choose her as a victim.[4]

Another way to reduce the opportunity for crime to occur is by modifying the built environment. This approach goes by the name of crime prevention through environmental design (CPTED) or Designing Out Crime (DOC). This is not a new program, but it has gained more popularity in recent years as a positive and proactive approach to crime and fear of crime.

---

[3] N. Rader. Fear of Crime. *Criminology and Criminal Justice.* http://criminology.oxfordre.com/view/10.1093/acrefore/9780190264079.001.0001/acrefore-9780190264079-e-10

[4] How can I explain the difference between the fear of crime and the actual risk of crime? https://www.quora.com/How-can-I-explain-the-difference-between-the-fear-of-crime-and-the-actual-risk-of-crime

Appendix B: The Title of This Book

We came up with the title *CPTED and Traditional Security Countermeasures: 150 Things You Should Know* and realized we probably should have called it 200 Things You Should Know. We regret, we could not write or say enough about traditional security countermeasures. (See Figures B.1 and B.2)

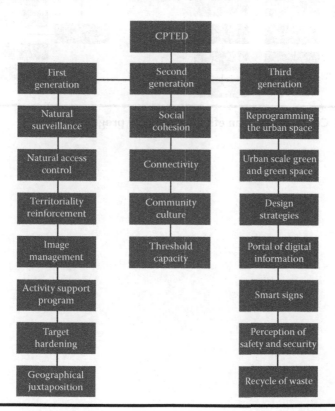

Figure B.1 The concepts of first-, second-, and third-generation CPTED.

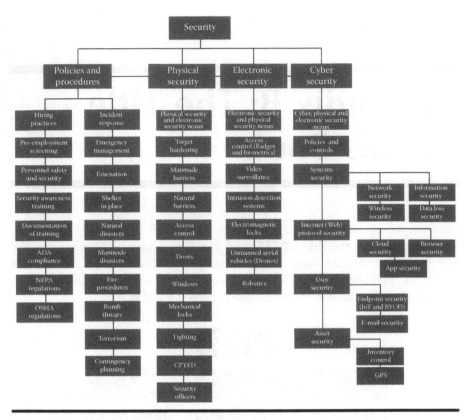

Figure B.2 Components of an effective security program.

Index

Printed in the United States
by Baker & Taylor Publisher Services

Printed in the United States
by Baker & Taylor Publisher Services